THE FLAWED PATH TO THE PRESIDENCY 1992

SUNY Series on the Presidency: Contemporary Issues
John Kenneth White, Editor

THE FLAWED PATH TO THE PRESIDENCY 1992

Unfairness and Inequality in the Presidential Selection Process

ROBERT D. LOEVY

STATE UNIVERSITY OF NEW YORK PRESS

Cover photo by Walt Loevy.

Published by
State University of New York Press, Albany

© 1995 State University of New York

For information, address State University of New York
Press, State University Plaza, Albany, N.Y., 12246

Production by E. Moore
Marketing by Theresa A. Swierzowski

Library of Congress Cataloging-in-Publication Data

Loevy, Robert D., 1935-
    The flawed path to the presidency, 1992 : unfairness and
inequality in the presidential selection process / Robert D. Loevy.
        p.   cm. — (SUNY series on the presidency)
    Includes bibliographical references and index.
    ISBN 0-7914-2187-2. — ISBN 0-7914-2188-0 (pbk.)
    1. Presidents—United States—Election—1992. I. Title.
II. Series: SUNY series on the presidency.   93-48105
JK5261992   CIP
324.973'0928—dc20

10 9 8 7 6 5 4 3 2 1

CONTENTS

Contents vii

FOREWORD

Most of the books about presidential elections in the United States have been "candidate-centered." Most writers approach the subject from the point of view of those who are running for the office of president, seeing the election process mainly as a game or contest in which the various candidates maneuver and manipulate in order to "win."

Credit for this candidate-centered approach goes to political analyst and writer Theodore H. White, whose landmark book *The Making of the President 1960* revolutionized the way the American people—and the news media—look at presidential elections. Teddy White took his readers to the inside of John F. Kennedy's and Richard Nixon's campaigns for president in 1960. Readers suddenly found themselves at that first strategic planning session of the 1960 Kennedy campaign, held at Robert Kennedy's vacation home in Hyannisport, Massachusetts, in late October of 1959. From there on the book was an insider's trip all the way: strategy making, manipulating the system, gaining advantage. Under White's influence these candidate-centered activities became the principal focus of the study of presidential elections in the United States.

White redefined running for president as "strategic campaign engineering." Much as a civil engineer designed and then built a bridge, candidates and their high-powered campaign advisers were to design and then build a successful election campaign. Questions of policy—for example, what the various candidates said they would or would not do once elected to the office of president of the United States—became secondary to the campaign itself. Policy positions were important only to the extent that they would attract this group of voters to Candidate A, or provide that crucial margin of victory in the New Hampshire presidential primary for Candidate B.

White applied his strategic campaign engineering approach in three additional *Making of the President* books, in 1964, 1968, and 1972. His way of looking at presidential elections has attracted many imitators, the most successful being Jack Germond and Jules Witcover, who singly or together have written books on several recent presidential elections.

Some of Teddy White's successors have applied the candidate-centered approach to specific elements of presidential campaigning. Thus Joe McGinniss took his readers to the inner sanctums where campaign advertising was generated for Richard Nixon in the landmark *The Selling of the President 1968*. Timothy Crouse gave a wonderful insider's view of how the press covers the candidates in his *The Boys on the Bus*, published in 1973.

Robert D. Loevy's *The Flawed Path to the Presidency 1992* represents a major effort to break away from the pattern so ably established by Theodore White. Loevy takes a fresh and unique approach to United States presidential elections. Instead of seeing the presidential campaign as a game played by the candidates, Loevy views it as an important experience for the average American voter. Thus Loevy replaces the candidate-centered approach with a voter-centered approach, seeing the presidential election as something every American participates in and, most important, has a right to participate in *equally*.

Loevy's overall approach is different and so also is the way in which he gathered his information about the 1992 presidential contest. Loevy did not emphasize setting up interviews with either the candidates or their high-level campaign staff members. He conducted such interviews when they came his way spontaneously, but he did not specifically seek them out. Instead, he mingled with the crowds who turned out to hear the candidates speak and shake the candidates' hands. Loevy was interested in how the public responded to the candidates and related to the candidates. Further, Loevy's focus is on the way the rules and regulations by which we conduct our presidential elections influence the way average citizens are able to participate in those elections.

In pursuing his theme of how the American people relate to and participate in presidential elections, Loevy is one of the first political analysts to highlight the relationship between the governors and the legislatures of the fifty states and the presidential selection process. Few Americans realize the quiet yet important role the fifty state governments play in the presidential nominating process. State legislatures decide whether a particular state will have a presidential primary or a caucus, the date of that primary or caucus, and the detailed rules and regulations under which the primary or caucus is carried out. In many states, the governor has the choice of supporting or vetoing the final product of the legislature in this important area of democratic activity. Loevy not only points up the key role of the states in the presidential nominating process but reveals how this process is carried out in a generally haphazard and uncoordinated way. His call for the rationalization of the nominating process through the adoption of a Model Calendar of State Presidential Primaries and Caucuses is a call worthy of serious consideration.

In highlighting for all to see the key role of the state legislatures and state governors in the presidential nominating process, Loevy reminds us of the *federal* character of our nominating system. The founders of the United States, working at the 1787 Constitutional Convention in Philadelphia, fashioned a government in which both the national government and the state governments share sovereignty. The president of the United States is the top official of the national government in Washington, yet the nominating system follows the federal idea and gives the individual states a key role to play. Sometimes, in the heat of a hotly contested presidential nominating campaign we neglect the critical role states still play in shaping the overall process. This book helps us regain a serious understanding of exactly how the fifty states fit into the operation of the overall nominating system.

The Flawed Path to the Presidency 1992 is notable for the bold way it prescribes reasonable, workable, and achievable reforms in the presidential selection process. These proposed reforms are specific and detailed. Political scientists and political analysts traditionally take the safe road of being merely *descriptive* rather than openly *prescriptive*. Many previous works have treated the subject of reform simply by listing the many reforms that have been proposed over the years for overhauling the presidential selection process. Often, little or even no effort is made to evaluate those reforms, either in terms of their workability or their achievability. Bob Loevy mentions other proposals for reform but also makes clear what workable, achievable reforms are required to improve our presidential selection process.

Loevy's valuable treatise on the flaws of our presidential selection process deserves a wide audience. He is a gifted political observer and a superb teacher. This well-researched, well-written study is a lasting contribution.

THOMAS E. CRONIN

PREFACE

This is not an insider's account of the 1992 presidential election campaign. This book will not tell you what President George Bush said to his top aides when he first learned that Pat Buchanan was going to run against him in the New Hampshire primary. It will not reveal what Bill Clinton said to Hillary Clinton during a game of Hearts late one night as their campaign bus sped across the Midwest.

This also is not a systematic review or summary of the many books and articles that have been written about presidential elections in the United States. This book does periodically refer to that vast body of able and erudite scholarly literature, and an extensive bibliography on presidential elections is provided at the end. One reason I did not rely heavily on the literature of the field is that the presidential selection process in the United States is changing so rapidly that previous works quickly go out-of-date.

This book is about the way the American people related to the 1992 presidential election campaign, and the way the campaign related to them. It will describe how the voters of New Hampshire, for instance, had a much different experience from the voters in California. It will put the case, convincingly I hope, that the current presidential selection process in use in the United States is unfair in the way it makes the citizens of some states much more important than the citizens of other states. In addition to pointing out such flaws, this book proposes a number of nonradical, incremental reforms for improving United States presidential elections.

One major reform is the simple but important idea that an objective and neutral deliberative body—such as the National Conference of State Legislatures—adopt a *Model Calendar of State Presidential Primaries and Caucuses.* Such a model calendar would set the date for each state's primary or caucus in such a way that the citizens of each state would have a chance of participating equally in the primary-caucus process.

A second major reform presented advocates that, prior to all the presidential primaries and caucuses, each party hold a *Preprimary National Mini-Convention.* At this mid-January national mini-convention, elected officials from each political party would vote on the various candidates running for the party nomination for president, thereby giving the voters some idea of which candidates the "party professionals" prefer. Party members could take this advice or not as they went about voting in their particular state primaries and caucuses.

A third reform advocated is the outright abolition of the electoral college and its replacement with direct popular election of the president. This reform would require the adoption of an *Amendment for the Popular Election of the President* to the United States Constitution. Although the electoral college has been a hallowed part of American presidential elections since the founding of the republic, it does treat the voters in the various states of the union in a highly unequal fashion.

This book, therefore, is a blow-by-blow and state-by-state description of the inequities in voter participation in the 1992 presidential election. It concludes that the three simple reforms summarized above would go a long way toward giving each American citizen an equal voice in the presidential selection process.

Virtually all books on United States presidential elections acknowledge that the process is characterized by change. This has been particularly true in recent years of the sequential series of state primaries and caucuses that now constitute the nominating system. Most of these books, however, focus only on what the changes are and how they affect the outcome of a particular presidential election.

This book takes a unique approach by focusing on how change in the presidential selection system comes about. It identifies some of the people who are making these changes and attempts to discover their motives and purposes. Why and how did Colorado decide to have an early presidential primary in 1992? Who made the decision that Georgia would abandon Super Tuesday and hold its presidential primary one week earlier on the first Tuesday in March? And, perhaps the most important question of all in 1992, why didn't California abandon its end-of-the-line presidential primary date in early June and hold a more meaningful primary on the first Tuesday in March?

Most books on presidential elections do not address in detail these kinds of questions. This book does.

This book is written from a *participationist* political perspective. If there is one theme that is playing strongly in American political life in the early 1990s, it is the theme that average citizens want to have more of a say—an *equal* say—in how their government is conducted and how their public officials are elected. This desire to enhance the role and the power of the individual in modern day American government can be found in any number of political movements—from the desire to have citizens vote on specific tax increases to the effort to limit the growing influence of political action committees (PACs). This book is part and parcel of the participationist perspective in that its eventual goal is to give every American voter who wants one a larger and more equal role in electing the president of the United States.

This book was written as the 1992 election was taking place. I purposefully avoided using hindsight to rewrite or recast what I had previously written. I wanted my readers to see the election the same way the voters of the United States saw it at the time it was taking place. If something seemed important to the election—and the electorate—at the time it happened, it is in this book. If it did not seem important or was not known, it likely was not included. Only in those few instances where subsequently revealed information appeared to be crucial to understanding what happened in the 1992 presidential voting did I go back and add new material.

I was present at many of the events described in this book, particularly those that took place in my home state of Colorado. As a result, the descriptions and evaluations of these events are my own and not heavily cited in the Notes. Thanks to a Faculty Research and Development grant from Colorado College, I was able to travel to Iowa, New Hampshire, Maryland, Massachusetts, Florida, Illinois, Pennsylvania, Oregon, and California to observe significant portions of the presidential caucuses, primaries, and general election campaigning that took place in those states.

Because the American people mainly experience presidential election campaigns through their television sets and their local newspapers, I made it a point to include materials from television news programs and daily newspapers other than just the *New York Times* and the *Washington Post*. Of course I checked the *Times* and the *Post* throughout the lengthy 1992 presidential campaign, but I also picked up information from *USA Today*, the *Miami Herald*, the *Chicago Tribune*, the *Los Angeles Times*, the *San Francisco Examiner*, and other periodicals. I also used wire service stories—from Gannett, Knight-Ridder, Cox, and others—as they appeared in my own two morning newspapers, the *Denver Post* and the *Colorado Springs Gazette Telegraph*.

Most helpful and important were the thoughts, the ideas, and the feelings of the many people—average citizens, news reporters, and campaign personnel—who took the time to talk to me and answer questions while the 1992 presidential election was taking place.

1. GEORGE BUSH: FROM GREAT TRIUMPH TO BIG TROUBLE

It was one of the most amazing, and one of the most successful, events in all of American history. In the year 1989, people throughout the world sat glued to their television sets and watched as young West Germans and young East Germans joined together to tear down the Berlin Wall. Erected in the early 1960s to prevent East Germans from fleeing to the political freedom of the West, the Wall had come to symbolize the totalitarian tyranny of Soviet-style Communism. It also symbolized the seemingly never-ending Cold War between the Soviet Union and the United States, a war which many believed could only end in a global nuclear war.

Assaulted by pickaxes and sledgehammers, in large chunks and small bits the Berlin Wall slowly came down. Observers could not miss seeing the international character of the young Germans doing the work, and the visible signs of how United States culture had already penetrated their lives. Many were dressed in U.S.-style clothing. One Wall-destroyer was wearing a Los Angeles Raiders warmup jacket.

The president of the United States during this historic event was George Herbert Walker Bush, a Cold War trench warrior if there ever was one. A combat veteran of World War II, Bush had served his country in such varied international duties as director of the Central Intelligence Agency, ambassador to the United Nations, and ambassador to

Communist China. Throughout his eight years as vice president during Ronald Reagan's presidency, Bush had steadfastly supported Reagan's policy of building up United States military strength and taking a combative and competing attitude toward the Soviet Union.

When he ran successfully for president in 1988 in his own right, Bush made the continuation of Reagan's hard-line foreign policy a central part of his own campaign.

The revolution that began with the fall of the Berlin Wall continued to spread. Soon the Soviet Union itself was coming apart, with Russia and most of the other former Soviet republics declaring themselves independent states. Most amazing of all, the new nations that rose out of the ashes of the Soviet Union abandoned the Marxist ideology of Lenin and Stalin and declared themselves ready and willing to adopt democratic forms of government and Western-style free market economic systems.

All of the time this cataclysmic revolution was taking place, it was George Bush who was manning the telephones and maintaining close personal contact with other heads of state. He took the lead in managing the Western alliance's response to the upheaval in the Soviet Union, working to guarantee that the final outcome would be a world built on peace and cooperation rather than distrust and destruction.

Of course, President Bush could not take all the credit for the breakup of the Soviet Union and the end of the Cold War, and he did not try to. He acknowledged that, since the end of World War II, Democrats and Republicans alike had labored to maintain a strong United States defense and respond both economically and militarily to Communist attempts to take over other nations. But Bush did make the claim that, ever since George McGovern ran unsuccessfully for president in 1972 as an antiwar Democrat, a substantial portion of the Democratic Party had opposed military preparedness and strenuously criticized United States military efforts to halt the spread of world Communism.

Then fate gave George Bush another opportunity to demonstrate his skills as a master designer of successful foreign policies. When Iraq launched a military attack against its close neighbor Kuwait, Bush took the lead and convinced the United Nations to build an international military force to roll back the Iraqi invaders. Being careful to repel Iraqi aggression but not overthrow the government of Iraq, Bush stripped the Iraqi leader, Saddam Hussein, of most of his weapons of mass destruction. Even more amazing, this swift and massive military operation was carried out with minimal loss of life on the part of the military forces opposing Iraq.

But that was not all. Working closely with his secretary of state, James A. Baker III, President Bush slowly and carefully pressed for peace talks between Israel and its hostile Arab neighbors. A Middle Eastern peace settlement, impossible to even contemplate in previous years, suddenly seemed a real possibility with Bush and Baker at the foreign policy helm.

And then, yet another giant step toward world peace: President Bush and Secretary Baker negotiated sweeping nuclear arms cuts with Russia, the largest and most powerful of the many republics that had previously constituted the Soviet Union. The cuts were highly beneficial to the United States, simultaneously reducing the threat of accidental nuclear war and allowing the nation to spend less money on military hardware. George Bush thus became the first American president to reap a "peace dividend," that is, to save the government money by reducing military expenditures now that the Soviet Union no longer existed and thus was no longer a major military threat to the United States.

One would expect that an American president who carried out such a phenomenally successful foreign policy would enjoy high standing in the eyes of his fellow citizens. At first that was the case with George Bush's presidency. In March of 1991, at the successful conclusion of the war with Iraq, Bush enjoyed a record 90 percent approval rating in the public opinion polls.[1] Some political commentators argued that Bush's popularity was now so great he could "sleepwalk" his way to a giant reelection victory in the 1992 presidential election.

The euphoria that surrounded George Bush's reelection prospects in the spring of 1991 slowly began to dissappear, however. The biggest problem was the national economy, which never had been very strong during Bush's presidency and continued to weaken throughout the remainder of 1991. Many well-known economists agreed with the Bush administration that economic recovery was just around the corner, but then the early signs of recovery faded. Each new set of statistics showed the economy remaining stagnant.

Unemployment continued to creep slowly but steadily upward, and as it did Bush's approval ratings moved just as steadily downward. By December of 1991, just as the 1992 presidential primaries and caucuses were about to begin, Bush's approval rating had dropped to 47 percent, an unprecedented 43-point drop from the 90 percent approval of the previous March. Even more disturbing for the Bush camp was the fact that seven out of ten Americans said they disliked the way the president was handling the national economy.[2]

A storm of controversy began to brew around Bush's economic policies. Many critics argued that he long ago should have begun stimulating the national economy by ordering massive increases in government spending and not worrying about the effects on the national debt or the rate of inflation. Bush's defenders, however, pointed out that his efforts to limit government spending had given the United States one of the lowest inflation rates in history and were setting the stage for a "real" recovery rather than a "fake" recovery based on profligate government spending.

The one area in which Bush was generally admired by economists was international trade. Bush pursued an aggressive policy of reducing tariffs and other barriers to international commerce whenever and wherever possible. At the Uruguay round of GATT (General Agreement on Tariffs and Trade), Bush successfully reduced world agricultural subsidies, thus opening foreign markets for American food products. He began the process of bringing Mexico into the North American Free Trade Agreement, hoping to create large numbers of high-paying industrial jobs by opening up vast new markets for United States industrial products in Mexico.

But even Bush's achievements in the area of free trade generated some vehement criticism. Organized labor claimed that reducing trade barriers with Mexico would cost many Americans their jobs, mainly because Mexican laborers would work for lower wages than workers in the United States. Long before the identity of the 1992 Democratic nominee for president was known, organized labor in the United States committed itself to the defeat of George Bush because of his free trade policies.

There were good historical reasons why George Bush's approval ratings fell so precipitously toward the end of 1991. Ever since the early 1930s, when the United States suffered through the worst economic depression in its history, the American people have tended to vote Democratic when worried about the national economy. The event which marked the beginning of the Great Depression, the Stock Market Crash of 1929, took place under a Republican president, Herbert Hoover, and the American populace very quickly blamed Hoover and the Republicans for both causing the depression and being unable or unwilling to do anything about ending it.

Herbert Hoover ran for reelection in the 1932 presidential race. Governor Franklin D. Roosevelt of New York was Hoover's Democratic opponent. Roosevelt condemned Hoover for causing so much economic suffering. He promised, if elected, to take swift action to end the depression. Roosevelt defeated Hoover easily and, once in office, launched his "New Deal" program of government regulation and government spending to restore the national economy.

Franklin Roosevelt and his New Deal program for ending the Great Depression proved exceptionally popular with the American people. Roosevelt was reelected president in 1936 by one of the largest percentages in American political history. His Republican opponent, Alf Landon of Kansas, won only two states—Maine and Vermont. Roosevelt's economic policies accomplished two things. They made the Democratic Party the most popular political party in the United States, and they branded the Republican Party as a party that could not be trusted to successfully operate the national economy.[3]

So when the economic indicators began to sag during George Bush's presidency in 1991, many Americans, particularly older Americans, went back to the old rule of voting for a Democrat, any Democrat, for president when the economy goes bad. Even though the Stock Market Crash and the Great Depression had occurred more than sixty years earlier, they would be a major factor in how many people would decide to cast their votes in the 1992 presidential election.

Ironically, not only was the bad economic situation harming George Bush, but so was the major foreign policy triumph of his Administration—the end of the Cold War. In the years following World War II, the Republican Party had done very well in presidential elections by blaming the Democrats for alleged foreign policy failures. Thus in the 1952 election, Republican presidential candidate Dwight D. Eisenhower blamed the Democrats for getting the United States into a war in Korea which the United States could not win. At the same time, Eisenhower criticized the Democrats for not being tougher with the Soviet Union and thereby allowing Communist governments to take over all of Eastern Europe as well as mainland China. Eisenhower won that election, and a Republican pattern of winning presidential elections by exploiting Democratic foreign policy failures was firmly established.

In 1968, Republican candidate Richard Nixon blamed the Democrats for the war in Vietnam in much the same way that Eisenhower had blamed them for the war in Korea. As had Eisenhower, Nixon won the election. In 1980, Republican candidate Ronald Reagan blamed the incumbent Democratic president, Jimmy Carter, for allowing a large number of United States citizens to be held hostage by the government of Iran. The United States nationals, most of whom were diplomatic personnel assigned to the United States embassy in Tehran, had been taken prisoner following a pro-Muslim revolution in Iran. Similarly to Eisenhower and Nixon, Reagan was able to ride this foreign policy problem of an incumbent Democratic president to yet another Republican victory.

The irony of George Bush's presidency was that, when the Soviet Union broke apart and the Cold War ended, the Republicans no longer had the foreign policy issue to use against the Democrats. A Republican candidate for president could not campaign against the Democrats for being "soft on Communism" if there was no longer a world Communist threat. The Republicans could not accuse the Democrats of failing to maintain a strong national defense if there was no longer a major enemy threatening the military security of the United States.[4]

The result was that George Bush faced a "double whammy" as he prepared to run for reelection to the presidency in 1992. The first "whammy" was that he was saddled with a weak national economy, and historically the American people have voted Democratic in recent decades when worried about economic problems, particularly the problem of increasing unemployment. The second "whammy" was that the Cold War was over, and President Bush therefore could no longer win votes by charging that the Democrats were soft on military defense and resisting Communist expansion.

By late 1991 many Americans had the feeling that President Bush was beginning his reelection campaign in a severely weakened condition. One of them was conservative newspaper columnist Patrick Buchanan, who on December 10, 1991, announced that he would challenge George Bush for the 1992 Republican nomination for president. Buchanan criticized Bush for being a "globalist" and called on the United States to embrace a "new nationalism" that would put "America First."[5] He also condemned the president's free trade policies, saying they would cost Americans their jobs, and he accused Bush of putting the American economy in "the dumpster."[6]

Buchanan also attacked President Bush for breaking his famous pledge from the 1988 presidential election campaign: "Read my lips: no new taxes!" Many conservative Republicans had voted for Bush in 1988 precisely because of his strong stand in opposition to tax increases. Bush broke the pledge when, during negotiations with congressional Democrats over the annual budget, he agreed to a tax increase to try to reduce the mushrooming growth of the national debt. Ed Rollins, a conservative Republican campaign consultant, subsequently called Bush's action "probably the most serious violation of any political pledge anybody has ever made."[7]

Buchanan announced his candidacy for the Republican nomination in a building lobby in Concord, New Hampshire, right across the street from the New Hampshire state capitol. He made it clear that his challenge to Bush would be mounted, first and foremost, in New Hampshire's "First in the Nation" presidential primary, now only slightly more than two months away.

2. BILL CLINTON: EMERGING FROM THE DEMOCRATIC FIELD

There is no set starting date for United States presidential elections. Long before the first caucuses and primaries are held, would-be Democratic and Republican nominees begin the political manuevering, the fund-raising, and the never-ending quest for news media coverage that are part and parcel of the presidential selection process.

Few persons in American history ever laid more careful plans for winning the presidency than Bill Clinton did in 1992. In a very real sense, his campaign for the White House began in 1985, when he and a group of other moderate southern Democrats, all of them elected officials, formed the Democratic Leadership Council (DLC).

Bill Clinton was born in Hope, Arkansas, in 1946. Several years later his family left Hope and moved to Hot Springs, Arkansas. As had many other young southerners, Clinton left the South to go to college, attending Georgetown University in Washington, D.C., and then winning a Rhodes Scholarship to study at Oxford University. He completed his education by earning a law degree at Yale Law School.

Returning home to Arkansas, Clinton entered Democratic politics and was elected governor of Arkansas in 1978. In his early thirties at the time he moved into the Arkansas governor's mansion, Clinton was the youngest governor in the nation. A number of his policies rubbed a lot of Arkansas voters the wrong way, however, and at the end of his two-year term, in 1980, he was narrowly defeated for reelection.

Clinton's loss of the governorship so early in his political career led to much soul searching and contemplation about how best to pursue a successful political life. The experience was said to have made him more cognizant of the wishes and needs of the voters and less concerned with pursuing his own agenda of political reform. Admitting openly to the voters that he had made lots of mistakes during his first term, Clinton successfully regained the Arkansas governorship in 1982. Repeatedly reelected thereafter, by 1992 he was the longest sitting governor in the country.[1]

Clinton thus was a very well-established political office holder when he and other southern Democrats formed the DLC in 1985. The council was created to help the Democratic Party redefine itself following Republican Ronald Reagan's forty-nine-state defeat of Democrat Walter Mondale in the 1984 presidential election. Clinton and his fellow southerners felt the Democratic Party was losing presidential elections because it had moved too far to the liberal left for the average southern voter. The group hoped to advance more moderate political ideas and more moderate political programs and thereby show the Democratic Party the way back to the White House.[2]

Among those programs and ideas were a strong emphasis on economic growth and outspoken support for the business community. The DLC proposed various plans for helping people work their way off the welfare rolls, and it stressed conventional values such as working hard to achieve success and practicing individual responsibility. It strove to reach beyond both the "left" and the "right" by finding pragmatic, workable, middle-way solutions to the nation's many problems.

One of the most notable achievements of the DLC was the creation, in 1988, of "Super Tuesday," a single day on which large numbers of southern states scheduled their presidential primaries. By having so many southern states hold primaries on the same day, the council hoped, the presidential candidacies of moderate southerners, or moderate candidates who would be appealing to voters in the South, would be advanced.

The DLC had good historical reasons for emphasizing the South as a crucial element in Democratic attempts to win back the United States presidency. The giant bloc of voters that put Franklin D. Roosevelt in the White House in 1932 consisted of two major groups. One group was the large number of working-class Americans, many of them members of minority groups, concentrated in the populous cities of the North and upper Midwest. The other group was White southerners, since the Civil War the most loyal Democratic voters in the nation. This alliance of urban northerners and White southerners was known as the "Roosevelt Coalition."

The major problem facing the Democratic Party in the 1980s, the DLC argued, was that the Republicans were getting the votes of White southerners in presidential elections. In other words, the Republicans were successfully splitting the White South out of the Roosevelt Coalition and thereby winning trip after trip to the White House. For emphasis, the council liked to point out that the last two Democrats elected to the presidency, Lyndon Johnson in 1964 and Jimmy Carter in 1976, were both southerners.

Bill Clinton became chairman of the DLC in 1990. It was a perfect platform from which to identify himself with the move toward moderation in the Democratic Party. When newspaper reporters and television commentators began mentioning Clinton as a possible candidate for the Democratic presidential nomination in 1992, Clinton's close identification with the DLC made his candidacy more believable and respectable.

Most important, close association with the DLC gave a rationale for how Clinton might win the presidency. He would win it by bringing the White South back into the Democratic Party, holding on to the ethnic and minority group Democratic vote in northern and midwestern cities, and thereby reviving the highly successful Roosevelt Coalition of the 1930s.[3]

Presidential elections in the United States begin with a lengthy but unclearly defined period during which would-be candidates for president drop hints to the press and the public that they are thinking of making a race for the White House. Some of these would-be candidates actually do go ahead and officially announce a campaign for the presidency. Others announce, equally officially, that they will not be running. Some even announce they are running but, when the early campaign does not go well or campaign contributions are not forthcoming, withdraw from the race.

This lengthy and ill-defined period of announcements, nonannouncements, and withdrawals begins in the spring and summer of the year before the presidential year. In the case of the 1992 presidential election, it began in the spring and summer of 1991 and lasted until the Iowa caucuses and the New Hampshire primary, the two events that officially begin the presidential caucus and primary season.

During this period the would-be presidential candidates, both announced and unannounced, tour the United States trying to attract audiences and generate news media attention. They give speeches, hold small campaign rallies, appear on local radio and television talk shows, and give interviews to newspaper reporters and sound bites to television news programs. This period of a would-be presidential candidate's campaign is a success only if the news media give the candidate at least some coverage and present him or her to the public in a favorable light.

Because this part of a presidential campaign is so dependent on the amount and type of attention that the news media give the presidential candidates, I call it the "News Media Candidate Evaluation and Promotion Period." Other writers and political commentators have their own names for this neglected but most important portion of the presidential selection process. Rhodes Cook of *Congressional Quarterly* referred to it as "The Exhibition Season."[4] Ross K. Baker of Rutgers University labeled it the "Prehistory" of the nominating process.[5] Whatever it is called, this lengthy period prior to the first primaries and caucuses can have a dramatic effect on who does or does not win a major party nomination for president.

Bill Clinton began the News Media Candidate Evaluation and Promotion Period at the DLC's annual convention in Cleveland, Ohio, in May of 1991. As chairman of the council, Clinton was able to dominate the proceedings and project the moderate image which he and the other DLC members had worked so hard to shape. The DLC convention made it crystal clear to the news media that Bill Clinton was going to be both a southern and a moderate Democratic presidential candidate in 1992.

Over the summer of 1991, a period when President Bush still was getting high favorable ratings in the public opinion polls, three of Clinton's major would-be opponents for the 1992 Democratic nomination announced they would not be running. They were United States House of Representatives Majority Leader Richard A. Gephardt of Missouri, United States Senator John D. "Jay" Rockefeller IV of West Virginia, and United States Senator Albert Gore Jr. of Tennessee. When these three potential candidates from the border states and the South declined to enter the race, Bill Clinton was left as the only White southerner seeking the Democratic nomination.

From the very moment it became known that Bill Clinton was running for president, his campaign was clouded by repeated rumors of marital infidelity. Joined by his wife, Hillary Clinton,[6] at a Washington press breakfast in September of 1991, Clinton confronted these rumors head on. Looking at Hillary Clinton, he said firmly: "We have been together for almost 20 years and we are committed to each other. It has not been perfect or free from problems, but we are committed to each other and that ought to be enough."[7]

Clinton officially announced his candidacy on October 3, 1991. Standing outside the Old State House in the Arkansas capital city of Little Rock, he declared to a crowd of three thousand cheering supporters his intention to run. "We must turn this country around and get it working again," Clinton said. "We've got to fight for middle-class Americans for a change."

Clinton used the phrase "middle class" twelve times in his thirty-two-minute speech.[8] He pledged to avoid the use of political labels in his upcoming campaign for the presidency. "The change I seek, and the change we must all seek, isn't liberal or conservative. . . . Out here, the people don't much care about the labels: left or right or liberal or conservative—all the words that have made our politics a substitute for action."[9] In pledging to eliminate the words "liberal" and "conservative" from his campaign rhetoric, Clinton was steering himself straight down the "moderate" course that had been so skillfully charted for him by the DLC.

Clinton immediately sought to gain credibility on the issues by giving a series of three speeches—on values, economics, and foreign policy. He gave the speeches at Georgetown University, his undergraduate alma mater. In a year of tight news media budgets, he hoped to get more news media attention by delivering the speeches in Washington. Since all the major newspapers and television networks already had reporters and camera operators stationed in the nation's capital, they could cover the Clinton speeches without having to spend much money.

Clinton then moved to secure his credentials with members of the liberal wing of the Democratic Party. At a meeting of the Association of State Democratic Chairs in Chicago in November of 1991, the Clinton campaign managers arranged for Clinton to be asked if he was not "a Republican in Democrat's clothing."[10] Not only did Clinton supporters plant the question, they loaded the meeting with large numbers of Clinton sympathizers. Clinton's response went right to the idea that the Democratic Party was the party of Franklin D. Roosevelt and that Democratic liberals and Democratic moderates needed to reunite to put the party of Franklin D. Roosevelt back into the presidency. Not surprisingly, Clinton's answer drew enthusiastic applause and began the process of making the Clinton candidacy more acceptable to liberal Democratic voters.

By late November of 1991 Clinton's fund-raising was beginning to accelerate. Between mid-November and the end of the year, Clinton raised $2.5 million. His campaign financial officers immediately released an optimistic fund-raising report, forcing rival candidates to release their own reports. The comparisons showed that Clinton was rapidly outdistancing his opponents in terms of money raised, thereby further enhancing the image of Bill Clinton in the eyes of the news media as the campaign front-runner.

The Clinton forces next decided to get some publicity mileage out of the December 15, 1991, Florida Democratic state convention. They built up the idea that it would be a tough fight for Clinton to win the straw poll of Democratic presidential candidates taken at the state convention, downplaying the point that a southern moderate like Clinton should win among Florida Democrats in a walk. Clinton's big victory in the Florida Democratic state convention poll earned him the additional favorable press coverage he sought.

As Bill Clinton built more and more momentum behind his drive for the Democratic nomination, additional powerful would-be opponents decided not to make the race. A possible Black candidate, Jesse Jackson, who had unsuccessfully run for the Democratic nomination in 1984 and 1988, announced in November that he would not be running in 1992. Another Black candidate, Governor L. Douglas Wilder of Virginia, officially announced his candidacy and began to campaign, but he failed to generate much support or financing and soon withdrew. With no Black candidates in the race for the Democratic nomination, Bill Clinton was able to begin bidding for the votes of moderate African Americans, both in the North and the South.

The most celebrated noncandidate of 1992 was Governor Mario Cuomo of New York. A northerner who was popular with ethnic and minority-group voters in the large cities of the Northeast, Cuomo spent ten weeks in November and December of 1991 agonizing over whether or not to run. Because of Cuomo's high name recognition, great fundraising skills, and proven ability as an eloquent public speaker, liberal elements in the Democratic Party strongly suppported his candidacy. Cuomo was particularly attractive to liberal Democratic politicians, and liberal Democratic news reporters, who regarded Bill Clinton and the DLC as too southern and too moderate for their taste.

Mario Cuomo took so long making up his mind, and fretted over the decision so publicly, that the news media became somewhat critical of the whole affair. Dan Rather, the anchorperson on the CBS TV evening news, began referring to Governor Cuomo as "the Hamlet on the Hudson," a sarcastic comparison to Shakespeare's indecisive prince.

Suddenly it was December 20, 1991, the day of the filing deadline for the 1992 New Hampshire primary. Cuomo aides had a chartered airplane waiting at the Albany airport, all set to whisk the New York governor from the New York capital to New Hampshire if he decided to announce his candidacy. A site near the statehouse in the New Hampshire capital of Concord had been selected as the spot for

Cuomo to give his announcement speech. The tension was building minute by minute.

When the New Hampshire filing deadline was just two hours away, Mario Cuomo announced that he would not be a candidate for president in 1992. His official excuse for not running was that New York State faced serious budget problems, therefore he would not have the time to both run for president and fulfill his gubernatorial responsibilities. "It seems to me I cannot turn my attention to New Hampshire," Cuomo told a hastily called news conference at the governor's mansion in Albany, "while this threat hangs over the head of the New Yorkers that I've sworn to put first."[11]

Mario Cuomo's last-minute decision not to run was a big break for Bill Clinton. Cuomo was Clinton's only potential opponent who, like Clinton, had established national stature as a Democratic Party leader. Many news personnel and longtime presidential campaign observers were dissappointed that there was not going to be a showdown in the 1992 Democratic primaries between Mario Cuomo, the darling of the old liberal wing of the Democratic Party, and Bill Clinton, the favorite son of the new moderate wing.

As it turned out, Bill Clinton had only four major opponents running against him in the 1992 Democratic presidential caucuses and primaries. They were United States Senator Tom Harkin of Iowa, former United States Senator Paul Tsongas of Massachusetts, United States Senator Bob Kerrey of Nebraska, and former California governor Jerry Brown. None of them had anywhere near the national stature or the potential vote-getting ability of Mario Cuomo, now nothing more than the Democratic Party's best known noncandidate.

There was no question that Bill Clinton had proven to be the big attention-getter during the News Media Candidate Evaluation and Promotion Period of the 1992 race for the Democratic nomination. Many observers were amazed at how little was required for the news media to declare Clinton the leading candidate. As Susan Feeney of the Washington bureau of the *Dallas Morning News* pointed out: "The press designated Bill Clinton the preprimary and precaucus front-runner on the basis of little more than three speeches at Georgetown, a successful fund-raising effort, and a victory in the Florida straw poll."[12]

As the news media and the public turned their attention to the Iowa caucuses and the New Hampshire primary, all the major national polls showed Clinton leading his four rivals.[13] The only question seemed to be whether any one of those four rivals—Tom Harkin, Paul Tsongas, Bob Kerrey, or Jerry Brown—could seriously challenge Clinton in the primaries and caucuses ahead.

3. Iowa

When it comes to choosing delegates to national party presidential nominating conventions, the fifty states of the United States have essentially two choices. They can hold a presidential primary election—or they can hold party caucuses followed by county and state conventions.

The details of what is done vary greatly from state to state, but in most states with presidential primaries the various candidates run against each other in a spring primary election. Any voter registered in the political party can go to his or her polling place on primary election day and cast a vote for his or her favorite candidate. After the votes are counted, the state's delegates to the party national convention are distributed to the various candidates in the same proportion as the votes received in the presidential primary.

In states that use the caucus system, registered voters in a political party gather at a meeting place in their voting precinct. They organize the meeting, discuss the various candidates for the party nomination for president, and then elect delegates to a county convention who in turn elect delegates to a state convention. The state convention then elects the delegates who attend the political party's national convention.

For years the state of Iowa held precinct caucuses that attracted very little media attention. Then, in 1972, Iowa political leaders scheduled the state's presidential caucuses a couple of weeks or so before the New Hampshire primary. Instantly the Iowa caucuses became the heavily publicized starting point on the presidential primary and caucus calendar.[1]

The brilliant part of this manuever was that Iowa chose to stay with caucuses rather than go to a primary. The state of New Hampshire has a law requiring that the New Hampshire presidential primary be scheduled one week earlier than any other state's presidential primary. By deciding to stick with caucuses, Iowa avoided having New Hampshire schedule its primary a week ahead of Iowa's time slot.

Iowa political leaders also did a good job of creating the kind of precinct caucuses that attract media attention. On a Monday night in late January or early February, Iowa Democrats and Republicans make their way to their separate precinct caucuses, usually held at the local public school or a nearby church hall. The caucus attendees then break up into smaller caucuses supporting particular presidential candidates. An important rule is that, for a presidential candidate to win any delegates at the caucus, he or she must have the support of at least 15 percent of the caucus attendees. Those caucus attendees who initially support a candidate who gets fewer than 15 percent of the caucus attendees can, if they wish, walk across the room and give their support to one of the more popular candidates.

The most important characteristic of the Iowa caucuses, from the point of view of the national press, is that they produce reportable results on election night. The number of delegates won by each presidential candidate in each precinct caucus is immediately reported to the state capital in Des Moines. The results for the entire state are totaled up, and the candidate who wins the largest number of delegates is declared the winner. It is this last fact, that the Iowa caucuses produce both a Democratic and a Republican statewide winner on caucus night, that makes the Iowa caucuses such a big event for the news media.

How big a media event is it? In 1984, all three major television networks broadcast their evening news from Des Moines on Iowa caucuses night. In 1988, ABC News prevailed on Iowa officials to light up the outside of the statehouse so it could serve as an exciting television backdrop as ABC reported the results of the Iowa caucuses to all of America throughout the late evening hours. On that night, forty of the seventy-four trucks in the United States capable of beaming a television signal up to a communications satellite were in use in Des Moines.[2]

The ultimate reason for all this attention and excitement is an elusive commodity nicknamed the "Iowa bounce." Sometimes winning Iowa has enabled relatively unknown candidates to "break out of the pack" of party presidential candidates and go on to win the nomination. On other occasions, Iowa winners have faded in subsequent presidential primaries and quickly disappeared from the race.

The most famous Iowa winner was Jimmy Carter, the relatively unknown former governor of Georgia who, in 1976, spent the better part of a year campaigning in Iowa. His surprise victory in the Iowa caucuses bounced him into the lead for the Democratic nomination and eventually into the White House.[3]

Four years later, in 1980, Iowa gained additional luster when underdog George Bush upset front-runner Ronald Reagan in the Republican caucuses. So much attention was paid to the Iowa caucuses that year that another Republican candidate, Senator Howard H. Baker of Tennessee, branded them the "functional equivalent of a primary." Unfortunately for both Bush and Baker, Reagan triumphed in the New Hampshire primary a few weeks later and went on to win both the Republican nomination and the presidency.[4]

Another Iowa phenomenon was Gary Hart, the 1984 candidate for the Democratic nomination who finished second in the Iowa caucuses but received a surprising 16 percent of the vote. This second-place "Iowa bounce" propelled Hart to another unexpected victory, a first-place finish a week later in New Hampshire. Although Hart eventually lost the nomination to former vice president Walter F. Mondale of Minnesota, the Iowa caucuses were credited with propelling Hart out of obscurity and into the role of a major contender.

By now it should be obvious that winning the Iowa caucuses can be either very important or totally meaningless. In 1988, the two Iowa winners—United States Representative Richard A. Gephardt of Missouri for the Democrats and United States Senator Bob Dole of Kansas for the Republicans—lost in New Hampshire and were soon completely out of the running.

The following rule thus appears to apply to the Iowa caucuses: They are an important stop on the presidential nomination trail, but nowhere near as important a stop as the New Hampshire primary.

In 1992, the Iowa caucuses were over before they ever began. One of Iowa's two United States senators, Tom Harkin, decided to run for the Democratic nomination. Once Harkin was in the race, all the other candidates and the news media acknowledged that Harkin would easily win his home state. The other candidates and the news media therefore decided to skip Iowa, let Harkin have it for free, and concentrate all their attention on New Hampshire.

Many Iowans were saddened by the way having a "favorite son" in the race made the 1992 Iowa Democratic caucuses a foregone conclusion. Over the years the party faithful in Iowa had become accustomed to personally meeting and hearing speeches by the major party presidential candidates as they campaigned in Iowa. "They miss it," said former Iowa Democratic Party Chairman Arthur Davis. "There are a lot of folks who miss it. It was a big highlight in their lives . . . to have presidential candidates around."[5]

Only Tom Harkin bothered to open a campaign headquarters in Iowa and campaign in the state. As interest in the caucuses dropped, Harkin found himself mainly working to get as many Iowa Democrats out to their caucuses as possible. Winning the Iowa caucuses would not give Harkin much of a boost if the turnout was very low.

Tom Harkin was considered a major contender for the 1992 Democratic nomination for president. The tough-talking son of a coal miner, the fifty-one-year-old Harkin described himself as a prairie populist who sought to represent the "have-nots" against the "haves." He was the one Democratic contender in the 1992 race who campaigned as a traditional hard-core liberal.

"This is a fight between Wall Street and Main Street," Harkin said when he announced his candidacy on September 15, 1991. "It's a straight economic populist campaign."[6]

Tom Harkin grew up in Cumming, a small Iowa town near Des Moines. Cumming is so small it is only seven blocks long and two blocks wide. It has a population of under two hundred. Harkin spent his youth in relative poverty. As one close associate pointed out: "Inside there's a very angry small-town kid who saw firsthand what poverty can do to you if you don't have the government as a last resort on your side."[7]

Harkin first made national news in 1970 when, working as a congressional aide, he released photographs of the South Vietnamese government mistreating political prisoners. The United States was fighting the Vietnam War at that time, and Harkin's actions were regarded by a number of observers as harming the war effort.

Returning to Iowa, Harkin soon was elected to the United States House of Representatives on the Democratic ticket. He continued to play the role of the critical outsider, however. In 1977 he led a successful drive to get the World Bank to stop lending money to countries that violated human rights. In 1980 he strongly attacked Democratic President Jimmy Carter for putting an embargo on Iowa grain bound for sale in the Soviet Union. Carter had stopped the grain shipments in response to the Soviet invasion of Afghanistan.

In 1984 Harkin was elected to the United States Senate. When he was reelected in 1990, he became the first Iowa Democrat ever to win two consecutive terms in the Senate.

As a senator, Harkin was as feisty and combative as ever. In January of 1991 he strongly opposed United States involvement in the Persian Gulf War. In order to dramatize his position, he tried to compel a vote on using force in the Persian Gulf before Democratic Senate leaders wanted one. As might be expected, an activist and outspoken liberal such as Harkin was not especially popular with his Senate colleagues.

A former aide to Harkin, who asked not to be identified, gave this somewhat unfavorable view of the Harkin approach to politics: "It's moral outrage combined with personal and political opportunism."[8]

With the United States economy showing obvious signs of weakness in late 1991, Harkin offered himself to the American people as an unapologetic liberal Democrat. He called for a "new New Deal" of government spending programs to quickly end the economic recession. His platform proposed a "new growth agenda" of government investment in roads, bridges, mass transit, medical research, and schools. It provided for paying for all that by cutting $150 billion in foreign military aid. Harkin opposed cutting taxes for business or the middle class, arguing that the money was badly needed for public investments.

As did all the Democratic candidates in 1992, Harkin attacked President Bush for failing to maintain a strong economy. He pledged to toss the "trickle down economics" of the Reagan-Bush years "on the trash heap of history." One time, surrounded by cheering supporters wearing "Give 'em hell, Harkin" T-shirts, he exclaimed: "I'm here to tell you that George Herbert Walker Bush has feet of clay, and I intend to take a hammer to them."[9]

To no one's surprise, Tom Harkin easily won the Iowa Democratic caucuses in 1992. There was no "bounce," however, because none of the other Democratic candidates campaigned in the state. A newspaper cartoon made perhaps the best comment on what happens when a hometown candidate runs in a key caucus or primary and all the other candidates stay out. The cartoon portrayed the Iowa caucuses as if they were the Iowa State Fair. Harkin was pictured finishing first. An Iowa cow finished second, and a pie-baking Iowa grandmother third. Harkin was saying dejectedly and sarcastically: "This is just what I need to propel me into the White House!"[10]

There was no Republican contest in the Iowa caucuses in 1992. Conservative newspaper columnist Patrick Buchanan got into the race too late to run in Iowa. President Bush won Iowa unopposed. Buchanan made it clear he would be making his major effort against Bush eight days later—in the New Hampshire primary.

4. NEW HAMPSHIRE

Way back in 1913 the New Hampshire state legislature enacted a presidential primary law and set the date for the election in the middle of May. Two years later, in 1915, it was decided to save money by holding the presidential primary on the same day as Town Meeting Day, when town officials were elected. Town Meeting Day was scheduled for early March so that voters could get to the polls before the spring thaw made backwoods New Hampshire roads impassable. It thus was a combination of New England frugality and muddy roads that gave New Hampshire its unique historical tradition of holding the nation's first presidential primary.[1]

From 1916 to 1952 the New Hampshire primary attracted little or no attention due to the fact that Granite State citizens voted for delegates to the national conventions rather than for the presidential candidates themselves. Things changed in 1949 when Sherman Adams, the Republican governor of New Hampshire, went looking for a way to boost the candidacy of World War II military hero Dwight D. Eisenhower for the 1952 Republican nomination for president.[2]

Governor Adams decided on having New Hampshirites vote directly for the presidential candidate of their choice rather than for convention delegates. He believed Eisenhower would easily win such an early "beauty contest." Adams prevailed on the New Hampshire state legislature to adopt this presidential-preference form of primary, for both the Republican and the Democratic parties, and the Granite

State has gained fame as the crucial "First in the Nation" presidential primary ever since.

Incidentally, Sherman Adams's strategy worked. General "Ike" Eisenhower won the 1952 New Hampshire Republican primary. The early victory gave the Eisenhower campaign the boost it needed, and Ike went on to win both the 1952 Republican nomination and the fall general election.

Over the ensuing years it became obvious that New Hampshire's early primary was having a major impact on who eventually received the Democratic and Republican party nominations for president. The boost that came from winning New Hampshire strongly influenced voters in other states, particularly states that held caucuses and primaries in the first three or four weeks after the New Hampshire voting.[3] Candidates for president, particularly little-known ones, began campaigning early in New Hampshire and spent lots of extra time there, hoping that a New Hampshire victory would produce enough momentum, or "Big Mo," to get them all the way to the nomination.[4]

The more emphasis presidential candidates placed on New Hampshire, the more the "First in the Nation" presidential primary benefited the Granite State, both economically and politically. The campaigning candidates were soon joined by large groups of news media personnel. Hotels, motels, restaurants, bus companies, and rental car companies all found themselves making extra money every four years servicing the candidates and their news media camp followers. New Hampshire's scenic mountains and picturesque villages became the backdrop for the various primary campaigns, thereby enhancing New Hampshire's image throughout the nation and the world as a beautiful place to visit.

New Hampshire state legislators became so entranced with the benefits of holding the first presidential primary that they passed that famous law requiring that New Hampshire's primary be one week before any other state's primary.[5]

Because the New Hampshire primary is such a critical part of the nominating process, its very existence inspires large numbers of New England politicians to run for president. New Hampshirites are more likely to vote for someone from a nearby state, so the logic goes, and this encourages New England political leaders to undertake a presidential campaign when they otherwise might not do so. A case in point was Michael Dukakis, governor of the immediately adjoining state of Massachusetts, who in 1988 entered the New Hampshire primary, easily won it, and went on to get the Democratic nomination for president. In the general election, Dukakis lost to George Bush, another native New Englander (from Connecticut), who also won his New Hampshire primary that year.

In 1992, the man who stood to gain the most from the "First in the Nation" New Hampshire primary was former United States Senator Paul Tsongas of Massachusetts. Tsongas's home was in Lowell, Massachusetts, a city located just seventeen miles from the Massachusetts-New Hampshire border. Tsongas could sleep in his own bed at home every night, thereby saving thousands of dollars in hotel and motel expenses, yet make the short drive north to New Hampshire each day and spend the entire day campaigning in the Granite State.

This proximity to the state with the first presidential primary gave Tsongas a tremendous geographical and financial advantage over the other 1992 candidates for the Democratic nomination, all of whom were from states far distant from New Hampshire. Tsongas's opponents had to rent expensive hotel and motel rooms for themselves and their staffs when campaigning in New Hampshire.

Being from Massachusetts gave Paul Tsongas another big advantage in the 1992 New Hampshire Democratic primary. Most of the population of New Hampshire lives in southern New Hampshire, much of which is immediately adjacent to the Boston metropolitan area. As a result, many New Hampshire citizens regularly read Boston-area newspapers and watch Boston-area television news. Because Paul Tsongas was a former United States senator from Massachusetts, many New Hampshire citizens already knew about him because they had followed his political career in the Boston-area news media.

Thus thousands of New Hampshire residents already knew the tragic yet inspiring story of how Paul Tsongas, at the end of a distinguished first term in the United States Senate, declined to run for reelection because he was suffering from lymph cancer. Given less than ten years to live, his life was saved in 1986 by a then-experimental treatment. Following a series of exhaustive medical checkups, his doctors declared him free of the disease.

Tsongas wanted his narrow escape from death to mean something. He therefore decided to run for president and, in the course of the campaign, raise tough issues that none of the other candidates were courageous enough to discuss. To Paul Tsongas, the big issue in 1992 was whether the United States would be able to compete with other nations in a newly-emerging global economy. The United States would not be able to keep up, Tsongas argued, unless government and business joined together in an all-out drive to modernize the country's manufacturing facilities.

"You can't really understand Paul Tsongas until you drive down to Lowell and see what he did down there." The man who made this observation was a New Hampshirite at a Tsongas rally in Nashua, the New Hampshire city closest to Lowell. He and his wife had been following Tsongas's career for years. Only in Lowell, they said, could one find the answer to why Tsongas was so concerned about economic competitiveness.

Lowell is a typical nineteenth-century New England mill city. In the early 1800s, private entrepreneurs in Lowell dammed the Merrimack River and diverted the falling water through large turbines. The power of the spinning turbines was carried by an elaborate system of drive shafts, gears, and rubber belts throughout giant red brick factory buildings. The power then was used to run automatic spinning machines and automatic looms that soon made Lowell one of the great textile manufacturing centers of the United States.

Lowell not only manufactured and exported its textiles, but it soon began manufacturing and exporting the spinning machines and power looms that made the textiles. This business was profitable at first, but then other cities in New England and the Midwest began using their Lowell-built machines to manufacture and export their own textiles. By the early twentieth century the economy in Lowell had gone into sharp decline, and Lowell's business leaders were either unwilling or unable to modernize their aging factory buildings and manufacturing equipment to keep competitive.

As a youthful member of the United States Congress, Paul Tsongas set out to revive his hometown. Emphasizing private enterprise as well as government programs, he convinced Lowell property owners to invest in their falling-down factory buildings and recycle them as residential and office condominiums. For the United States government's part of the job, Tsongas had the National Park Service declare downtown Lowell the first "national industrial park."

A number of typical red brick mill buildings were restored, complete with the spinning water turbines and drive shafts and gears, and used to show tourists how a typical New England textile mill operated. Stylish shops and fashionable restaurants soon opened to serve the large tourist trade that began coming to downtown Lowell. A quaint trolley car, running on its own rails, was used to haul visitors from tourist site to tourist site in the city.

As the grimy, collapsing mill buildings were turned into upscale riverside condominiums, Paul Tsongas became famous as the man who helped Lowell become "the city that rose from the dead." By 1992, however, Tsongas could see that the entire United States was beginning to suffer from the same industrial obsolescence that had wrecked the economy in his hometown. So Paul Tsongas, the man who rebuilt a dying city, set out to rebuild the nation's troubled economy. He felt the United States, like Lowell, could only be as strong as its manufacturing foundation.[6]

Despite the close proximity of his Massachusetts home to New Hampshire, Paul Tsongas was viewed by the press as the longest of long shots for winning the 1992 New Hampshire primary. The early favorite of the news media was Arkansas governor Bill Clinton, who clearly had won the precaucus, preprimary portion of the campaign. Three weeks before New Hampshire's primary day, however, the Clinton campaign stumbled—and stumbled badly.

Gennifer Flowers, an acquaintance of Bill Clinton's in Little Rock, charged in a paid interview in a supermarket tabloid newspaper that she had had a twelve-year affair with the Arkansas governor. Her accusation was supported by tapes of telephone conversations between herself and Bill Clinton that could be interpreted as indicating she and Clinton had something to hide. Clinton immediately and vehemently denied the charge of a twelve-year affair.

Media coverage of Gennifer Flowers's accusation of marital infidelity was so extensive that Clinton felt he must answer publicly.[7] He asked for and received ten minutes of time on the Sunday evening CBS television news magazine, *60 Minutes*. Clinton was joined by his wife, Hillary Clinton, as he answered a series of questions from reporter Steve Kroft.

Clinton took the general position that questions about the stability of his marriage and rumors of possible marital infidelity were irrelevant to his ability to be a good president. "I have acknowledged wrongdoing. I have acknowledged causing pain in my marriage," Clinton told the *60 Minutes* audience. He described his relationship with Gennifer Flowers as "very limited."

At that point Hillary Clinton stated that she and her husband would not be more specific about the accusation. "I don't think being any more specific about what's happening in the privacy of our life together is relevant to anybody besides us," she said. "We're proud of our marriage, we've kept it going, and we hope that's what we can convey to the American people."

Bill Clinton argued that the majority of *60 Minutes* viewers would understand his and his wife's position. He concluded: "I think most Americans who are watching this tonight, they'll know what we're saying, they'll get it, and they'll feel we have been . . . candid."[8]

Before the New Hampshire Democratic electorate had much time to absorb these marital infidelity charges, the *Wall Street Journal* printed a story charging that Clinton used unusual means to avoid being drafted into military service at the time of the Vietnam War. Apparently Clinton received a draft deferment for promising to join the Reserve Officers' Training Corps (ROTC) at the University of Arkansas. Shortly thereafter, however, Clinton decided not to join the ROTC unit, but the deferment he was given protected him from being drafted for two crucial months.[9]

The immediate result of both the marital infidelity charge and the draft dodging charge was that Bill Clinton quickly sagged in the New Hampshire public opinion polls. As Clinton's fortunes rapidly waned, those of Paul Tsongas steadily increased. By one week before the New Hampshire presidential primary election, Tsongas was running a strong first in the polls with Clinton coming in a weak second.

Tsongas did everything in his power to exploit his newfound lead over Clinton. At a particularly memorable news conference, Tsongas showed up with a child's toy—a stuffed panda bear. This is a "Pander Bear," Tsongas told the assembled news personnel, and it symbolizes the way Clinton "panders" to the voters by promising almost every conceivable government program ever thought of. Instead of promising things to voters, Tsongas concluded, a responsible candidate for president would be telling them they were going to have to work harder and sacrifice more to keep up with international competition.

Tsongas's "Pander Bear" tactic worked. Newspapers throughout the country carried a photograph of him holding the panda bear on his lap and talking about Bill Clinton's "Pander Bear" ways.

As the day of the New Hampshire primary drew ever closer, more and more news reporters and political commentators began to arrive in the Granite State. The week before election day, on one airplane winging its way from Chicago to Manchester, the largest city in New Hampshire, the upper storage bins on the plane were almost completely filled with the large television camcorders and tripods used by TV news personnel. As a result, most of the passengers had to ride with their hand luggage stuffed under the seat in front of them, where it uncomfortably reduced the available leg room.

One camera crew on the plane was from Davenport, Iowa. They were heading to New Hampshire to cover Iowa's favorite son, United States Senator Tom Harkin, in his bid for the Democratic nomination for president. Across the aisle from them, a similar crew from Little Rock, Arkansas, was preparing to trail Arkansas governor Bill Clinton in the final stretch before New Hampshire's "primary day." Many of the media were from places far from New Hampshire. One crew was from Dublin, Ireland. Another was from Osaka, Japan.

On the main road leading away from the Manchester airport, there were immediate signs that an election was going on—roadside signs. The two-foot-by-one-foot cardboard signs were stapled to a pointed wooden stick and driven into the ground at the edge of the road. In most cases the signs were in the front yards or attached to the mailbox mounts of people whose homes were located on the main road. Occasionally, however, overzealous supporters of various candidates erected the signs on public property along the edge of the highway or on empty building lots. Since such signs are often placed in the middle of a homeowner's front lawn, they are often referred to as "lawn signs."

Clearly, Republican challenger Pat Buchanan was winning the Republican battle of the lawn signs in New Hampshire in 1992. Particularly in the Manchester area, Buchanan signs were almost everywhere. Incumbent Republican president George Bush had his share of roadside signs, but Bush signs were more likely to be found on the spacious and well-tended lawns of large and expensive homes located in the Manchester suburbs and the outlying small towns. It was further proof that the most loyal Republican voter is the upscale, upper-income voter.

For the Democrats, Paul Tsongas of Massachusetts and Bill Clinton of Arkansas both had plenty of lawn signs on display. There were some Tom Harkin and Bob Kerrey signs as well. There were no roadside signs at all for former California governor Jerry Brown. Limited finances prevented the Brown campaign from having much of the customary campaign paraphernalia, such as campaign brochures, large numbers of roadside signs, lapel pins, and so forth.

New Hampshirites appeared to be perfectly adjusted to being the center of national and international media attention. In a picturesque village about thirty miles west of Manchester, the high school had one of those signs that usually says "Friday, 7:30 P.M., Grizzlies vs. Wildcats." This particular weekend it nonchalantly read "Saturday, 10 A.M., President Bush."

Anyone attending a Bush rally found much more than President Bush. A particularly notable rally in Derry included a thirty-minute baton twirling demonstration by thirty or more junior high school students that could only be described as spectacular. C-SPAN, the national cable channel that covers only politics, carried the baton-twirling demonstration live in its entirety.

Then there was Arnold Schwarzenegger, star of the film *Terminator II*, warming up the audience for the President. *Terminator II* was a science-fiction adventure film that still was playing to large movie theater audiences throughout the nation. Using a famous line from the film, Schwarzenegger would look knowingly at the audience and then shout, "Pat Buchanan! Hasta la vista, Baby!" In the film, the actor had used the line when he attempted to kill a particularly relentless alien invader.

Although an obvious ploy for media attention, Schwarzenegger's theatrics worked. The major networks all put the movie star on their evening newscasts, unanimously choosing "Pat Buchanan! Hasta la vista, Baby!" for live quotation.

The final weekend before primary day, a walk or drive down any major street in any major New Hampshire city was likely to produce a campaigning presidential candidate. Anyone who was in Nashua, New Hampshire, on the Sunday morning before the election soon became aware that President Bush was in town attending local church services. Both sides of the street in front of the church were filled with a permanent army of protesters who were following the President everywhere he campaigned in New Hampshire. One could name almost anything anyone might want to complain about and then find a Bush protester holding up and waving the appropriate sign. Were supporters of Croatian independence being killed by Serbian troops in what used to be Yugoslavia? Clearly it was President Bush's fault, or at least that was what one group of protesters seemed to think. Child pornography was another evil being blamed on the President, along with a sagging national economy and too much spending for military defense. Wherever the President went, his permanent retinue of protesters was ever with him—or at least standing and yelling and signwaving in a street or park nearby.

Democratic contender Bill Clinton was traveling first class. The Clinton campaign had a great deal of money to spend, and the Clinton campaign managers knew how to spend it well. There were two Clinton campaign headquarters in Manchester, one downtown for the news media and a second one, in a white house west of town, for door-to-door campaigning. The Sunday before election day, two big buses pulled up at the westside headquarters and began disgorging college students who had been recruited from nearby colleges and universities. Each student was given a precinct list with the names of all the registered Democrats in a particular neighborhood. They also were loaded down with as many short videos about Bill Clinton as they could possibly carry.

The instructions were to *not* ring the doorbell of the intended video recipient. Ringing the doorbell, the youthful volunteers were told, wastes time and gives the recipients the opportunity to refuse to accept the video. The video was to be left between the screen door and the front door, thus guaranteeing that the voters in the household would find the video and, it was hoped, watch it. There appeared to be no concern whatsoever that some of the homes receiving the video might not have a VCR on which to play the video.

In the Clinton camp, there seemed to be a virtually endless supply of both videos and college students to deliver them. Dropping Clinton videos at the front door the way other candidates drop a campaign brochure or flyer suggested the Clinton campaign was about as well-financed as a campaign can get.

(A disturbing result of such practice is this: Campaign innovations in one presidential election tend to become standard operating procedure in the next election four years later. In 1996, all the candidates will have to do "video drops" in order to keep up, which means they will have to raise even more money and make even more promises to various interest groups to get the money.)

Republican challenger Pat Buchanan was a fun candidate to follow around on the campaign trail in New Hampshire in 1992. Operating on a tight financial budget, Buchanan emphasized the idea of the "porta-crowd." Buchanan and a group of avid supporters rode around New Hampshire on a bus. At selected towns and shopping centers along the way, the bus stopped and Buchanan and his band walked down the street, looking for New Hampshirites who wanted to meet and talk with the candidate.

Once a voter or a group of voters was found, the porta-crowd gathered closely around as Buchanan laid his message out one more time. The image that played on television was one of Buchanan talking, the voter listening, and the adoring porta-crowd taking it all in. The camera did not show, or rarely showed, that the porta-crowd was made up of only about twenty people who did not live in that particular town.

The porta-crowd technique was effective as well as inexpensive. For the price of one rented bus and driver, Buchanan could make a supporter-surrounded appearance in town after town without having to go to the time and expense of turning out a crowd of local supporters in each town.

Pat Buchanan had another wrinkle working in his campaign. A small microphone connected to a small radio transmitter was permanently attached to Buchanan's necktie. All the television and radio people covering Buchanan were equipped with radio receivers that enabled them to hear and record every word Pat said. A television camera operator could be 150 feet from Buchanan, get the visual shot, and still pick up what Buchanan had to say. The total focus was on the man and his words, not the crowd noise and crowd enthusiasm that was being emphasized in better-financed rival campaigns.

More than most of the other candidates, Buchanan proved to be very skillful at giving the kind of short, pithy answers to questions that made the evening news. Asked by one citizen to react to Bush's internationalist and interventionist foreign policy program, the New World Order, Buchanan thought for a moment and then mockingly intoned, "It's *globaloney!*"

The crowd told a great deal about the candidates. Iowa Senator Tom Harkin staged a Sunday-night-before-election-day rally in an old brick Manchester textile mill that was being recycled as an extension campus of the University of New Hampshire. Right on cue, just as the rally began, two buses pulled up and out stepped more than 100 members of a local AFL-CIO labor union. To make sure onlookers and the media got the message, all were dressed in the same blue and gold United Auto Workers union jacket. ABC television news had a camcorder crew at the rally. Both Harkin and the crowd of union members "made the tape."

Former Massachusetts Senator Paul Tsongas had the best crowd gimmick. Since his home—and home constituency—were located just a few miles over the southern border of New Hampshire in Lowell, Massachusetts, it was very easy for his many Massachusetts supporters to cross the state line and swell the crowds at Tsongas rallies in New Hampshire.

Every Tsongas rally was the same. At one end of the room was a raised platform loaded with television cameras and news reporters. At the other end was the platform on which members of Tsongas's family would appear, often joined by important local New Hampshire political leaders supporting Tsongas, and from which Tsongas would give a short speech. The area between the two platforms was filled with supporters, most of whom had been provided with Tsongas signs and banners to wave. The television cameras thus could shoot the adoring crowd, the waving signs, and the candidate, thereby catching the appropriate "crowd going wild" atmosphere. Tsongas had a paid staff member, a young woman from Los Angeles who knew a great deal about television and very little about Paul Tsongas, to see that the television crews and news reporters got everything they wanted.

Tsongas was running what might best be described as a "message" campaign. Every time he spoke he showed the audience a book he had written which purported to correctly diagnose the ills of the United States economy and proposed a series of wide-ranging economic reforms. Entitled *A Call to Economic Arms*, a copy of the book was given to anyone who showed the least bit of interest in the Tsongas campaign. Everyone in the Tsongas organization mentioned and referred to the book, although it was very difficult to find anyone, even committed Tsongas supporters, who had read the book and could succinctly summarize its main ideas.

Despite that, the idea got across to the media and the public that Tsongas was a thoughtful person with definite ideas about what he would do if elected president. At a well-attended rally in Nashua the day before election day, Tsongas looked committedly at his audience, cited recent public opinion polls showing that he was leading in the New Hampshire Democratic presidential primary, and said: "The message is—the message counts!" The audience seemed to know what the "message" was. It went wild with enthusiastic cheers.

As had Pat Buchanan, former California governor Jerry Brown had perfected the art of low-cost presidential campaigning. Essentially, he went from college campus to college campus, using his appeal to young adults to gather the seemingly adoring crowds that are required to get a candidate on the evening news. Brown was an impressive speaker who received authentic adulation and support from his young audiences. An observer who was not seeing Brown constantly described in the news media as "Governor Moonbeam" would have found Brown to be a believable candidate for president.

The center of action in the New Hampshire presidential primary is Elm Street in downtown Manchester. The weekend before election day, roving bands of supporters for the various presidential candidates were walking up and down Elm Street "waving corners." To wave a corner is to stand at the corner of a busy intersection and wave a sign for your candidate at passing motorists. The technique is thought to be particularly effective with motorists who are stopped at a red light. They essentially have nothing to do for up to a minute of time, and they will spend these otherwise wasted seconds watching the antics of the corner wavers and, in the process, see the candidate's name.

Motorcades for the various candidates also become part of the Elm Street scene just before primary day. A particularly noticeable motorcade was organized in behalf of Ralph Nader, a well-known consumer advocate of the 1960s who was a write-in candidate for the Democratic nomination in Hew Hampshire in 1992. Each car in the motorcade was a tan-colored compact with an enlarged wooden pencil mounted horizontally, front to back, on the roof. Emblazoned on both sides of the pencil were the words, "Write in Ralph Nader!" For more than an hour on a cloudy Sunday afternoon, the Nader motorcade, ten to twenty vehicles long, drove and honked its way up and down Elm Street.

On the west side of Elm Street stands the high-rise downtown Manchester Holiday Inn. During the week before the primary election, the south end of the parking lot was filled with television equipment trucks with dish-shaped antennae on the roof. These antennae connected the sights and sounds of the New Hampshire primary to communications satellites, which in turn beamed the visual images and the oral statements of the candidates and the political analysts to radio and television broadcasting facilities all over the planet.

Inside the Holiday Inn, in a large open area behind the hotel lobby and the various conference and meeting rooms, NBC News maintained its main communications center. Here editors looked at live camera shots and reviewed camcorder tapes of what the candidates had been doing and saying at various locations throughout New Hampshire on that particular day or evening. Here, for NBC News, a most important process was well under way. Editors were beginning to decide which candidates, which campaign events, which shots of cheering crowds or admiring porta-crowds, and which tidbits of political interpretation and analysis would actually be included in a television or radio newscast. A small part of the filtering process, that crucial but little understood process by which a relatively small number of news editors determine exactly what millions of people will see or hear that particular day, was taking place in that room.

Even more impressive were the operations of Cable News Network (CNN). The cable news giant considered the New Hampshire primary so important that it moved its anchor desk and anchorpersons from Atlanta, Georgia, to Manchester in an effort to provide total on-the-spot coverage. The CNN operation was so large that it occupied two entire floors of a large high-rise office building located on Elm Street several blocks north of the Holiday Inn. CNN subscribers throughout the planet could tune in at any hour of the day and soon get a complete and detailed report on what was happening in New Hampshire.

In addition, CNN was using its satellite transmission system to allow reporters from affiliated stations to beam personal reports back to their home stations throughout the United States. A television camera had been set up and pointed at a high stool in one of the rooms in the high-rise office building overlooking Elm Street and downtown Manchester. Day or night, the Elm Street background made it clear to faraway hometown audiences that their hometown reporter really was "on the scene" in Manchester.

The reporters all stood in a line waiting for their brief period on the satellite. As the previous reporter was speaking to his or her folks back home, the next reporter in line was being wired with a micro-phone and an earplug. When the previous reporter finished his or her spot, the next reporter stepped before the camera, sat down on the stool, and plugged his or her microphone and earphones into the audio sys-tem. Suddenly the voice of the hometown news director was coming out of the earplug, setting up the spot. "You're on in thirty seconds," the camera operator would say, and in exactly that time the hometown news anchorperson would begin talking to the reporter, even though that anchorperson could be as far as three thousand miles away.

In most cases, the hometown reporters analyzed what was going on in New Hampshire in terms that would interest their particular hometown audience. This was especially true when one of the candi-dates was from that particular state or if the hometown state had an upcoming presidential primary.

Once the spot was over, the reporter would quickly disconnect his or her audio equipment and give up the stool and the camera to the next reporter. The microphone and earplug were removed while the next reporter was on the satellite. The entire process went on for hours, each hometown reporter assigned exactly three minutes of satel-lite time to talk to the audience back home. The process perfectly sym-bolized the extent to which the media and media coverage are the driv-ing forces in the presidential primary and caucus system.

On election night, the ballroom at the downtown Manchester Hol-iday Inn became "George Bush for President" headquarters. An inter-esting feature was a small platform erected immediately in front of the platform with the television cameras. Particular individuals, such as leading New Hampshire Republicans and well-known political observers, could be brought up to this platform and interviewed per-sonally by the television reporters with all of the television cameras having a tight close-up shot.

In addition to all the television cameras, the "George Bush for President" ballroom was equipped with two cash bars, a small musical group playing a never-ending medley of well-known songs, and four or five television sets scattered throughout the room. Those who wished to do so could stand near one of the television sets, all of which were car-rying network coverage of the New Hampshire primary results, and compare what Bush supporters were saying live in the room with what the network reporters and analysts were saying over the airwaves.

As election night got underway, the ballroom began to fill with exactly what one would have expected—well-dressed Republican men in suits and ties and equally well-dressed Republican women in dresses, pants suits, and, occasionally, expensive jewelry. The general atmosphere was one of an upscale cocktail party at which people were more interested in talking to each other in small groups than in standing and listening to speeches and the reporting of election results. Cheering and sign waving were present but subdued.

At one point during the evening the musical combo began playing "Happy Days Are Here Again." This would not have been notable except for the fact that "Happy Days Are Here Again" is the national theme song of the Democratic Party. Was the person who chose the musical selections for the evening a Democrat who decided to play a not-too-subtle joke on his or her Republican customers? Or was the musical combo merely playing its standard repertoire and too politically naive to know that "Happy Days Are Here Again" is not a good choice for a Republican shindig? Whatever was going on, the Republicans at the Bush for President election-night party were either too engaged in their private conversations to notice this musical boo-boo or were too polite to even remark on it, let alone do anything about it.

New Hampshire governor Judd Gregg, a Republican, was the master of ceremonies. With unfailing enthusiasm, he began reporting from the speaker's platform that incumbent President George Bush was getting about 56 percent of the Republican vote in New Hampshire and challenger Pat Buchanan was getting only 44 percent. Governor Gregg and other Republican speakers interpreted this as a big win for President Bush, noting that, traditionally, a win of 55 percent or more is considered a landslide, almost a blowout. Later in the evening Judd Gregg began reading a long list of New Hampshire towns that had voted strongly for Bush over Buchanan, some of them by as much as a two-to-one margin. With the reading of each town's name and the Bush margin of victory, the Bush Republicans in the packed ballroom smiled and applauded as if it were a truly successful evening.

To anyone who was watching the televison sets in the ballroom, however, there seemed to be two different elections under discussion. The networks were interpreting Buchanan's 44 percent of the vote as a victory for Buchanan. Anchorpersons and analysts alike knowingly suggested that President Bush was in big trouble. Buchanan had been saying all along that, if he received 40 percent or more of the Republican vote in New Hampshire, he would consider it a victory. The networks clearly were buying the Buchanan spin that 40 percent or more for Buchanan was a Buchanan victory. They were not buying the Bush spin that 55 percent or more for Bush was a Bush landslide.

To their credit, the networks had done some impressive homework. They presented statistics that suggested that incumbent presidents can win the New Hampshire primary but, if they do not win by

60 percent or more of the vote, they are likely to lose the general election in November. The best case in point was Republican President Gerald Ford, who narrowly won the Republican primary in New Hampshire in 1976 and then lost the general election to Democrat Jimmy Carter the following November.

Did George Bush or Pat Buchanan win the 1992 New Hampshire Republican presidential primary? In the end, the news media decide who wins or loses presidential primaries, no matter what the actual mathematical results. Both the candidates and the press play what is called the "expectations game." A particular candidate starts spinning the idea that getting above a certain percentage of the vote will be a victory. If the news media buy that particular spin, and they often do, then the candidate who exceeds the expected percentage of the vote can characterize himself or herself as a "winner" despite the fact that he or she may have fewer votes than some other candidate. In the final analysis, primary election results mean what the news media say they mean.

The day after election day, a number of news sources found a way to make Bush's showing in New Hampshire appear even weaker. There had been several fringe candidates on the Republican ballot in addition to Bush and Buchanan, and they had drawn a small but statistically significant number of votes. In addition, many New Hampshire Republicans had chosen to write in the name of a candidate rather than support one of the candidates on the official ballot. Taking all these votes into consideration, Bush had received only 53 percent of the vote. The end result was a number of Wednesday morning newspaper headlines saying that "47 percent of New Hampshire Republicans do not support President Bush."[10] Less notice was taken of the fact that, with fringe candidate and write-in votes counted, Pat Buchanan's vote total dropped from that "magical" 44 percent to only 37 percent, three points less than the 40 percent Buchanan said would constitute a "victory."

The Democratic candidates all had victory celebrations too. They were held at various places in the Manchester area—a downtown hotel, a bar and restaurant just outside the city limits, and elsewhere. All were similar in that there was a cash bar, either one big-screen television or a series of regular-size televisions on which to watch the results come in, and a place where television cameras could be set up to interview the candidate as he either claimed victory or acknowledged defeat. Television is the most important guest at these celebrations, both for receiving information about how the election is going and for sending out information about how the candidate and his or her campaign personnel interpret the results.

Exactly as the polls had predicted, Paul Tsongas from nearby Lowell, Massachusetts, won the 1992 New Hampshire Democratic primary. Instantly the little-known ex-senator became a major candidate for the 1992 Democratic nomination for president. According to historical tradition, if the Democrats were going to win the presidency in 1992, it would have to be with Paul Tsongas. Since 1952, the first year the New Hampshire primary was held, no candidate of either party had been elected president of the United States without first winning the New Hampshire primary.

But many news reporters and news analysts were quick to point out that the Tsongas victory was not as sweet as it might have been. In the first place, Tsongas had not done as well in the actual voting as the pre-election polls had said he was going to do. He finished first in the primary voting, but not by the expected margins. More importantly, Bill Clinton, who finished second, did much better in the actual voting than the polls had predicted. The result was a final impression that the Tsongas campaign was sagging while the Clinton campaign was gaining momentum.

Tsongas's victory in New Hampshire also was diminished by the fact that early returns showed Pat Buchanan getting more than 40 percent of the vote in the Republican primary. The attention which Buchanan received for his surprise showing in New Hampshire took attention away from Tsongas's Democratic win. If Bush had had little or no opposition in New Hampshire, Tsongas's victory over Bill Clinton would have been the top story of the election. As it was, Tsongas had to share the main media spotlight in New Hampshire with Pat Buchanan. The front page of the *Boston Herald* was typical. The major headline, in large bold type, screamed: "Bush whacked!" A much smaller headline said: "Tsongas defeats Clinton."[11]

Winning New Hampshire did give the Tsongas campaign the surge in national interest and attention that Tsongas was hoping for. Proximity to New Hampshire had been turned into victory in New Hampshire and made the Tsongas candidacy important and believable. Suddenly Paul Tsongas was deluged with requests for news interviews and became a most desired guest on radio and television news analysis and discussion programs. Tsongas received exactly the "media rush" that one would expect for winning the "First-in-the-Nation" New Hampshire Democratic primary.

Over in the Clinton camp, the Clinton spin doctors were hard at work making it appear that their man was a winner too. Because he finished second and did much better than the polls had predicted, Bill Clinton described himself to the news media as the "comeback kid."[12]

Clinton even worked at turning his recent problems with charges of marital infidelity and draft avoidance into assets. He noted that he took a severe beating from the press and still finished a strong second in New Hampshire. As for Paul Tsongas, Clinton dismissed the Massachusetts ex-senator as a regional candidate who only had appeal in New England and who would quickly fade when the primary election calendar shifted to the West and the South.

Tsongas campaign workers were irate at the extent to which the national press played up Clinton's second-place finish in New Hampshire and thereby minimized the impact of Tsongas's victory. "All you had to do was look at the *New York Times*," said Noel Eisenberg, a Tsongas staffer. "Bill Clinton was quoted in the second paragraph of the *Times*'s morning-after-election-day story and given a small headline, 'Clinton Looks Ahead.' The reader was forced to read through 34 paragraphs of copy and turn to page A16 to get to the first quotation attributed to Paul Tsongas from the night before. That to me represents blatant press favoritism."[13]

Tom Harkin, Bob Kerrey, and Jerry Brown were weak also-rans in the 1992 New Hampshire Democratic primary. None of the three received a substantial proportion of the vote, therefore all three received minimal media attention on election night. As far as most of the media were concerned, the 1992 race for the Democratic nomination was now essentially a two-person race between Paul Tsongas and Bill Clinton.[14]

Of passing interest was an unauthorized write-in vote campaign in New Hampshire for New York governor Mario Cuomo. Hoping that general dissatisfaction with the field of announced Democratic candidates could be turned into a substantial write-in vote for Cuomo, a small group of Cuomo supporters began the campaign without getting the governor's permission. The results were a disaster. Cuomo finished sixth as an unwilling write-in candidate, garnering fewer votes than even fifth-place finisher Jerry Brown.

A hapless Cuomo organizer, who had just given an election-night statement to CNN, was cornered by a group of newspaper reporters as he waited to catch the elevator down and out of the building from which CNN was doing its broadcasting. The reporters were unusually harsh with him. One said, more as a statement than a question, "The Cuomo write-in campaign really backfired, didn't it?" Another reporter picked up the thought with this question: "Isn't Cuomo in worse shape now than he would have been if you had not started the write-in campaign?" A third reporter finished the encounter: "The write-in campaign destroyed Cuomo's candidacy instead of helping it!"[15]

The reporters proved to be right. Cuomo's name was hardly ever mentioned again as a possible fall-back candidate for the 1992 Democratic nomination.

In retrospect, one can only describe the New Hampshire primary as a marvelous event, both to witness personally or over the television set. Most of the campaigning takes place in a thirty-mile urbanized strip from Nashua to Concord, with Manchester, the center of all the activity, located right in the middle. The result is that reporters and onlookers can follow all the candidates without having to drive very far and without losing much time driving from campaign event to campaign event. Occasionally candidates stray over to Portsmouth on the New Hampshire coast, or to Keene to the west or Berlin to the north, but by and large most of the action is in the Nashua-Manchester-Concord strip. The result is a very intense and concentrated political experience for all concerned—candidates, campaign workers, media people, and campaign observers.[16]

One has to wonder why the television reporters and the newspaper columnists put up with all the phoniness and contrivance of the staged media events—the orchestrated campaign rallies and the skillfully manipulated porta-crowds. The answer is: the media put up with it because it is contrived for them. What television news editors fear most is "talking heads." To prevent the boredom of only candidates presenting ideas, television demands the crowds, the handshaking, and the voter interviews that now make up the steady diet of those involved in presidential campaigns.

Thus it is clear that the New Hampshire primary belongs to the press and the public as well as the people of New Hampshire. Some analysts argue that, although New Hampshire has fewer than 1 percent of the convention delegates at the Democratic and Republican national conventions, 40 percent of the press coverage of the presidential primary season is focused on New Hampshire's opening-gun primary. Two reporters for Cox News Service summarized the point this way: "Unfair as it may be, the winners and losers are picked only in part by New Hampshire's 560,000 voters. Their message will be promptly translated by an unelected yet potent jury of the press and party activists. Together they form a rolling consensus that has been shown to deeply influence other voters [in other states] and, at times, even the final outcome [i.e., who finally wins the nomination]."[17]

The morning after the primary found New Hampshire covered with a light fog, a fog that was not heavy enough to stop airplanes from flying in and out of the Manchester airport but that was heavy enough to slow things down. Throughout the day the airport was crowded with media personnel and campaign workers turning in their rental cars and preparing to catch a flight out of town. Once again television camcorders and radio cassette recorders were everywhere.

As each jet airplane roared down the runway and lifted off into the sky, there was only a very brief period that the airplane was visible before it disappeared into the fog. It was the same way with the New Hampshire primary. There had been moments of clarity, but the final results were murky and indistinct. George Bush had won the Republican primary, but Pat Buchanan's strong showing suggested the President was in a weak, if not possibly fatal, position. Paul Tsongas, a valiant but little-known ex-senator, had won the Democratic primary, but it was unclear whether he could now mount a nationally effective and successful campaign. Bill Clinton had taken an unbelievable battering from the news media in the weeks prior to New Hampshire, but by finishing second in the voting he had at least survived to fight another day. In the final analysis, the Tuesday night New Hampshire results were as foggy as the Wednesday morning weather.

5. MAINE

Before the long and complicated presidential primary and caucus season gets underway, it is difficult, if not impossible, to tell which states will turn out to be important and which ones will have little or no effect on the final result. Except for New Hampshire, with its traditional exclusive privilege of holding the first presidential primary, any state can be a critical turning point in the primary-caucus process. A good case in point was the state of Maine in 1992.

Maine's Democratic Party presidential caucuses were scheduled for Sunday, February 23, 1992, only five days following the New Hampshire primaries. In the two decades since 1972, the Democratic winner in New Hampshire had always followed up with a clear-cut victory in Maine. The tremendous surge in publicity and the aura of being a winner that followed a triumph in New Hampshire had always been enough to guarantee a comfortable win in Maine.

The caucus process used by the Democrats in Maine was particularly suited to coverage by the news media. In each of the state's 665 voting precincts, Democratic Party activists gathered in living rooms, public schools, town halls, and firehouses to elect delegates to a state party convention scheduled for mid-May. Because each delegate elected at a caucus was either firmly committed to one of the candidates or to supporting an uncommitted delegation, it was possible for the news media to total up the number of delegates committed to each candidate and declare a winner.

Maine's actual twenty-three delegates to the Democratic National Convention would be chosen at the state party convention in May. That event would be anticlimactic, however. By mid-May the eventual Democratic nominee probably would already be known. The real significance of the Maine caucuses was that winners and losers could be determined the same night the caucuses were held. Who won and who lost in the Democratic caucuses in Maine thus would be factors in building momentum for the winner in subsequent primaries and caucuses. The Maine results would slow the campaigns of the losers.

All of the attention in Maine was focused on the Democratic caucuses. The Republican caucuses were scheduled to be held over a two-month period (February and March) and would elect unpledged rather than committed delegates. Furthermore, Republican challenger Patrick Buchanan made little or no effort to contest President Bush for Maine's Republican delegates.

The outcome of the Maine Democratic caucuses was a shocker. Everyone had expected New Hampshire winner Paul Tsongas to win by a comfortable margin. Instead, Tsongas ended up in a close race with former California governor Jerry Brown. By late Sunday evening Tsongas had 29.5 percent of the elected delegates and Brown was a whisker's thickness behind with 29.3 percent. Even more surprising, Arkansas governor Bill Clinton, who was supposed to have a strong organization in Maine, finished fourth (15 percent) behind an uncommitted delegation (16 percent).

Tsongas and Brown each claimed victory, but Brown's surprise showing gave Paul Tsongas much less to cheer about. Brown, after all, had finished last among the five major contenders in New Hampshire. In addition, the Brown campaign was not taken seriously by experienced political observers, partly because Brown put a $100 limit on contributions to his presidential campaign. The Associated Press concluded that "Brown was the big winner in Maine's caucuses."[1]

Brown's surprise showing in Maine appeared to prove that personal campaigning, particularly in small states that hold caucuses rather than primaries, can pay big dividends. More than any other candidate, Brown worked hard in Maine, campaigning throughout the state the five days before caucus day. In addition, he appealed for support from voters who shared his strong opposition to nuclear power.

"It's certainly an upset," Brown told the Associated Press. "It has to be a shock to the pundits in Washington, who early on believed that only $1,000 checks and obscene campaign war chests could propel a candidacy."[2]

The close finish in Maine was a great dissappointment to Paul Tsongas, who was struggling to nurture the momentum he had gained by winning in New Hampshire. Once again the "expectations game" had taken a Tsongas victory and made it appear to be something less than a victory. Even more important, what briefly had looked like a two-person race between Tsongas and Clinton was now something of a three-person race among Tsongas, Clinton, and Brown.

It is important to note that only about 13,000 of Maine's 272,079 registered Democrats, or 4.8 percent, actually went to and voted at their precinct caucuses.

6. SOUTH DAKOTA

The 1992 presidential election year found the state of South Dakota occupying a meaningful place in the primary election calendar. Prior to 1988, South Dakota held its presidential primary the first Tuesday in June, the same day as California and a number of other states. With a population even smaller than New Hampshire's, South Dakota was almost totally ignored when the high-profile California primary was going on at the same time. As one South Dakota political operative put it: "Nobody's going to pay any attention to us when California's at stake."[1]

In 1988, South Dakota did the logical thing for a state with a small population hoping to enlarge its role and importance in the presidential nominating process. It moved its presidential primary date as far forward as possible, from early June to the last Tuesday in February. South Dakotans ended up in an enviable position in 1988 and 1992. Their primary was scheduled just one week after New Hampshire's, and no other state picked that particular date for either a primary or even a caucus. South Dakota thus got to have an important primary date with no competition from any other states, large or small.

South Dakota's problem in 1992 was that two of the five major Democratic candidates were from states bordering on South Dakota. Tom Harkin was from Iowa, a state whose northwestern corner touches the southeastern corner of South Dakota. Bob Kerrey was from Nebraska, a state whose northern border runs for hundreds of miles along the southern border of South Dakota. Both Harkin and Kerrey campaigned in South Dakota as near native sons who, unlike the other three major candidates, really understood the problems of a northern Farm Belt state like South Dakota.

The odds-on favorite to win in South Dakota was Bob Kerrey.[2] This forty-eight-year-old son of the American prairie grew up in Lincoln, Nebraska. After graduating from the University of Nebraska at Lincoln in 1966, Kerrey enlisted in the United States Navy and joined the SEALs, an elite special forces underwater attack team. Sent to Vietnam in March of 1969, Lieutenant Kerrey led a seven-man team on a mission that involved climbing down a 350-foot cliff and attacking some Vietcong intelligence officers operating on a ledge beneath the cliff.

Spotted by the enemy when they were halfway down the cliff, Kerrey and his men came under heavy fire. A hand grenade exploded near Kerrey's feet, badly wounding his right leg. Bleeding profusely and in great pain, Kerrey continued to command his men, directing their fire into the heart of the enemy camp until it was wiped out. For his courage and tenacity under fire, Kerrey was awarded the nation's highest military honor, the Congressional Medal of Honor.

Bob Kerrey paid a high price for his heroism. At the Philadelphia Naval Hospital, his right leg was amputated beneath the knee. Kerrey knew other Vietnam veterans had suffered more, however, so he took his cue from his mother. He asked her at the hospital, "How much did they leave?" She looked at him, not his leg, and replied, "They left a lot!"[3]

Following a nine-month recuperation, Kerrey became the successful co-owner of a restaurant chain and a fitness center business. In 1982 he ran for governor of Nebraska as a Democrat and surprised everyone by winning in such a strongly Republican state. As governor he gained national celebrity of a different sort by dating sultry movie star Debra Winger.

Kerrey stepped down after one four-year term in the Nebraska governor's office, but he was elected to the United States Senate two years later in 1988. On Capitol Hill in Washington he championed improved education and health care reform. His Medal of Honor, his movie star social life, and his rugged good looks and friendly speaking style gave him genuine star quality. One of his rivals for the 1992 Democratic nomination for president, Governor Bill Clinton of Arkansas, dubbed him "Hollywood's candidate."[4]

Perhaps the best description of Bob Kerrey's allegedly phenomenal popular appeal was given by David Karnes, the Republican senator from Nebraska who Kerrey defeated in 1988: "People ask how a guy from Nebraska who is so liberal in his voting can be so popular. Well, it's a wonderful story—unless you have to run against it: An injured, decorated war veteran becomes one of the youngest governors of a solid midwestern state. Hollywood comes to Lincoln, Nebraska, and makes a movie, *Terms of Endearment*. The young governor invites the leading lady to the Governor's Mansion for dinner. They fall in (and out of) love. The film wins an Academy Award. He runs for senator—and wins."

"And now everybody wants to write the next chapter," Karnes concluded, "where he's president of the United States."[5]

The major campaign event prior to the South Dakota primary was a Sunday-before-election-day debate among the five Democratic candidates. Although the debate was not carried on any of the major television networks, it was presented live on South Dakota public television and nationally on C-SPAN, the exclusively politics and government network. Perhaps more importantly, the debate was well-covered by the print media, with most of the next day's newspapers running a major story about it.

Former California governor Jerry Brown scored the biggest media coup at the South Dakota Democratic debate. He arrived at the debate hall in Sioux Falls just at the time it was being announced that he had made such a surprisingly strong showing in the Maine caucuses. Brown walked into the debate hall and up to his place at the debate table flashing a V sign. A photographer snapped Brown just at that moment of triumph, and the Associated Press transmitted the photo along with its coverage of the debate. The Brown photograph played on the front pages and the political pages of hundreds of newspapers throughout the country the next morning.

Brown thus successfully pulled off what every presidential candidate hopes will happen at a campaign debate. The various candidates strive to come up with that one pithy statement or that one tart retort or that one photogenic or telegenic move or gesture that will be the dominant item in the media coverage the next day. Can such a tiny thing as a well-timed V sign be a candidate's ticket to a lot of front page photographs? Brown's actions at the South Dakota Democratic primary debate showed that it can be.

Because Paul Tsongas won the primary in New Hampshire and was now considered the front-runner for the Democratic nomination, rival candidates Kerrey and Harkin both attacked him for knowing next to nothing about the agricultural issues that are so important to a farming state such as South Dakota. Tsongas endeavored to take the sting out of the charges by owning up to them and then trying to change the subject to fiscal responsibility. "I acknowledge that Bob Kerrey and Tom Harkin know more about agriculture than I do, but I'm here to listen," Tsongas said, "[and] there are some things I stand for, like fiscal discipline, that are relevant here."

Jerry Brown used the South Dakota debate to develop his viewpoint that concerns at home in the United States should take precedence over concerns overseas. Brown promised South Dakota, which is considered by many to be a midwestern state, that he would redirect government spending from the "Mideast to the Midwest." Brown added: "I wouldn't give a penny in foreign aid until every family farmer and small businessman . . . in America was taken care of."[6]

It often happens in early presidential primaries that candidates from nearby states do well; now, the two candidates from states close by South Dakota finished at the top. Bob Kerrey of Nebraska came in first with 40 percent of the vote, and Tom Harkin was second with 25 percent. There also was good news for Bill Clinton, who finished third and well ahead of Paul Tsongas, the man who had beaten him in New Hampshire. The South Dakota voting lent credence to Clinton's charge that Tsongas was a regional candidate who could not win anywhere but in New England.

In South Dakota the results of news media-designed exit polls received as much media attention as the actual primary election results. Three out of every ten Democrats who voted, mindful of the marital infidelity and draft avoidance charges against Bill Clinton, said they did not think Clinton had the "honesty and integrity" needed to be president. The news media clearly had decided to make Clinton's character an issue in the primary elections by including such a question in the election day exit polls.

In the end, the South Dakota Democratic primary results proved as foggy and inconclusive as the results from New Hampshire. The top two vote getters, Kerrey and Harkin, were subject to the same "regional candidate" charges that had been used to deflate Tsongas's win in New Hampshire. Jerry Brown had almost all of the glitter from his cliffhanging finish with Tsongas in the Maine caucuses obliterated by his fifth-place finish, garnering only four percent of the vote in South Dakota. As in New Hampshire and Maine, no one candidate in the South Dakota Democratic primary could claim to be an all-out winner.

There was one interesting analysis point once the South Dakota Democratic primary was over. Each of the major Democratic candidates but one could claim a victory somewhere in the primaries and caucuses to date. Tom Harkin had won the caucuses in his home state of Iowa. Paul Tsongas had won the primary in his almost home state of

New Hampshire. Jerry Brown had "won" the Maine caucuses by finishing neck-and-neck there with Tsongas. And Bob Kerrey had just won in his neighboring state of South Dakota. Ironically, although Bill Clinton was the only major Democratic candidate who had not won at least one primary or caucus to date, he was still considered by most observers to be the front-runner. As the only southern candidate, Clinton was expected to win big in the large number of southern states that hold their presidential primaries on Super Tuesday, then just two weeks away. For that reason, most commentators and analysts continued to see him as the front-runner despite the fact that he had not won any of the early primaries and caucuses.

On the Republican side in South Dakota, Pat Buchanan was not on the ballot, so South Dakota Republicans had a choice between President Bush or "uncommitted." Bush received 69 percent of the vote; 31 percent of voters chose to be uncommitted. As with the Democratic primary, however, the story that received equal play with Bush's easy victory was the exit polls. Two-thirds of the Republicans who said they chose to be uncommitted told the exit pollsters they would not support Bush in the November general election.

The South Dakota exit polls thus began developing something that would be a favorite theme of the news media throughout the 1992 presidential primary season. It was the idea that the leading candidate in each party, George Bush for the Republicans and Bill Clinton for the Democrats, was very unpopular with a significant portion of his party's primary election voters.

7. COLORADO

From the time it entered the Union in 1876 up through 1988, the state of Colorado used precinct caucuses and state conventions to pick its delegates to political party national conventions. In 1992, in a stunning break with history and tradition, Colorado held its first ever presidential primary.

The idea of holding a presidential primary in Colorado got rolling when state senator Mike Bird read the manuscript of a proposed book on Colorado politics.[1] Bird accepted the book's argument that the caucus/convention system traditionally used in Colorado left the state's voters completely out of the presidential nomination process. Colorado's June state conventions were scheduled so late in the spring that, by the time the conventions were held, the presidential nominees of both political parties had already been determined in early presidential primaries held in other states.

The Colorado presidential primary thus began with a state legislator who, almost accidentally, read a critique of the caucus-convention system and decided to use his power and influence to try to do something about it. It is important to note at this point what did *not* cause the drive for a Colorado primary. It was not started, as happened with presidential primaries in many other states, to advance the candidacy of this or that particular candidate for the Republican or Democratic nomination for president. Also, it was not started by a governor or United States senator who wanted to create a home state presidential primary to advance his or her own candidacy for president.

In late January of 1990, state senator Bird introduced SB 162 (Senate Bill 162), a proposed law creating a Colorado presidential primary, in the Colorado senate. Working carefully, he lined up twenty-six co-sponsors for the bill, more than one-fourth of the 100 members of the Colorado state legislature. In drawing up the proposed law, Bird had carefully adhered to two guiding principles. The first principle was to establish a primary that involved the citizens of Colorado in the most meaningful way possible in the presidential nominating process. The second was to see that Colorado, a medium-sized state in terms of population, voted as early in the primary process as possible.

The most interesting thing about the proposed Colorado presidential primary was the almost total lack of controversy which it generated. The newspapers in Denver, the state capital, were quick to point out that, by selecting an early date in the primary process, Colorado was making its bid to enter the unofficial competition over which state can have the biggest voice in who gets nominated for president. The newspapers also seemed to like the idea that, if other Rocky Mountain region states would join Colorado in selecting an early caucus or primary date, more attention might be paid by presidential candidates to Rocky Mountain political and economic issues.[2] The newspapers did not appear to be particularly enthusiastic about the proposed presidential primary, but none of them boldly criticized or attacked it.

About this time a key strategy decision was made by state senator Bird. He decided to have the presidential primary proposal submitted to a popular vote at the time of the 1990 general election. By holding a referendum on whether or not to have a presidential primary, the voters of the state could be brought into the approval process and thereby become more involved with and informed about the presidential primary process.

There was another benefit from submitting the proposed primary to a vote of the people. In Colorado, a bill passed by the state legislature that is submitted to the voters for final approval does not have to be signed by the governor. State senator Bird was a Republican, and the governor of Colorado, Roy Romer, was a Democrat. Although Bird was reasonably confident that Governor Romer would sign a presidential primary bill, he was not completely certain about it. Submitting the proposal to a popular vote was a convenient way of totally avoiding the question of whether or not the governor would climb on the presidential primary bandwagon.[3]

Only one person testified in favor of the presidential primary bill when it came up for committee hearings in the state senate. The senate committee listened politely to the testimony and had very few questions to ask.

Sherrie Wolfe, the Democratic national committeewoman from Colorado, made a surprise appearance at the senate committee hearings. She pointed out that Colorado could not hold its presidential primary *one* week after New Hampshire's because a new national Democratic Party rule required that no new primaries be held before the first Tuesday in March, a date that came *two* weeks after New Hampshire's primary. Furthermore, Wolfe pointed out, there was some question as to whether national Democratic Party rules would permit Colorado to absolutely bind delegates to vote for those presidential candidates who did well in the Colorado primary. In addition, Wolfe said, Democratic officials in Colorado had been talking with Democrats in New Mexico, Arizona, Nevada, and Utah about having a Rocky Mountain regional primary and caucus day in April rather than March.

The senate committee quickly postponed action on the presidential primary bill and gave state senator Bird and Democratic national committeewoman Wolfe the time they needed to work things out. Senator Bird agreed to hold the Colorado primary no earlier than the first Tuesday in March, thus bringing the primary date into line with national Democratic Party rules. If other Rocky Mountain states wanted to have a Rocky Mountain region primary and caucus day, Bird said, they could join with Colorado on an early March date.

After a number of calls to the Democratic National Committee in Washington, D.C., suitable language was found to loosely connect the first ballot votes of Colorado delegates to the Democratic National Convention to the vote which various Democratic candidates had received in the Colorado presidential primary. At a future meeting, the senate committee readily approved the new language. The Colorado primary had successfully leaped over what turned out to be its only serious legislative hurdle.

State senator Mike Bird's dealings with the Democratic National Committee illustrated a very important point about the presidential nominating process in the United States. The United States Supreme Court has ruled that national political party rules take precedence over state election laws.[4] It is true that state legislatures establish the detailed procedures under which states conduct presidential primary elections, but the state legislatures are required by the courts to always operate according to the rules laid down by political party national committees.

In effect, this means that states have to operate both their Democratic *and Republican* presidential primaries in accordance with rules laid down by the Democratic National Committee. Of the two national political parties in the United States, it is the Democrats who make more numerous and stricter rules. Because most states do what Colorado did and set up their Democratic and Republican presidential primaries together on the same date, the Republicans are forced to join the Democrats in conforming to most of the rules laid down by the national Democrats.

Following passage in the Colorado senate by a wide margin, the presidential primary bill proceeded to the Colorado house of representatives, where it also was quickly passed. The proposal then went directly on the 1990 general election ballot for approval or rejection by the voters.

The general election campaign for approval of the Colorado primary can best be described as a noncampaign. Although state senator Bird formed a small political committee to provide information to the press and public about the Colorado primary, very little information was requested. No money was raised or spent either for or against the presidential primary. The voters of Colorado were allowed to make a choice in a statewide referendum without having to watch and listen to a barrage of television and radio commercials.

Newspaper coverage mainly consisted of publishing public opinion polls. One month before election day, a *Denver Post* poll found 63 percent of voters for the presidential primary, 23 percent against, and 14 percent undecided. A *Rocky Mountain News* poll showed 52 percent for, 13 percent against, and 35 percent undecided.[5] That strong support never faded. In the 1990 November general election, the voters of Colorado approved a presidential primary by a vote of 70 percent to 30 percent. The presidential primary calendar in 1992 was going to be a little bit different from what it was in 1988.

What lessons can be learned from this story of how Colorado got its first ever presidential primary?

First, it is the clear responsibility of the state legislature in each state to determine whether a state will have a presidential primary and, equally important, on what date the primary will be held. Colorado gained its early March primary only because a powerful and influential legislator, state senator Mike Bird, was willing to take the time and make the effort to get a majority of the legislature to follow his lead and pass a presidential primary bill.

Second, there is little press or public understanding of or interest in the details of how presidential primaries are created and scheduled. The remarkable thing about SB 162 going through the Colorado legislature was the general lack of interest and concern about the bill, even on the part of most of the state legislators. Some of this can be attributed to the trust and confidence many of the Colorado legislators had in state senator Bird, but most of it probably came from the fact that everyone thought a presidential primary was an acceptable idea but not something they were very excited about.

Third, the fact that a presidential primary was adopted overwhelmingly by Colorado voters suggests that the American public has bought the idea that state primaries are the correct way to go about nominating major party candidates for president. Since there was no major campaigning either for or against the presidential primary in Colorado, the voters were left to make up their own minds, primarily on the basis of how they had observed the presidential primary system working in other states. The landslide adoption of the Colorado primary indicates that presidential primaries are now an accepted fact of United States political life.

Fourth, other states might want to follow the Colorado model of trading in the caucus-convention system for a presidential primary. Unless a state is holding the first caucuses in the nation, as Iowa does, caucuses get minimal attention from the press when compared with the attention that is given to presidential primaries. Fifteen of the fifty states continued to use some variant of the caucus-convention system in 1992.[6] If these states really wanted to involve their voters in the presidential nominating process in a meaningful way, they would consider adopting a presidential primary.

Fifth, states adopting a presidential primary for the first time should consider following the Colorado example and submit the proposed primary to a vote of the people. This can occur, of course, only in states that already provide for a popular referendum on laws passed by the state legislature. The Colorado experience suggests that, given the opportunity to vote themselves a more meaningful role in the presidential nominating process, a solid majority of voters will support a state presidential primary.

Colorado voters overwhelmingly approved the Colorado primary in November of 1990. Six months later, on May 1, 1991, Colorado received its first visit from an announced candidate for the 1992 Democratic nomination for president. Former Massachusetts senator Paul Tsongas flew into Denver and outlined his ideas for reforming the United States economy at a luncheon meeting of about 100 Colorado business executives.

Tsongas came to Denver only two days after he announced his candidacy. Colorado was his first stop after a one-day swing through Massachusetts (his home state), New Hampshire (the first presidential primary), and Iowa (the first presidential caucuses). When asked by the *Denver Post* what he was doing in Denver so early in the campaign, "Tsongas cited Colorado's primary . . . as a reason for his interest in Colorado."[7]

Almost immediately following his New Hampshire primary victory in February of 1992, Paul Tsongas launched a major television advertising campaign in Colorado. On the Friday after New Hampshire, a full ten days before the actual voting in Colorado, thirty-second television spots for Tsongas began appearing on both Denver and Colorado Springs area television stations.

The TV spots were upbeat and personal. They emphasized Tsongas's successes as a United States senator and his pro-business economic views. A particularly memorable TV ad showed Tsongas vigorously swimming a butterfly stroke up and down a swimming pool. An announcer's voice noted that this presidential candidate liked to "swim against the current."[8] Close-ups of Tsongas's face while swimming portrayed a man who was both physically fit and determined to succeed. The swimming pool advertisement clearly was designed to overcome voter doubts that Tsongas might not have fully recovered from his bout with lymphatic cancer.

The Tsongas TV commercials never mentioned his opponents for the Democratic nomination. The ads were classic examples of *positive* campaigning.

Clearly Tsongas had decided to pursue an "early and often" strategy for winning the Colorado primary. He was the first Democratic candidate to visit the state. He was the first Democratic candidate to launch a major television advertising campaign in the state. These efforts, coupled with his victory in New Hampshire, paid off in the public opinion polls. By the Thursday before election day, polls by the *Denver Post* found Tsongas solidly in first place in Colorado with 28 percent. Bill Clinton was fading at 21 percent. Jerry Brown was a distant third at 14 percent but gaining.[9]

Perhaps because of his strong lead in the polls, Tsongas did not emphasize personal campaigning in Colorado the week before primary day. Two other important states, Maryland and Georgia, would be voting the same day as Colorado, and each had more delegate votes than Colorado. Tsongas came to Denver for a Saturday-night-before-election-day debate with the rest of the Democratic candidates, but otherwise he concentrated much of his personal campaign time elsewhere.

There was the expected sharp contrast between the Paul Tsongas campaign organization in Colorado and the Bill Clinton operation. The Tsongas state headquarters was the dining room table in the Denver home of one of the candidate's cousins, Theodora Tsongas. The kitchen telephone was the state campaign hotline. Only a few miles away—but light years away in terms of funds available—was the Bill Clinton Denver headquarters. There also were Clinton headquarters in the outlying cities of Greeley and Pueblo. In Denver alone five paid staffers worked at directing the efforts of a large number of full-time volunteers. Heading the Clinton effort in Colorado was an experienced wife-husband team of political consultants, Mary Alice Mandarich and Chip Spreyer.

Mandarich said that a good state organization serves as a "gas station" for the candidate, pumping up the campaign in the state by raising money and turning out local supporters at campaign events. Completing her gas station image, Mandarich said it was her task to "keep the Clinton campaign on the road to the nomination."[10]

On Sunday, February 23, 1992, that road led to Pueblo, Colorado. A caravan of hired buses brought Bill Clinton and his Colorado entourage to the Sangre de Cristo Arts and Conference Center, a modern red brick and cement structure in the heart of downtown Pueblo.[11] On the way into town, the buses took a short detour so that Arkansas governor Bill Clinton could cross the Arkansas River, the same river that, almost eight hundred miles further downstream, flows through the Arkansas capital city of Little Rock. In his speech, Arkansas governor Clinton made it a point to say that seeing the Arkansas River again made him feel right at home in Pueblo.

A city of steel mills and railroad yards located 110 miles south of Denver, Pueblo was an ideal place for Bill Clinton to give a speech. Furnace by furnace, job by job, the steel mills had been slowly closing down for more than two decades. As a result, Pueblo had one of the highest unemployment rates of any major city in Colorado. It also was a community where nearly 30 percent of the voters were Hispanic. If there was a perfect place to draw an enthusiastic Democratic audience in Colorado, surely Pueblo was it.

Not ones to leave anything to chance, however, the Clinton campaign managers bused in additional supporters from Greeley, Denver, Colorado Springs, and Canon City. It was a good way of guaranteeing that the vast majority of people in the crowd were avid Clinton supporters. As usual, neither the print nor the electronic media bothered to mention that many of the three hundred or so cheering admirers at Clinton's Pueblo speech were hauled in from all over Colorado rather than being from Pueblo.

The Clinton rally in Pueblo was blessed with beautiful weather. Although it was late February at the foot of the Rocky Mountains, a bright sun in a cloudless blue sky made it a pleasant winter's day to be outside.

The speaker's rostrum was placed halfway up a long set of cement steps leading up to the arts and conference center. From the rostrum, Clinton faced directly into the midday sun, thereby lighting his face perfectly for the television cameras and news photographers located on a raised platform directly opposite but some distance away. As usual, the crowd of mostly bused-in supporters stood in the space between Clinton and the media platform.

Signs of a well-financed campaign were everywhere. Portable posts connected with yellow plastic tape channeled the crowd into exactly the right places between the candidate and the media. Clinton signs and posters had been put up everywhere. Anyone who wanted a Clinton sign to wave during the speech was given one.

In many ways the setting symbolized Bill Clinton's place in the contemporary Democratic Party. The Sangre de Cristo center itself was new and modern, a physical testimonial to the efforts of the citizens of Pueblo to stimulate the arts and bring convention business into a slumping downtown. Across the street, however, stood a typical row of old nineteenth-century business buildings, some in good repair but many in dilapidated condition. About half were empty and for rent. Pueblo was an old city trying to make itself new again, exactly as Bill Clinton hoped to take the old Democratic Party, revive its major coalition, and make it new again.

Clinton's speech probably was one he had given many times to pro-Democratic, pro-Clinton audiences. He said he wanted to bring a "New Covenant" to the American people, a New Covenant under which government would help people solve their problems, but without taking complete responsibility for the people's lives and livelihood. The New Covenant, of course, was highly reminiscent of the New Frontier theme that John F. Kennedy had used in his successful campaign for the presidency in 1960. Kennedy, on the other hand, had borrowed the New Frontier from Franklin D. Roosevelt's New Deal programs for ending the Great Depression of the 1930s.

Clinton hammered hard on the idea that he would look to the needs of the "forgotten middle class," and he emphasized that a "middle class tax cut" would be the best way to achieve that goal. He then ran down a list of the current problems facing the American people and detailed the ways in which government should be used to solve those problems. Health care is a problem! Clinton called for a United States government-supported health care program. The poor quality of education in public schools is a problem! Clinton called for more government aid to education. America's infrastructure—her highways and bridges and water mains and sewer lines—is getting old and falling apart and creating a problem! Clinton called on the government to begin a massive program of repairing and replacing the infrastructure, creating large numbers of good jobs at the same time.

In short, Clinton's speech went back to the old Democratic Party philosophy of using government spending to solve social and economic problems. A critic might have heard the cash register ringing loudly as Clinton proposed and supported United States government program after United States government program, but the crowd did not. Although Clinton had begun his speech by calling for a middle class tax cut, and had later on mentioned the need to balance the budget, his speech was mainly built around the old Democratic concept of the "share-out," the idea that the Democratic Party wins elections by pledging to solve people's problems with effective United States government programs.[12] Every time Clinton mentioned yet another government program he was prepared to support, the crowd gave him an enthusiastic cheer and a big hand. It was everything an old-style Democratic rally ought to have been.

Clinton's speech in Pueblo seemed to suggest that Clinton was moving to the political left as the presidential primary season got underway. Originally Clinton had believed he would be the moderate, middle-of-the-road Democratic candidate running against left wing, liberal Democratic candidates such as Tom Harkin and Bob Kerrey. Paul Tsongas's unexpected victory in New Hampshire had changed all that. On economic issues and government involvement in the economy issues, Tsongas was a conservative, not a liberal. In order to sharpen the difference in the average Democratic voter's mind between himself and Paul Tsongas, Bill Clinton was moving to the left economically and sounding much less like an economic moderate.

Clinton also used a variant of the "America First" position to differentiate himself from Tsongas. Tsongas was a strong supporter of free international trade and the United States government helping American companies improve their competitiveness in the international business world. Clinton told his Pueblo audience that he, too, supported government aid to American business, but he made a pointed remark that such aid should only go to firms that invest those funds in the United States, *not* overseas.

At the end of his formal speech, candidate Clinton came down the cement steps of the Sangre de Cristo center and began to shake hands with the audience. In the highly controlled manner of the Clinton campaign, those who wanted to shake Clinton's hand had to line up along a long rope. Clinton started at one end of the rope and moved along, shaking the extended hands and responding to greetings and questions from the handshakers as he went along. The rope was stretched along a north-to-south line so that, as Clinton worked his way down it, he was perfectly lit by the sun. Exactly as the Clinton campaigners had planned, TV camcorder operators and press photographers took videos and pictures of Clinton as he "pressed the flesh" and chatted with the Clinton faithful.

A middle-aged woman, old enough to remember John F. Kennedy in the heyday of his New Frontier, shook Clinton's hand and spontaneously said, "You are the Kennedy of Arkansas!" In any other Democratic campaign in any previous presidential year, such a remark would have been taken as a great compliment. By 1992, however, there had been much publicity given to the fact that Kennedy had indulged in a number of extramarital affairs, even while serving as president and living at the White House. Clinton himself was struggling with the burden of the many rumors about his own infidelities, rumors which he had more or less confirmed to a national television audience two weeks earlier on the CBS News program *60 Minutes.*

Was this woman praising him because his New Covenant so closely resembled John F. Kennedy's New Frontier? Or was she taking a none too subtle dig at the moral values of both Clinton and Kennedy? Whatever she was saying, Bill Clinton could not handle it. His head jerked back and his eyes flashed. He mumbled a response, but his voice was so low that neither the woman nor others standing close by her could hear it. Clinton quickly moved on down the handshaking line. This was not the time in American political history to be compared *personally* with John F. Kennedy. (The woman said she had meant the statement "You are the Kennedy of Arkansas" only as a compliment. She was not referring to Kennedy's personal life, or Clinton's.)

This one small incident dramatizes why presidential candidates work so hard at drawing favorable, rather than unfavorable, audiences to their public events. If even well-intentioned members of the audience can occasionally ask embarrassing and damaging questions, imagine what the openly hostile and critical could do. Clinton probably considered himself most fortunate that none of the news media picked up on the "You are the Kennedy of Arkansas" statement.

A week later, two days before election day, a crowd of about 100 persons gathered at the Hillside Community Center in Colorado Springs. Hillside is a prime example of the classic neighborhood center that American cities built in the 1960s and 1970s to try to cure the nation's urban problems. Athletic facilities, primarily a basketball court, attract youngsters from the "mean streets" to team sports and physical development. A series of meeting rooms provide a place where the various constituent groups in the neighborhood—senior citizens, teenagers in social clubs, and others—can meet and plan community activities.

The Hillside Center was a perfect place for a campaign visit from Hillary Clinton, wife of Democratic presidential nomination contender Bill Clinton. Colorado Springs presents a problem to Democratic candidates for office. An overwhelmingly middle-class and suburban-style community, Colorado Springs is the most Republican city in Colorado. Large and favorable Democratic audiences are difficult to muster in such a Republican setting. The Hillside Center, however, is located in a small part of Colorado Springs that has a large number of low-income residents and a high percentage of minority groups. If there was a Democratic audience to be found in Colorado Springs, it would be around the Hillside Center.

The immediate vehicle for drawing a crowd for Hillary Clinton was the Sunday services of the New Hope of the Rockies Church. This neighborhood church, apparently unaffiliated with any of the major national religions in the United States, used the main meeting room in the Hillside Center for its Sunday hymn singing, Bible reading, and sermonizing. Those who came to hear Hillary Clinton give a political speech on this particular Sunday morning could, if they wished, meet their religious obligations at the same time.

As almost always happens with political campaigners, Hillary Clinton was a little late arriving for her talk. The minister and congregation of the New Hope of the Rockies Church solved the problem by singing more hymns and reading more Scripture. Television camera crews and reporters looked at each other nervously as even more hymns were sung and little mini-sermons were given. Hillary Clinton still did not appear.

The result, as intended, was a great rush of excitement when Hillary Clinton at last appeared at the back of the meeting room and walked up the center aisle to a portable podium—a podium which only minutes before had served as the pulpit from which the Sunday sermon had been given. Hillary Clinton looked every inch the successful Yale Law School graduate and lawyer that she was. Her good clothes and fine grooming instantly set her apart from the much more informal and occasionally threadbare dress of the congregation of New Hope of the Rockies Church. Around her neck hung a gold necklace with a gold Christian cross. On her lapel was a red, white, and blue "Bill Clinton for President" button.

Hillary Clinton spoke to the varied audience gathered at the Hillside Center in a formal style more suited to the courtroom than the campaign hall. If her words and manner of speaking were upscale, however, what she had to say was not. She began by condemning the Reagan and Bush administrations for encouraging Americans to be self-centered rather than caring about community needs. "For more than 12 years," she charged, "we have had a philosophy that has really allowed each one of us to go our own way and has allowed us to turn our backs on the problems about us."[13]

Continuing in her lawyerlike style, Hillary Clinton listed point by point some of the specific programs which her husband would support when elected to the presidency. A national service trust fund would permit any young American to borrow money for college and then pay for it with two to three years of national service, thereby helping to solve United States social problems. Houses and apartments taken over by the government through foreclosures (for nonpayment of government-backed mortgages) would be turned over to charitable organizations and used to house the homeless. "Conversion programs" would be established to help workers in defense industries find new jobs when anticipated large cuts in defense spending began to take effect.

Echoing what her husband had said a week before in Pueblo, Hillary Clinton made it clear she had no problem using the United States government as the primary vehicle for solving the nation's social and economic problems. As a conservative nationally syndicated columnist later put it, Hillary Clinton's "politics are suspected of being refried '60s activism.'"[14]

When her speech and a brief question period were over, Hillary Clinton and the political junkies in the crowd drifted out to the wide cement sidewalk in front of the Hillside Center. Anyone who wanted to meet Hillary Clinton, shake her hand, and ask an additional question or two could easily do so. A local television station got a brief, close-up personal interview. The photographer from the local newspaper took a few more photographs. When every last voter had been greeted and every last interview given, Hillary Clinton stepped into the large passenger van that was her mode of transportation that day and departed for Denver. More speeches, more handshakes, and more media interviews and photo opportunities lay ahead.

Hillary Clinton's visit to Colorado Springs was a complete media success. As in most American cities these days, Colorado Springs has only one newspaper. The next morning that newspaper ran a front-page color photograph of Hillary Clinton shaking hands with voters and an inside black-and-white photograph of her addressing the religious service. Accompanying the black-and-white photograph was a short but comprehensive newspaper article summarizing what Hillary Clinton had to say.

At the same time Hillary Clinton was campaigning for her husband the last weekend before Colorado's presidential primary election, something much more important was taking place on each Coloradan's television set. Beginning on Friday night of that final weekend, a veritable barrage of Bill Clinton television spot ads hit the airwaves. The ads were directly aimed at rival candidate Paul Tsongas, who as of Friday night had a substantial lead over Clinton in Colorado in the public opinion polls.

The Clinton camp labeled the ads "comparative," but that was a pleasant sounding euphemism for classic *negative* campaigning. They began with a photograph of Paul Tsongas, and not a particularly flattering photograph. An announcer's voice would state the Tsongas position on an issue, always in negative terms. Then Bill Clinton's smiling face would appear on the screen, and the announcer would present the Clinton position on the same issue, but always in positive terms. Then Tsongas's photograph would reappear, and a negative spin would be placed on another Tsongas issue position. Then back to the smiling face of Bill Clinton, and the Clinton position on the issue would get a positive spin. The net effect of the ad was to give the distinct impression that Paul Tsongas was going to create a lot of problems for the viewer while Bill Clinton was advocating solutions that would work and would favorably affect the viewer.

The ad suggested that Tsongas's conservative fiscal policies might lower senior citizens' Social Security payments. It hinted that Tsongas's internationalistic economic views might cause working American men and women to lose their jobs. The ad tied Tsongas to the evils of "big business" on Wall Street. It charged Tsongas with giving too much support to the idea of generating more electricity with nuclear power.

The ad dealt with easily understood issues, such as Social Security and unemployment, that are vitally important in the daily lives of many Colorado voters. The ad was very well done and very effective. Most of all it saturated all four network television channels the weekend before election day. It left an enduring final impression. Paul Tsongas and his new economic ideas: BAD! Bill Clinton and his economic and social programs: MUCH BETTER!

While Paul Tsongas and Bill Clinton were battling it out with television advertisements, former California governor Jerry Brown was pursuing a completely different strategy in Colorado. Because Brown put a cap of $100 on campaign contributions and would not accept support from political action committees, he was forced to pursue a low-budget strategy. As he had done in New Hampshire, Brown built that strategy around college and university students, giving major speeches at the University of Colorado in Boulder and at Colorado College in Colorado Springs.

Jerry Brown's advance work in Colorado was handled by a young woman in her early twenties named Caroline. She set up speeches for Brown by telephoning professors and students at various colleges and universities around the state, trying to find someone to handle the local arrangements. After shopping around a bit at Colorado College, she eventually found a professor who was willing to find her a place—for free—for Brown to talk.

Jerry Brown's speech at Colorado College was scheduled for February 26, 1992, in Gates Common Room, a large room with folding chairs seating about two hundred, but plenty of standing room around the sides and the back if an unusually large crowd turned out. The room was equipped with a handheld microphone because, as Caroline put it, "Jerry likes to move around and get close to the people he is talking to."

Caroline arrived at Colorado College the day before the talk to check out the lecture hall and begin the process of turning out a crowd to hear Brown speak. The only campaign materials she brought with her were several hundred flyers giving the time, date, and place of Brown's address. The flyers had black print on plain white paper and obviously had been turned out quickly and cheaply on a borrowed copy machine. The copy machine reproduction of a photograph of Brown on the flyer was, as one would expect, vague and indistinct. It had a delightfully amateurish and slipshod quality to it. A small note at the bottom of the flyer said it was printed with volunteer labor. It looked like it, perhaps intentionally so.

There were none of the other expensive paraphernalia of a campaign appearance. There were no slick paper signs to be posted on the walls and waved by the audience. There were no campaign buttons to be given out. There would be no raised platform for the TV camcorder operators and newspaper photographers. They would have to get their videos and still photographs at audience level. Caroline was given the names of some politically active students on campus. She recruited them to hand out and post her small stack of flyers for free.

After checking out the lecture hall and making the arrangements for distributing the flyers, Caroline headed over to the campus radio station, where she introduced herself to the staff and left a press release publicizing the date, time, and place of Brown's talk. She made similar visits to the major television and radio stations in Colorado Springs and the daily newspaper. In every case she was hunting up free advertising, keeping all costs to an absolute minimum.

Caroline said she had attended a lecture by Jerry Brown during her senior year at the University of Southern California and at that time realized she wanted to work in his campaign for president. She had more or less been on the road for Brown ever since graduating from USC, making contacts on college and university campuses and turning those contacts into free lecture halls for Brown. When she first appeared at Colorado College to recruit student helpers to distribute her flyers, Caroline was wearing a pair of old Levi's with a worn patch and a hole here and there. Her appearance was indistinguishable from that of the students she was so avidly recruiting.

On the afternoon of Jerry Brown's talk at Colorado College, students began pouring into Gates Common Room around 4:00 P.M., half an hour before the activities were scheduled to begin. Word had spread quickly on campus that Brown was coming, the talk was going to be popular, and seats might be hard to come by. By 4:15 P.M. additional chairs were being set up to accommodate the crowd. By 4:20 P.M. all the chairs were taken and the crowd was filling the standing room, which included the area behind where Brown would be speaking. By 4:30 P.M. the place was packed to capacity and latecomers were being turned away. As planned, a sense of excitement and expectancy filled the room with so many people crowded into it.

Unusually for a political candidate, Jerry Brown and his small entourage arrived fifteen minutes before the talk was scheduled to begin. Ten minutes after that Caroline hurried into the building. "It's not a good thing for the candidate to arrive well ahead of the advance person," she grumbled.

Caroline was carrying a large "Brown for President" banner that she wanted to hang on the wall at the back of the room. Like everything else about the Brown campaign, the banner was inexpensive, made by volunteers, and looked as if it had been used many, many times. Running late as she was, Caroline had nothing with which to stick the banner to the wall. Quickly some masking tape was located and two students recruited to help her put it up.

At 4:30 P.M. Jerry Brown walked from a nearby classroom, where he had been waiting, into Gates Common Room to give his talk. The crowd of standees was so thick that a path had to be cleared for him through all the people. A major campaign event was about to begin, and it had all been done at a fraction of the cost usually associated with such events.

Candidate Brown was dressed in a black double-breasted suit with a white turtleneck sweater. He thus looked well dressed but not like a typical businessman in a coat and tie, which is what all the other candidates tended to wear. On his lapel Brown sported a red ribbon, the well-known symbol of solidarity with people who are suffering from AIDS.

In the course of his talk Brown presented a wide range of new ideas that would provide innovative solutions to national problems. He recommended cutting the United States military budget by 50 percent and using the savings to build high-speed trains and harness solar and wind power. "We doubled the military budget because of the Soviet Union," Brown said. "Now we can cut it in half."[15]

Brown suggested creating a centralized national health care program that would provide health care to every citizen. He supported setting national standards for educational achievement and greatly increasing funding for the Head Start program, the United States government program that provides preschool education for poor children. He proposed a conservation corps to put troubled youth to work in the outdoors improving public parks, forests, and recreation areas.

Brown's major economic proposal was the flat tax, which would replace the present graduated scale of income tax rates with a flat rate of 13 percent. Most current tax loopholes, particularly tax deductions that help the wealthy, would be eliminated, thereby generating the additional tax income needed to make up for setting the flat rate at only 13 percent. Brown said he would allow deductions for charitable donations, rent, and mortgage payments because those deductions benefit poor people and the middle class.

Most of all, Brown condemned big money politics and the way giant economic interests in America dominate the national government by making large campaign contributions. His overall message was strongly pro-environment and antinuclear. He exhorted his audience of basically young admirers to join him in becoming "moral agents of change." He also mentioned his "800" number, which people could call if they wanted to make a contribution to his campaign to "Take Back America!" At the end of his talk, Brown received a prolonged ovation from the crowd.

Later, a local newspaper reporter asked Brown why he was spending so much of his time in Colorado campaigning on college and university campuses, particularly when college students tend not to vote in very large numbers. Brown replied: "It's their future."[16] But there was more to it than just the students' future. As his visit to Colorado College so clearly indicated, Brown had developed an inexpensive way of generating large and enthusiastic young audiences to listen to his bold plans for America's future. His college and university campus talks were covered by the news media just as extensively as the more expensive speaking events staged by rival candidates. Brown was effectively using his college and university student constituency to reach the larger constituency that watches television news and reads newspapers, and he was reaching that larger constituency for a very cheap price.

One had to wonder about the amateur atmosphere and "poor boy" feel of the Brown campaign as it passed through Colorado. Back in the 1950s, a political scientist from California named Eugene Burdick wrote a novel entitled *The Ninth Wave*. In this fanciful account of an outsider's campaign for the Democratic nomination for governor of California, political professionals perfected a technique of intentionally making the campaign look amateurish and unprofessional. In one particularly memorable scene in the novel, a roomful of paid campaign workers laboriously produced handmade lapel signs for their candidate using cheap white cards and soft pencils. Everything looked amateurish and spontaneous, but the entire campaign was being run by slick professionals who really knew what they were doing.[17] A few days before election day a lawn sign for Brown appeared on a telephone pole on a heavily traveled street in Colorado Springs. Someone had used a stencil and cans of spray paint to make an amateurish sign that read, "Empowerment! Vote Brown." Had the sign been the dedicated work of a lone volunteer truly inspired by the Brown campaign and the Brown message? Or had many of them been produced as part of one of the slickest professional campaigns for president ever conceived? There was no way the average citizen observer could know for sure.

As primary election day in Colorado neared, dedicated politics watchers began to notice two things about Jerry Brown. First, he was spending a great deal of time campaigning in person in Colorado, and that had to start having an effect, even if he was mainly working colleges and universities. Second, though Brown was way behind Tsongas and Clinton, he was starting to move up rapidly in the polls.

The Saturday night before election day, all five major Democratic candidates came to Denver for a television debate. Because Paul Tsongas was leading in the polls in Colorado, the other four candidates tended to gang up on him. Bill Clinton opened the attack. "We do not need to do what . . . Tsongas wants to do," Clinton said, "to build hundreds of more nuclear plants."[18]

"That is a lie! That is a lie!" Tsongas charged back. He said he favored building new-generation nuclear power plants, not the big, older models that are dangerous and inefficient.

Clinton then jumped on that statement by Tsongas. "You don't want to build more nuclear plants?" Clinton asked mockingly. "Say you don't then. Let's get you on the record for the first time."

Tsongas responded by reiterating his well-known position that nuclear research must be continued as a necessary energy option and as a possible way to reduce global warming.

Clinton dramatically pointed his finger at Tsongas as he made his charges concerning the Tsongas position on nuclear energy. The *Denver Post* noted that the crowd—or at least part of the crowd—let out a whoop at that stage of the proceedings. A photograph of Clinton pointing at Tsongas was printed in the *Denver Post* the next day. Clearly, the argument over nuclear energy had been the "defining exchange of the debate."

For his part, Tsongas called on the other four candidates to make a pledge to stop attack television advertisements against each other. "Put your hand up, Bill, no negative ads," Tsongas said to Clinton, who at that very moment was inundating Colorado television with attack ads against Tsongas. Clinton declined to make such a pledge, however, noting that it was Tsongas himself who ran the first negative ads of the campaign.

Tsongas's "make a pledge" gambit did pay off in one way. At the same time he called for Clinton to make a pledge against negative ads, Tsongas raised his own right arm as if taking a solemn oath. As Tsongas surely hoped would happen, the Associated Press circulated to its member newspapers a photograph of Tsongas with his right arm in the air.

As he had done throughout the Colorado campaign, Jerry Brown carefully positioned himself as the outsider among all the candidates, repeatedly condemning the corrupting influence of big money in politics.

On Tuesday, March 3, 1992, Colorado Democrats went to the polls to participate in their first ever presidential primary. The results of the election were startling. In a stunning upset, former California governor Jerry Brown won the Colorado primary by the narrowest of margins. He nosed out Bill Clinton, who came in a close second. Clinton in turn narrowly outran Paul Tsongas, who finished a close third. Bob Kerrey and Tom Harkin came in far behind the three front-runners.

Political analysts hurried to explain how Brown, whose candidacy had not been taken seriously by the news media, could win in Colorado. The most obvious reason was that Brown had spent almost all of the last week before election day campaigning in Colorado. If nothing else, Brown had demonstrated that being physically present in a primary state and getting as much free publicity as possible can, upon occasion, compensate for not having a lot of money for expensive television commercials.

Another reason for Brown's Colorado victory was his strong stand against nuclear power. Northwest of Denver, on a high plain overlooking the city, stands the Rocky Flats nuclear weapons plant. For years this facility had been manufacturing highly radioactive plutonium triggers for detonating nuclear bombs. Environmentalists long had charged that the Rocky Flats plant was emitting radioactivity and endangering the health of the many Denver suburbanites who had moved into the immediate vicinity of the plant. Whether or not Rocky Flats was indeed dangerously radioactive was a vigorously debated point, but one result of the debate was to create a strong antinuclear constituency in the northwest Denver suburbs.

Analysis of the election results showed that Brown had drawn his strongest vote in the area around Rocky Flats. He easily carried Boulder County, which is located just to the north. He also carried Denver, which is located to the east, and Jefferson County, the large suburban county in which Rocky Flats is located.[19]

The unusually heavy vote for Brown in Boulder County also was attributed to the fact that the University of Colorado is located there. As Brown's advance person, Caroline, had put it: "Jerry is red hot on college campuses."

The Colorado win was a tremendous boost for Brown. He had done well in Maine, but that was in a caucus state, not a primary state such as Colorado. In addition, the Colorado victory enabled Brown to qualify for more government campaign matching funds, a source of money he greatly needed given his $100 limit on personal campaign contributions. Because he did not get 10 percent or more of the vote in the New Hampshire or South Dakota primaries, Brown had to get at least 20 percent in Colorado to keep those campaign dollars coming his way. He ended up with 28.7 percent of the Colorado vote.[20]

The big loser in Colorado was the former Massachusetts senator Paul Tsongas. Once again Tsongas had suffered miserably at the hands of the expectations game. He had been leading in the polls the week before primary election day and had been predicted at one point to easily win Colorado. When he came in third, albeit a close third, Tsongas lost all claim to be gaining momentum and growing in stature with Democratic voters.

Clearly Tsongas was the victim of two forces. One force was Brown's growing popularity in the Denver area because of his strong antinuclear statements. The second force was the impact of Bill Clinton's negative advertising campaign, which was directly targeted at

Tsongas. The net result of these two forces was to shove Tsongas back into third place and push Jerry Brown into the Colorado winner's circle.

Tsongas "tsupporters" in Colorado were openly disappointed. Meridith Farnham, a coordinator for Tsongas, tried to put as bright an interpretation on things as possible. "We expected to be third three weeks ago," she noted. She then pointed out that, before his win in New Hampshire two weeks previously, Tsongas was near the bottom of Colorado public opinion polls and virtually unknown in the state.[21] Judged in that light, a close third-place finish was a big improvement.

The Clinton forces were able to make their usual claim of victory, even though Clinton did not come in first in Colorado. By finishing a close second to Brown, it was argued, Clinton demonstrated, as he did in New Hampshire, that he can run well in a nonsouthern state. "What [Colorado] demonstrates is [Clinton] has strength in the West, in a state outside the South," said Polly Baca, the Colorado co-chair for Clinton.[22]

Although no one in the Clinton camp would say so publicly, the Brown victory in Colorado enormously helped Clinton by making Paul Tsongas, Clinton's real competition for the Democratic nomination in 1992, look bad. Because Tsongas had won New Hampshire, it was Tsongas that Clinton wanted to knock out of the race first. Clinton could easily deal with an underfinanced and overly liberal candidate such as Jerry Brown once he had Tsongas out of the way.

The Colorado primary was most unkind to Nebraska senator Bob Kerrey. The northeast corner of Colorado is contiguous with southwest Nebraska, so Kerrey was able to make the same "close to home" claim in Colorado that had worked so well for him in South Dakota. The Kerrey campaign never really got off the ground in Colorado, however, because Tsongas, Clinton, and Brown received almost all the media attention in the state. Kerrey's weak fourth-place finish in "close to home" Colorado indicated that Bob Kerrey's campaign for the Democratic nomination for president in 1992 was just about over.

As for Tom Harkin, the Iowa senator gave up on Colorado very early and did next to no campaigning in the state. Colorado is not a strong labor union state, and much of the Harkin campaign strategy was oriented to winning support from labor union members.

The major message that Brown's Colorado victory sent to the general public was that it definitely was no longer a two-way race for the Democratic nomination between Paul Tsongas and Bill Clinton. It was now a three-way race among Paul Tsongas, Bill Clinton, and Jerry Brown. "The Democratic field is wide open," said Walter Stone, a professor of political science at the University of Colorado at Boulder. "It's not the case that any candidate has been able to seize the day and define himself as the front-runner."[23]

The daily newspaper in Colorado Springs summed up the race for the Democratic nomination for president in one good headline: "Surprising Colorado Muddles Race."[24]

On the Republican side of the ledger in Colorado, the Pat Buchanan campaign looked at first as if it might get some action going. A $250-a-plate dinner with Buchanan was scheduled to be held in Denver followed by a $100-a-plate luncheon with him the following day in Colorado Springs. Both events were canceled, however, when ticket sales lagged badly. Only twenty people in Colorado Springs signed up and paid their $100 to have lunch and hear a speech by Pat Buchanan.[25]

Once the Denver and Colorado Springs fund-raisers were called off, Buchanan decided to skip Colorado completely. Georgia was having its presidential primary on the same day as Colorado. Buchanan decided a conservative southern state like Georgia was probably a more lucrative place to hunt for anti-President Bush votes than Colorado.

Although President Bush himself did not campaign in Colorado, the Bush campaign made quite an effort at bringing "Bush-surrogates" into the state. Ten days before primary election day, Vice President Dan Quayle flew into Denver for a $500-a-plate fund-raising breakfast, a news conference, a speech to the heavily Republican Colorado state legislature, and a speech to some five hundred Republican supporters gathered at the Hyatt Regency Hotel in downtown Denver. Quayle told his audiences there was a big difference between making America "No. 1 in the world," which was what presidents Reagan and Bush accomplished, and trying to put "America First," Pat Buchanan's recommended policy of trying to protect United States manufacturing industries with high import tariffs on foreign goods.[26]

One week later, a member of President Bush's cabinet, Housing and Urban Development Secretary Jack Kemp, campaigned for Bush at a luncheon in Colorado Springs. As had Vice President Quayle, Kemp attacked Buchanan for his "America First" approach to international trade issues. Kemp quipped: "He's the only guy I have ever seen who has a Mercedes-Benz with a 'Buy American' sticker on it!"[27]

The Saturday before primary election day, Barbara Bush, the president's wife, paid an all-day visit to Colorado. The First Lady concentrated her time in Colorado Springs and Golden, two of the more Republican cities in Colorado, and avoided Denver, which is heavily Democratic. Her visit to Colorado Springs was typical of how top celebrities often are handled in political campaigns.

Twenty-four years earlier, in Richard Nixon's successful 1968 campaign for the presidency, his managers came up with a new theory of how to handle a well-known personality on the campaign trail. Voters do not particularly like to hear speeches, this theory holds, and radio and television stations only cover a few sentences, or at most one paragraph or two, of a political speech. Most voters are content just to see the famous person and, if possible, shake hands and perhaps exchange a few words. Nixon's managers in 1968 encouraged him to reduce the number of formal speeches he gave and spend more time simply walking past, and being seen by, large numbers of people. Because he had been vice president for eight years and an unsuccessful candidate for president in 1960, Nixon was well enough known to voters by 1968 that just to "see Nixon" was enough.[28]

Barbara Bush's visit to Colorado Springs appeared to have been designed directly by this philosophy. At the Citadel Mall, a large and busy regional shopping center, a long stretch of wide hallway, with stores and shops on both sides, was divided in half length-wise by red plastic taped to the floor. Those who wanted to see and shake hands with Barbara Bush were told to stand along the red tape but to be careful not to step over it.

By the time Barbara Bush was scheduled to arrive at the Citadel Mall, thousands of people were lined up to see her. The more committed Republicans were waving "Bush-Quayle 1992" signs. The hoped-for "wave of excitement and anticipation" swept through the crowd when the First Lady appeared and began making her way along the red tape, taking her time as she shook hands, cuddled babies, admired Girl Scouts, accepted a rose from a little girl, and answered people's questions.

At the end of the long shopping center hallway, the red tape took a hard right turn. The area just past the hard right turn was designated for the press, particularly the television cameras and camcorders. This location enabled the television cameras, some of them equipped with telephoto and zoom lenses, to film Barbara Bush as she walked the entire length of the line. As she passed the press area, the First Lady stopped and gave brief personal interviews to the television reporters and camerapersons who wanted them.

Obviously, such a setup was designed to give both the voters and the media exactly what they wanted. The voters did not have to listen to a long speech or pay a great deal of money for a mediocre hotel banquet dinner, but they did get to see and meet the First Lady, and that would be enough to be able to go home and tell family and friends about it. The news media, particularly television, got a well-known personage who was constantly in motion (never a stationary talking head) and continually interacting with local citizens. The locale, a busy regional shopping center where almost everyone in the community had been at one time or another, would add even more local interest to the news coverage.

To no one's surprise, George Bush defeated Pat Buchanan by more than a two-to-one ratio in the Colorado Republican primary. Bush received 67.6 percent of the vote to Buchanan's 29.9 percent. It was a big improvement for the president over the New Hampshire primary, held only two weeks earlier, in which Bush received only 53 percent of the vote.

In retrospect, the citizens of Colorado got a good deal when they voted themselves their first ever presidential primary. All of the major Democratic candidates except Tom Harkin campaigned in the state. Those Coloradans with a mind to do so, particularly those who lived in Denver, Colorado Springs, and Pueblo, could get out and hear candidates speak, meet them personally and shake their hands, and even ask them a question or two. In addition to the candidates themselves, the Colorado primary attracted a number of candidate spouses, including First Lady Barbara Bush, as well as the vice president and a member of the president's cabinet.

Although some people might not consider it a plus, the primary election brought presidential primary television advertisements to Colorado for the first time. More than $280,000 was spent on TV commercials in Colorado by the various presidential candidates.[29] Realistically, it was through Paul Tsongas's and Bill Clinton's television ads that many Democratic voters in Colorado related to and were informed about the issues in the Democratic presidential primary. Nothing like that would have happened if Colorado voters had not adopted themselves an early presidential primary.

More importantly, Colorado got to have a big say in the outcome of the presidential nominating process, something that had never happened before. On the Democratic side, Colorado gave a big boost to Jerry Brown. It also dealt a damaging blow to Paul Tsongas, a result which significantly advanced the candidacy of Bill Clinton.[30] On the Republican side, Colorado gave President Bush a much higher percentage of the vote over Pat Buchanan than he had received in New Hampshire, thereby smoothing Bush's path toward renomination. All in all, the Colorado primary turned out to be more important than even its most committed supporters had expected.

8. MARYLAND

Colorado was not the only state voting on the first Tuesday in March. Three other states—Maryland, Georgia, and Utah—joined Colorado in holding a presidential primary on the earliest date allowed by national Democratic Party rules.

Historically, Maryland had been one of the earliest states to hold a presidential primary, traditionally voting on the second Tuesday in May. Back when very few states held presidential primaries, Maryland occasionally found itself in the center of the presidential primary spotlight. In 1960, a young United States senator from Massachusetts, John F. Kennedy, scored a big win in the Maryland primary and the resulting publicity helped propel Kennedy to the 1960 Democratic nomination and, the following November, the presidency.

In 1964, Maryland again attracted national attention when Alabama governor George Wallace ran for the Democratic nomination for president on an anti-civil rights platform. Incumbent Democratic president Lyndon Johnson declined to run in any primaries that year, so a pro-Johnson Marylander, United States Senator Daniel B. Brewster, ran in Johnson's place. Many people feared that Wallace, famous for his outspoken support of racial segregation, just might win the primary in a quasi-southern state such as Maryland. As it turned out, Brewster defeated Wallace by 57 percent to 42 percent on Maryland's presidential primary day. The Wallace threat to Lyndon Johnson's renomination quickly evaporated.[1]

Maryland legislators were so embarrassed by the Wallace campaign of 1964 they abolished the Maryland presidential primary for 1968. It was reinstituted in 1972, but with somewhat meaningless results. Governor Wallace, again running for the Democratic nomination on a pro-segregation platform, was shot and critically wounded by a would-be assassin (not a Marylander) the day before primary election day. The bullet struck Governor Wallace in the spine and left him paralyzed from the waist down for life. A wave of sympathy for Wallace swept Maryland Democrats, and he easily won the 1972 Maryland primary.[2]

After 1972 Maryland voters began developing a "nonsouthern" preference for Democratic presidential candidates. The rest of the nation was genuinely surprised in 1976 when then Governor Jerry Brown of California upset former Georgia governor Jimmy Carter in the Maryland primary voting.[3] In 1984, a majority of Maryland Democrats cast their ballots for Walter F. Mondale of Minnesota, and in 1988 they went for Massachusetts governor Michael S. Dukakis. Maryland Democrats, it appeared, were abandoning their quasi-southern past and favoring candidates from north of the Mason-Dixon Line.

Despite Maryland's new northward political perspective, in the mid-1980s Maryland state legislators jumped on the Super Tuesday bandwagon and moved the Maryland primary date from the second Tuesday in May to the second Tuesday in March. Michael Gordon, a member of the lower branch of the Maryland legislature, the house of delegates, recalled that joining with the South in voting on Super Tuesday was highly controversial. "At the time we joined the Super Tuesday fiasco," Gordon said, "I promised to move the Maryland primary back to the middle of May if, as many legislators suspected, Maryland was eclipsed by so many large southern states voting on the same day."[4]

Super Tuesday in Maryland in 1988 fulfilled Michael Gordon's worst fears. "There was no candidate participation in Maryland in 1988," Gordon said. "The candidates spent all their time and money in states like Florida and Texas. Voter turnout in the primary went way down. As soon as I could, I introduced legislation to move the Maryland primary back to mid-May."

At this point Nathan Landow, chairman of the Maryland Democratic Party, intervened. Rather than going back to mid-May, which might result in the Maryland presidential primary being too late in the process to make any difference, Landow pushed for Maryland to adopt the earliest date permitted by the national Democratic Party. Landow and Gordon reached political agreement on the issue. Gordon changed the date in his presidential primary bill to the first Tuesday in March in return for Landow agreeing to use his influence to get the bill through the upper house of the legislature, the Maryland senate.

"I felt strongly about this," Landow said. "I was angry at the way Iowa and New Hampshire were getting so much attention just by going first. Maryland is a microcosm of the entire country, much more representative of the American people than either Iowa or New Hampshire. We were completely lost in the Super Tuesday shuffle. I thought Maryland should be in a more important place. I knew we could accomplish that by moving the primary date forward."[5]

Landow pointed out that the Democratic National Committee allowed presidential primaries on the first Tuesday in March in 1992 because, at one time in early 1991, California was looking for an early primary date and did not want to join the southern states on Super Tuesday. "I figured that if that early date is good enough for California," Landow said, "it's good enough for Maryland."

With Landow's strong support, the bill changing Maryland's presidential primary to the first Tuesday in March easily passed the Maryland legislature, which had large Democratic majorities in both houses. "We did not care whether the Republicans liked it or not," Michael Gordon said. "They have very little input in the Maryland legislature."

As one of the lawmakers who was chiefly responsible for the new early Maryland primary date, Michael Gordon was very pleased with the way the primary turned out. "Nathan Landow was absolutely correct. The early date gave us tremendous candidate play. All the candidates campaigned and spent money in Maryland. There was an unusually large amount of voter participation. Maryland had an exciting presidential primary in 1992."

The Democratic candidate for president who looked most longingly at Maryland in 1992 was Paul Tsongas. Maryland is not a New England state, but it is located on the East Coast, and that gives it something in common with Massachusetts. More important, because Maryland contains both the Baltimore suburbs and the northern and eastern suburbs of Washington, D.C., it is full to overflowing with the same kind of young, upscale suburbanites who voted so strongly for Tsongas in New Hampshire. The Tsongas camp also was aware that, in most recent Democratic primaries, Maryland had been voting for northern candidates such as Paul Tsongas rather than southern candidates such as Bill Clinton.[6]

For its part, the Clinton campaign could not abandon Maryland to Paul Tsongas, even when early polls showed Tsongas with a big lead in the state. Clinton campaigned in Maryland and, as he had done in Colorado, flooded prime time television the weekend before election day with anti-Tsongas advertising. Brown, Kerrey, and Harkin all made an effort in Maryland also.

When the votes were counted in the Maryland primary, Tsongas emerged a comfortable winner. Clinton came in second with Brown, Harkin, and Kerrey trailing behind. The Maryland win was vitally important to Tsongas. It counterbalanced his unexpected loss to both Brown and Clinton in Colorado. It also demonstrated that Tsongas could win in a state that was not, like New Hampshire, immediately adjacent to Massachusetts.

The Republican portion of the Maryland primary was dull and uneventful. Conservative Republican candidate Pat Buchanan bypassed Maryland to concentrate his campaign in the southern state of Georgia, which also was holding its presidential primary on the first Tuesday in March. As a result of Buchanan's neglect, President Bush won all forty-two of Maryland's Republican delegates.

Maryland's experience with Super Tuesday in 1988 is instructive. A midsize state in terms of population, Maryland found itself getting no candidate visits and press attention whatsoever when it shared the same primary date in 1988 with states as large as Florida and Texas. Maryland political leaders were much happier in 1992 when they shared their primary day with only two other midsize states, Colorado and Georgia, and one small state, Utah. The lesson seemed to be that no state with a small or midsize population can expect to play a significant role in the presidential nominating process if it holds its primary on the same day a populous state, or a group of populous states, is voting.

9. GEORGIA

Georgia, a Dixie state if there ever was one, voted on Super Tuesday in 1988 along with most of the rest of the southern states. Instead of boosting the candidacy of a moderate White southern candidate, Senator Al Gore Jr. of neighboring Tennessee, Georgia Democrats gave first place to a Black candidate, Jesse Jackson of Illinois. Al Gore finished a strong second, followed in third place by Michael Dukakis, the candidate who eventually won the Democratic nomination in 1988.

Up until early December of 1991, Georgia was scheduled to stick with Super Tuesday, the second Tuesday in March, as its 1992 presidential primary day. Then, with no advance warning, Democratic Governor Zell Miller appointed a commission of Georgia citizens to review the idea of moving the Georgia primary ahead one week to the first Tuesday in March. The commission held two public hearings, one in Macon and one in Atlanta, and in early January of 1992 recommended that Georgia switch to the earlier primary date.

Bob Holmes, a member of the Georgia house of representatives from Atlanta, saw that it would be very difficult, starting as late as January of 1992, to introduce a new bill in the Georgia legislature to change Georgia's primary date. There simply was not enough time to get such a bill through both houses of the legislature and signed into law by the governor in time for a "first Tuesday in March" primary.

Holmes had a bill already working in the legislature that dealt with setting the dates for county sales tax elections. He suggested to

Governor Miller that his bill, which was ready for final passage, be quickly amended to set the earlier presidential primary date. Governor Miller agreed to this high-speed legislative strategy, and virtually overnight the Georgia legislature moved the Georgia presidential primary to the first Tuesday in March.

State representative Holmes, who teaches political science at Clark Atlanta University when not attending to his legislative duties, said there were two reasons why Georgia moved its presidential primary ahead one week. "One reason was so Georgia could be 'First in the South,'" Holmes explained. "The other was that it was well known that Governor Miller strongly supported Bill Clinton."[1]

Moving the Georgia primary ahead one week would provide Bill Clinton with a bridge to Super Tuesday. One reason a moderate White southern candidate had not won a big victory on Super Tuesday in 1988, it was argued, was that a northern candidate, Massachusetts governor Michael Dukakis, won a number of primaries and caucuses in northern states before the Super Tuesday voting in the South took place. By the time the southern states voted on Super Tuesday, northerner Dukakis already had enough momentum to eventually win the nomination.

The way to prevent that from happening in 1992, so the logic went, was to move one southern state forward a week and thereby give Bill Clinton a chance to win an early southern state victory. This would give Clinton some badly needed momentum before the Super Tuesday voting in the South took place.

Governor Miller publicly denied that he was pressing for an earlier Georgia primary date just to help Clinton, his fellow southern Democratic governor. Cynthia Wright, the executive counsel to Governor Miller, stated the governor's position succinctly: "On any number of occasions, Governor Miller has firmly denied that he supported changing the Georgia primary date to help Bill Clinton."[2]

Representative Holmes made it clear there were more good reasons for moving the Georgia primary ahead than just furthering the Clinton candidacy. He noted: "There was this feeling of being overwhelmed by Texas and Florida. Instead of being one of the southern 'many' voting on Super Tuesday, it would be better for Georgia to be the only southern state voting a week earlier. No one ever said we were going to make Georgia the 'New Hampshire of the South,' but that was what we were trying to do."

It is interesting to review the situation faced by the Clinton forces in early December of 1991, when Georgia governor Miller began his drive to change the date of the Georgia primary.

The Iowa caucuses would be first, and Iowa "favorite son" Tom Harkin surely would win there. New Hampshire, a New England state, would hold the first primary, quickly followed by the Maine caucuses, another New England show. It was unlikely Clinton would win either of those two contests. South Dakota would vote next, and certainly either Kerrey or Harkin would win there, thus producing another Clinton loss. Colorado, Maryland, and Utah were scheduled to hold their primaries next, the Tuesday before Super Tuesday, but again there was no reason to think that Clinton, with his main base of support in the South, could win in any of those three states. Clinton probably would win the South Carolina primary, which would take place the Saturday before Super Tuesday.

Unless something was changed and changed quickly, Clinton would arrive at Super Tuesday having lost six primaries and the Iowa and Maine caucuses. His only victory would be South Carolina. That meant there would be little or no Clinton momentum as voting began on Super Tuesday in the South. It would be 1988 all over again, and a northerner or westerner would end up with the 1992 Democratic nomination for president. By speedily advancing Georgia's primary date by one week, Governor Zell Miller and the heavily Democratic Georgia legislature gave Clinton the opportunity for another early southern victory to add to South Carolina.

The 1992 Georgia Democratic primary centered mainly around the issue of Bill Clinton's character. The South is the most conservative section of the nation, and it is particularly conservative on the issues of patriotism and morality. To many Georgia Democrats, Clinton's candidacy represented a head-on collision between their desire to vote for a fellow southerner and their conservative outlook on military service and marital fidelity.

Clinton's attempts to avoid the Vietnam-era military draft and his admission that he "caused pain in my marriage" hurt him with Georgia voters. But for most Georgia Democrats, there was no other choice. Georgia state senator Earl Echols expressed the dilemma clearly when he told the Associated Press: "I don't like Clinton's position on the draft deal. But I haven't got anywhere else to hang my hat."[3]

Both Nebraska senator Bob Kerrey and former Massachusetts senator Paul Tsongas campaigned against Clinton in Georgia. Mable Thomas, a Georgia state legislator, endorsed Kerrey, a Vietnam War hero, and told a Kerrey rally that Americans "want somebody who'll be commander in chief, not commander in chicken."[4]

United States Senator David Boren, an Oklahoma Democrat, spoke at a Georgia rally for Paul Tsongas. Introducing Tsongas to a standing room-only crowd at Manuel's Tavern in Atlanta, Boren described Tsongas as a man of impeccable morals. "I don't have to wonder what his personal qualities are like," Boren said. "I know about his character."[5]

Clinton tried to deflect attention from the draft issue and the marital infidelity issue by advertising himself on television as a man of "old-fashioned values." In order to get the votes of economically conservative Georgians, he hammered away on his position that "welfare recipients should be preparing to go to work." Clinton argued that voters were getting tired of the character issue. He predicted he would win the Georgia primary and said that "people are beginning to get back to the issues and are listening to my message again."[6]

On election day the hastily advanced Georgia Democratic primary did the job it was designed to do. Bill Clinton won his first Democratic primary, and he won it by almost a two-to-one margin over the man who was now his chief rival, Paul Tsongas. Clinton came away from the Georgia Democratic primary with fifty-four delegates to the Democratic National Convention. Tsongas won only twenty-two.

Clinton thus got the big southern victory he needed as a prelude to Super Tuesday the following week.[7] His Georgia victory also gave him something to crow about on a day when he was finishing second to Paul Tsongas in Maryland and second to Jerry Brown in Colorado.

Exit polls conducted by CNN indicated that Clinton was, as he hoped to do, beginning to unite both Black and White southern Democrats behind his candidacy. CNN reported that 70 percent of Blacks in Georgia cast their ballots for Clinton and 53 percent of Whites.[8]

The last-minute shift in the date of the Georgia Democratic primary was the most blatantly manipulative act of the 1992 Democratic primary season. State legislatures control the calendar of presidential primary elections, and in this case the Georgia state legislature changed the calendar to give a big boost to Clinton's drive for the Democratic nomination. One of the oldest rules of politics is: "If you cannot win under the present rules, change the rules." This was done for Bill Clinton in Georgia in 1992.[9]

When Georgia's Democratic state legislature moved the Georgia presidential primary forward one week, no attention whatsoever was given to what effect this might have on the Republican presidential primary. According to Democratic state representative Bob Holmes, some Republicans in the legislature did complain about moving the primary on such short notice, charging that it was "too partisan." As is typical in such cases, the majority Democrats in the Georgia legislature paid no attention to the Republican minority and set the date of the Georgia presidential primary to suit themselves.

As it turned out, the change in date of the Georgia primary had a significant effect on the race for the Republican presidential nomination in 1992. Basking in the glow of the large amount of press coverage he had received following his strong showing in New Hampshire, Pat Buchanan looked around for another state where he could hope to demonstrate Republican dissatisfaction with President Bush. The conservative South was the place to look. Because Georgia had moved its primary forward one week, Georgia was holding the first southern primary in the Republican Party as well as the Democratic.

Buchanan decided to bypass Colorado, Maryland, and Utah, which also were voting on the first Tuesday in March, and concentrate all his attention on Georgia. If he could get a substantial number of Georgia Republicans to vote for him—enough to improve on his showing in New Hampshire—Buchanan could maintain his momentum and perhaps make an even stronger showing in more of the conservative South one week later on Super Tuesday.

The weekend before election day, Buchanan began running a large number of attack ads against President Bush in Georgia. One Buchanan TV spot accused Bush of continuing to allow the National Endowment of the Arts, a United States government agency, to subsidize paintings and dramatic productions that "glorified homosexuality, exploited children and perverted the image of Jesus Christ." The ad opened with particularly graphic scenes that portrayed naked gay Black men singing and dancing, scenes the ad said were from a film partially subsidized by the federal arts agency. The ad concluded by condemning taxpayer funding of "pornographic and blasphemous art."

Speaking to about five hundred enthusiastic supporters in an indoor shopping mall in the city of Rome in northwest Georgia, Buchanan said he would abolish the National Endowment of the Arts if he were president. He added: "I will have the building padlocked and fumigated."[10]

Buchanan also ran television ads in Georgia that attacked President Bush for signing into law a civil rights bill that eased the way for employees to win court battles against job discrimination. Buchanan charged the new rights law would lead to minority hiring quotas, a practice thought to be particularly unpopular with conservative White southerners.

The Bush campaign was quick to respond to Buchanan's charges, both those in the television ads and those delivered by Buchanan in person. Torie Clarke, a Bush spokeswoman, characterized Buchanan's charge that Bush subsidized pornography as "disgusting lies," "a strategy of desperation," and "garbage." She added: "The [Buchanan] ads are a real insult to people in this country and to the people of Georgia."[11]

The Bush camp also responded to the Buchanan TV ad charging that the civil rights bill Bush signed was a job quotas bill. Spokeswoman Clarke pointed out that President Bush had opposed earlier versions of the bill that really would have ushered in job quotas. Clarke said Buchanan "should stop stretching the truth so much. . . . George Bush worked for three years to get civil rights without quotas."[12]

Not to be outdone, the Bush campaign began running attack TV ads of its own. In one particularly noteworthy commercial, Bush was endorsed by Marine Commandant P. X. Kelley, who strongly criticized Buchanan for initially opposing United States military involvement in the Persian Gulf War.

The Sunday before election day, the Bush organization pulled out all the stops in its sizzling battle with Buchanan for Georgia's Republican voters. A leading Bush surrogate campaigner, former drug policy director William Bennett, charged Pat Buchanan with "flirting with fascism." Appearing on ABC televison's *This Week with David Brinkley*, Bennett was asked if he agreed with commentators who said that Buchanan's opposition to immigration into the United States by "non-English" peoples was a kind of fascism. Bennett replied: "I think that Pat certainly flirts with it—it being fascism."

"Pat has a mighty heart," the former drug czar continued, "but I am very disappointed with the character and quality of the approach he is making."

Another surrogate Bush campaigner in Georgia was Carroll Campbell, the Republican governor of South Carolina. Speaking on the CBS television show *Face the Nation*, Campbell attacked Buchanan for his "America First" campaign against President Bush's free trade policies. Campbell said that Buchanan, in his right-wing appeal for Georgia votes, was making the South look more "reactionary" and "isolationist" than it actually is. "We are not talking about building a wall around America," Campbell said. "We are talking about taking our place in the world."

The Bush forces even got some gratuitous help from Zell Miller, the Democratic governor of Georgia, who was appearing on *Face the Nation* with South Carolina governor Campbell. He also thought Pat Buchanan's intensely conservative campaign was a misreading of contemporary sentiment in the South. He concluded: "I think the Georgia that Pat Buchanan knows about is evidently the Georgia that he read about in 'Tobacco Road.'"[13]

The Bush managers decided that the Georgia showdown with Pat Buchanan merited some personal campaigning by the President himself. George Bush made a two-day swing through Georgia the weekend before election day with major campaign stops in Atlanta and Savannah. Speaking to thirteen hundred Republicans at a state party banquet in Atlanta, Bush said that Georgia had much to lose from Buchanan's proposed efforts to prevent foreign products from being imported into the United States. The President claimed 165,000 Georgia jobs are linked to international trade. "So get past all the tough talk out there," Bush said, "all the patriotic posturing about fighting back by shutting out foreign goods."[14]

The heavy campaigning by President Bush and his many surrogate campaigners worked. On primary election day, Georgia Republicans gave George Bush 64 percent of their votes compared to 36 percent for Pat Buchanan. Bush had triumphed by almost a two-to-one margin, significantly better than he had done against Buchanan in New Hampshire. Because the Georgia Republican party has a "winner-take-all" rule, Bush was awarded all fifty-two of Georgia's Republican National Convention delegates.

The Georgia Republican primary was bad news for Pat Buchanan. If the conservative challenger could not win in conservative Georgia, he probably was not going to win anywhere in the conservative South a week later on Super Tuesday. If, as a conservative, Buchanan could not win in the conservative South, he probably could not win anywhere in the nation.

10. An Evaluation of "Junior Tuesday"

About one week before voters went to the polls for the presidential primaries in Colorado, Maryland, Georgia, and Utah, the news media in the United States slowly began to realize that the first Tuesday in March was going to be a significant day in the 1992 race for the presidency. Someone nicknamed the day "Junior Tuesday" on the theory that it was a mini-version of Super Tuesday, the really big day of primaries and caucuses scheduled one week later for the second Tuesday in March. The nickname stuck, and Junior Tuesday became an exciting new addition to the presidential primary calendar.

And there was more than just presidential primaries on Junior Tuesday. American Samoa, Idaho, Minnesota, and Washington State all decided to hold their presidential precinct caucuses on that date.

Junior Tuesday illustrated some interesting things about presidential primaries and caucuses. One was that very little attention is paid to precinct caucuses scheduled the same day as a series of exciting presidential primaries. The presidential candidates paid only token visits to the Junior Tuesday caucus states, and the news media almost totally ignored them.

A big part of the problem in the Junior Tuesday caucus states was that, in Minnesota and Washington State, no clear-cut results were available on election night. In the Democratic race, Washington State never produced any results showing one candidate to be doing better than another. The best thing Minnesota could come up with was a straw poll showing Senator Tom Harkin, from the bordering state of Iowa, with 27 percent of the vote.

The Idaho caucuses selected six convention delegates for Harkin and five for Paul Tsongas, but those results were of questionable value because five of the state's convention delegates were not clearly determined in time for election night news reports. In American Samoa, where Democrats had to fly from the outlying islands to Pago Pago to cast their caucus votes, a somewhat ineffectual result was produced when three uncommitted delegates were chosen.

The conclusion is obvious. Caucuses are miserably poor competitors against presidential primaries when it comes to attracting candidate visits and media coverage. Only caucuses scheduled very early in the primary-caucus calendar, such as Iowa's and Maine's, have any real influence on who does or does not receive a major party nomination for president.

Junior Tuesday also illustrated the point that states with small populations, even when they conduct presidential primaries, will not receive much attention if those primaries are scheduled the same day as primaries in states with larger populations. This is what happened to Utah's Democratic presidential primary in 1992. Utah was the one Rocky Mountain state to join Colorado in holding a presidential primary on the first Tuesday in March. Utah had so few delegates at stake—23 compared to Colorado's 47, Maryland's 67, and Georgia's 76—that both the candidates and the news media tended to overlook it.

The election results from Utah's Democratic presidential primary somewhat reflected Colorado's. Jerry Brown won Utah with 34 percent of the vote, just as he had finished first in Colorado. He was closely trailed by Paul Tsongas, the third-place finisher in Colorado. Bill Clinton, who came in second in Colorado, finished a weak third in Utah.

For Colorado, Maryland, and Georgia, all of which are somewhat close to the same size in terms of population and numbers of convention delegates, Junior Tuesday was a very successful primary day. The major Democratic candidates split their campaigning more or less equally among the three states. Brown particularly emphasized Colorado, and Tsongas spent extra time in Maryland and Georgia, but the voters in all three states got to see a great deal of the candidates and had lots of campaign advertising playing on their television sets.

The final message seems to be that states can successfully hold presidential primaries on the same day as long as all the states are roughly the same size in terms of population and numbers of convention delegates.

The most interesting thing about Junior Tuesday was that it was something of a "nationally balanced" primary day rather than a regional primary day. Unlike Super Tuesday, which has an unusually large number of southern state primaries and caucuses, Junior Tuesday had its four presidential primaries scattered nicely around the country. Colorado and Utah are Rocky Mountain states, Maryland is an East Coast state, and Georgia is a southern state. Because no region of the nation was overly favored on Junior Tuesday, all three of the major Democratic candidates were able to score a win—Brown in Colorado and Utah, Tsongas in Maryland, and Clinton in Georgia.

Junior Tuesday thus could serve as a model "nationally balanced" presidential primary day. It really is unfair to give a particular region of the country undue influence on an early primary day, as Super Tuesday does for the South. The "nationally balanced" primary day, as represented by Junior Tuesday in 1992, is a more equitable option.

Junior Tuesday produced the first casualty of the five Democratic candidates who ran in primaries and caucuses in 1992. Senator Bob Kerrey from Nebraska, following his failure to place third in even one state on Junior Tuesday, withdrew from the race. Although a decorated hero of the Vietnam War and the only candidate with a comprehensive and well-thought-out health care plan, Kerrey failed to attract votes anywhere but in his neighboring state of South Dakota.[1]

The Saturday after Junior Tuesday, March 7, 1992, was the date of the South Carolina primary. Bill Clinton added more luster to his Georgia victory by winning South Carolina with 63 percent of the vote. Tsongas trailed badly with 19 percent and Brown and Harkin each had 6 percent.

That same Saturday, Tsongas narrowly defeated Clinton in the Arizona caucuses, but Clinton countered with a solid victory in the Wyoming caucuses. The next day, Sunday, Nevada Democrats caucused and gave first place honors to their next-door neighbor, Californian Jerry Brown.

Following his fourth-place finish in the South Carolina primary, Senator Tom Harkin of Iowa withdrew from the race for the Democratic presidential nomination. Harkin had made a concerted effort in South Carolina to attract Black voters, but despite that finished tied for last place with Jerry Brown. Harkin had beamed his campaign at traditional elements in the Democratic Party, particularly organized labor, but his campaign never succeeded in generating any momentum. Harkin's sorry showing and early withdrawal were inter-preted by many observers as a sign that organized labor had lost most of its punch in Democratic Party politics in the United States.

Harkin ended his campaign with a joke. "My advisers told me not to peak too soon," he said. "I took their advice too seriously."

11. SUPER TUESDAY

New Hampshire's "First-in-the-Nation" presidential primary is small and personal and intense. Super Tuesday is just the reverse. So many primaries are taking place in so many states, and a number of those states are so populous, that there is nothing at all personal about the process. On Super Tuesday, candidates resort much more to what is known as "wholesale" politics—a heavy emphasis on television advertising and "big city" media events. There is much less of the "retail" politics—volunteers going door to door, candidates shaking hands in shopping centers, and so forth—that is so extensively used in New Hampshire.

There also is very little candidate campaign time devoted to the Super Tuesday states compared to the candidate campaign time given to New Hampshire. Because New Hampshire votes first, candidates spend anywhere from ten to seventeen weeks campaigning there. Super Tuesday occurs only one week after Junior Tuesday (Colorado, Georgia, Maryland, and Utah) and a mere three days after the South Carolina primary. Big and important as Super Tuesday is, it is essentially a one-week campaign due to its location in a crowded part of the primary and caucus schedule.

Six southern states voted on Super Tuesday in 1992, including two of the largest and fastest-growing states in the nation, Florida and Texas. The other four southern states were Tennessee, Mississippi, Louisiana, and Oklahoma. Missouri, a border state midway between

North and South, held its caucuses on Super Tuesday, as did another border state, Delaware. There also were two New England states holding primaries on Super Tuesday, Massachusetts and Rhode Island. The state of Hawaii held precinct caucuses, but due to the fact that Hawaii is located in such a distant time zone, the Hawaiian results were not reported in time really to be part of the Super Tuesday scene.

Having a large number of southern states vote on the same presidential primary election day was the mid-1980s brainchild of the Democratic Leadership Council, the moderate southern Democrats who wanted to see the Democratic Party nominate more southern-oriented and more moderate candidates for president. If a large number of southern states voted on the same day early in the primary schedule, the logic went, this would give a boost to candidates from southern states. Even if a southerner failed to win in the South on what came to be called Super Tuesday, so many southern states voting on the same day would boost the more moderate Democratic candidates who would be expected to run well in the South.[1]

The Democrats found it easy to implement Super Tuesday because most of the state legislatures in the South have heavy Democratic majorities in both houses. As the Super Tuesday bandwagon started rolling in the mid-1980s, more and more Democratic-dominated southern state legislatures adopted the second Tuesday in March as their primary day. As so often happens in presidential nomination matters, the Republicans had no choice in the decision; in this case, southern Republicans had to go along with Super Tuesday. At the same time Democratic majorities in the state legislatures in southern states decided to hold the Democratic primary on Super Tuesday, they selected the same date for the Republican primary.

Super Tuesday did not work well for moderate southern Democrats in the 1988 primary season. One problem was that a Black candidate for the Democratic nomination, Jesse Jackson, received most of the Black vote in the South on Super Tuesday, thus denying those Black votes to the moderate southern White candidate, Tennessee Senator Albert Gore. This splitting of Black and White southern votes between Jackson and Gore enabled a northern liberal, Massachusetts governor Michael Dukakis, to win a number of key southern states on Super Tuesday in 1988, the most important of which were the populous states of Florida and Texas. Dukakis went on to win the Democratic nomination in 1988 but lost the general election, including all of the South, to Republican George Bush.[2]

The creators of Super Tuesday hoped that having so many southern states hold primaries on the same day would attract more southern candidates to run for the Democratic nomination for president. This part of the plan worked in 1992. Bill Clinton's candidacy was oriented around the idea that Clinton, a moderate southerner, would do well on Super Tuesday and thereby gain enough momentum to win the Democratic nomination.

Clinton's strategy was aided by the fact that, by the time the 1992 primaries and caucuses began, there were no Black candidates for the Democratic nomination for president. Jesse Jackson decided not to run in 1992. The only other prospective Black candidate, Virginia governor L. Douglas Wilder, dropped out of the race long before the New Hampshire primary. Clinton thus found himself in the beneficial position of being the only moderate southern candidate, White or Black, on the ballot in all of those southern states on Super Tuesday.

On a day when so many states are holding primaries and caucuses, both the candidates and the news media have a vested interest in concentrating on key states with large numbers of delegate votes and where the polls show the candidates are running closely. In the 1992 race for the Democratic nomination for president, candidate and press interest for Super Tuesday very quickly settled on Florida. The other Super Tuesday states were deemed uninteresting through the following process of elimination.

Massachusetts was Paul Tsongas's home state, a state he had previously represented in the United States Congress for a decade. Neither Bill Clinton nor Jerry Brown had a chance of coming anywhere close to Tsongas in Massachusetts. The same was true of Rhode Island, a state which bordered on Massachusetts and which Tsongas could claim as New England's "favorite son." Although Delaware, which would be holding caucuses, was not located in New England, it was an East Coast state and shared a long border with Maryland, a state that Tsongas had won easily on Junior Tuesday. Massachusetts, Rhode Island, and Delaware thus were all seen as "tsafe for Tsongas."

Four of the southern states slated to vote on Super Tuesday—Tennessee, Mississippi, Louisiana, and Oklahoma—all shared a common border with Bill Clinton's home state of Arkansas. Proximity was working so strongly for Clinton in these four states that neither Paul Tsongas nor Jerry Brown decided to campaign in them very much. The same "solid for Clinton" logic applied to Missouri, the state located just north of Arkansas, which would be holding caucuses on Super Tuesday.

There was some thought for a while that Tsongas might possibly give Clinton a close race in Texas. A large state, Texas has significant suburban populations living outside of Dallas, Houston, and San Antonio. Tsongas had shown himself to be particularly popular with these kinds of upscale suburban Democrats. In addition, a long-running depression in the oil and gas industry had caused a great deal of economic hardship in Texas, perhaps enough that Tsongas's hard-nosed economic reform plans could attract him a sizable number of votes.

Perhaps more important were Clinton's shortcomings. The many newspaper stories about Clinton's alleged marital infidelities and draft avoidance were thought to be particularly damaging in a state where morality and patriotism are important political issues.

Tsongas was encouraged enough by such reports to make a political swing through Texas, giving a major speech and providing plenty of photo opportunities at the Alamo, the historic symbol of Texas independence located in San Antonio. He also made a bid for Hispanic votes by having his eighty-six-page campaign manifesto, *A Call to Economic Arms*, translated into Spanish, *Un Llamado A Las Armas de la Economia*. Probably no more voters read the Spanish version than read the English, but the fact that Tsongas's major campaign statement was known to have been translated into Spanish probably did earn Tsongas some Hispanic votes.

Jerry Brown came to Texas, grabbing a handheld bullhorn and addressing a large outdoor crowd of students and townspeople at the University of Texas in Austin. *USA Today* reported that a group of middle-aged women in Austin were organizing in behalf of Brown using the name "Matrons for Moonbeam."

By four days before Super Tuesday, however, the pollsters and political analysts had given Texas to Bill Clinton. True, Texas had a significant number of Tsongas-prone suburbanites, but Texas also had a large "Bubba vote," conservative White working-class voters who are deeply committed to the South and southern values. "'Bubba' probably will swallow hard and vote big for Bill Clinton," was the way *USA Today* wrote off Texas as solid Clinton country.

As would be expected in a southern state, Clinton had an impressive organization in Texas headed by the state land commissioner, Garry Mauro. Clinton also lined up key endorsements from Texas members of Congress, important state legislators, and ethnic groups such as the Mexican American Democrats. The fact that Arkansas shares a small portion of its border with Texas also helped. Clinton worked in Texas in 1972 coordinating George McGovern's successful quest for the Democratic nomination for president that year. He made many connections in the Texas Democratic Party at that time, connections which were working strongly for him in 1992. As one Texas political commentator put it: "Not only is [Clinton] familiar here, but people have a comfort level with him. He speaks the language."[3]

In the end, then, Super Tuesday came down to a one-state race, and that state was Florida. The major reason for this was the large number of former northern voters who had moved to South Florida, either to retire or to make a good living and enjoy the outdoor lifestyle of one of the fastest growing states in the nation.

These former northerners were viewed as ripe targets for the Paul Tsongas campaign. His heavy New England accent would not sound quite so strange to them, and his New Hampshire and Maryland primary victories already had demonstrated his strong appeal to people from the northern part of the nation. Furthermore, Florida had voted for Michael Dukakis, another Greek from Massachusetts, on Super Tuesday in 1988. A state Democratic Party official summed up the political situation in Florida this way: "The saying here is, the more south you go, the further north you are."[4]

By the weekend before election day, newspaper polls showed Clinton and Tsongas running dead even in Florida. As Paul Tsongas flew into West Palm Beach on the Friday before election day, aides announced that he would campaign almost full time in Florida prior to the Super Tuesday primaries. "He has picked his battleground," bragged the *Miami Herald*, "and it is here." Tsongas desperately needed at least one win in a southern state on Super Tuesday. Clearly, Florida was his best shot.[5]

The Clinton camp was equally emphatic that, on this particular Super Tuesday, the Clinton-Tsongas showdown was going to be in Florida. "We have a fight on our hands with Paul Tsongas," said Jeff Eller, the Clinton state campaign director. "Florida is where the action is."[6] Clinton, who at one time had been the clear front-runner in Florida, wanted to block Tsongas completely out in the South. It was particularly important to do this because, one week after Super Tuesday, the primary trail led north again—to Michigan and Illinois.

To further illustrate Florida's importance, Jerry Brown, running third but, as usual, running hard, campaigned in Miami the weekend before election day with Black political leader Jesse Jackson. If Brown could do well in one or two of the heavily Black and Hispanic congressional districts in Miami, he could win some delegates.

All three candidates concentrated their campaigning on the many retirement complexes found throughout Florida. Bill Clinton, for instance, courted older voters the Friday before election day at a large waterfront retirement community in Tampa. The next day, Paul Tsongas met with the residents, many of them retired, of a large condominium on Collins Avenue in Miami Beach. The Monday before election day, Clinton's wife Hillary Clinton campaigned through a number of retirement condominiums in the North Miami Beach and Pompano Beach areas.

Retirement complexes are particularly desirable places to campaign because retired people have a great deal of spare time on their hands and enjoy attending political events. Furthermore, retirement facilities have comfortable lobby areas or, in the case of larger facilities, big assembly halls that make convenient and inexpensive places to hold candidate rallies. Bill Clinton and Paul Tsongas spent so much time campaigning in the large retirement condominiums that stretch up Florida's east coast from Miami Beach through Fort Lauderdale to Palm Beach that reporters began referring to "the condo wars" of South Florida.

Century Village is a typical retirement community in South Florida. Located in the small city of Deerfield Beach near Fort Lauderdale, it is a low-density apartment-style development that sprawls over acres and acres of landscaped grounds. Thousands of elderly persons, singles and couples, have resettled from all over the United States to this spacious and relaxing "senior city." Century Village is so large it has three separate community recreation centers to serve the social needs of its elderly residents.

On the Monday night before Super Tuesday, the Century Village Democratic Club held its regular monthly meeting in the auditorium of one of the recreation centers. Over three hundred residents gathered to hear United States Representative Joseph Kennedy of Massachusetts give a speech in behalf of Paul Tsongas. Joe Kennedy, the nephew of former President John F. Kennedy and the son of former Attorney General and Senator Robert Kennedy, was doing some surrogate campaigning in Florida for Tsongas.

One of the officers of the Century Village Democratic Club began the somewhat lengthy process of calling the meeting to order and introducing Congressman Kennedy. The accent of the man doing the introductions was unmistakably New York City. So, it seemed, was almost everyone else's accent in the audience that night. One man in his seventies volunteered the fact that, for more than forty years, he and the man introducing Joseph Kennedy had served together on the same Democratic Party central committee in New York City.

Those who bothered to listen closely to the introduction learned that Bill Clinton had personally attended and addressed a previous meeting of the Century Village Democratic Club. Supporters of Paul Tsongas complained about this show of favoritism to Clinton and demanded that Tsongas be invited to speak at a subsequent meeting. The night before Super Tuesday election day was offered, but

Tsongas had a previous engagement, thus necessitating Joe Kennedy's appearance as a celebrity replacement. One got the distinct impression that only the necessity to give equal time to all the candidates that requested it had led the leadership of the Century Village Democratic Club to give any exposure at all to the Tsongas campaign.

Joseph Kennedy gave an entertaining, workmanlike speech that March evening in Florida. He warmed up his audience with marvelous stories of the Kennedy family life that he experienced while growing up. He related Tsongas's underdog campaign for the presidency in 1992 to his uncle's well-known underdog campaign for the presidency in 1960. Above all, he emphasized that Tsongas had the economic ideas that would prepare the United States to compete effectively in the international economic sphere.

During the entire time Kennedy was speaking, however, well-dressed young men in suitcoats and ties stood at various places around the auditorium holding up "Bill Clinton for President" signs. The youthful appearance and more formal dress of the Clinton workers caused them to stand out in contrast to the obvious age and casual clothing of the residents of Century Village. Two of the Clinton signholders stood at each side of the stage, even while Kennedy was speaking, not waving their Clinton signs but making certain they were plainly visible to everyone in their half of the auditorium. No southern hospitality here. This was "in your face" politics New York City style!

Before, during, and after Kennedy's speech for Tsongas, Clinton workers were busy passing out to the audience a yellow leaflet entitled *The Record on Israel*. Many of the New Yorkers and other northerners who have resettled in South Florida are Jewish and strong supporters of Israel. According to newspaper estimates, Jewish voters account for as much as 25 percent of the vote in Florida Democratic primaries.[7] Clinton's yellow leaflet described him as strongly supporting Israel while noting that Paul Tsongas, when serving in the United States Senate, had supported United States military aid for Syria, one of Israel's enemies in the Middle East. The yellow flyer also charged that, when a senator, Tsongas had criticized Israel for launching a daring aerial bombing raid that wiped out an Iraqi nuclear reactor. The Israelis had feared the nuclear reactor might be used by the Iraqis to build nuclear weapons to be used against Israel.

By the time it was all over, Paul Tsongas Night at the Century Village Democratic Club ended up seeming a great deal more like a second Bill Clinton Night. It was true that Tsongas had an excellent surrogate speaker in Joseph Kennedy, but it was very obvious that Clinton had by far the better organization, both at Century Village and, by implication, throughout the state of Florida.

Clinton's yellow flyer entitled *The Record on Israel* became one of the most famous campaign artifacts of the 1992 Democratic presidential primaries. Clinton's army of Florida campaign workers distributed the flyer, it seemed, in every retirement condominium in the state the weekend before election day. Most important, the news media picked up on the flyer and summarized its "anti-Israel" charges against Tsongas for all to see.[8]

At the same time Clinton workers were bombarding the condos with the famous yellow flyer, the Clinton organization was flooding prime time television in Florida with the same negative ads against Tsongas that had worked so effectively in Colorado and the other Junior Tuesday states. Once again television watchers saw Paul Tsongas described as "Wall Street's best friend" and the enemy of increased Social Security benefits. The anti-Social Security charges were thought to be particularly damaging to Tsongas in a state with such a high percentage of retired residents living on Social Security.

Time magazine subsequently criticized Clinton for his attacks on Tsongas's Social Security proposals: "In Florida he [Clinton] showed a harsh streak in his character, assailing Tsongas most unfairly—but effectively—for supposedly planning to cut Social Security benefits."[9]

Clinton also attacked Tsongas for wanting to raise gasoline taxes, a sensitive issue in a state such as Florida where so many visitors drive to and through the state, either in their own automobiles or in rental cars.

By the time of the Florida primary, the Tsongas campaign appeared to be reeling from two simultaneous blows. One blow was the fact that, virtually overnight after his New Hampshire victory, Tsongas had to build a large national campaign staff. The other blow was the damaging effects of the storm of negative campaigning being unleashed on Tsongas by the Clinton camp.

In retrospect, it appeared that the Tsongas campaign really was not prepared to take advantage of Tsongas's big win in New Hampshire. In the three weeks that separated the New Hampshire primary from Super Tuesday, the Tsongas campaign staff had doubled from forty to eighty people. The result was poor coordination and missed opportunities as more and more inexperienced people joined the rapidly expanding Tsongas team.

It was pointed out that the *Atlanta Constitution* had endorsed Tsongas in the Georgia primary the previous week, but the Tsongas managers had been too inept to properly exploit such an important endorsement. In an effort to achieve more identity with Jewish voters in Florida, Tsongas took a tour of the Holocaust Memorial in Miami Beach, which was dedicated to the millions of Jews who had been killed by Nazi Germany during World War II. Newspaper and television photographers waited in a roped-off area near the entrance to the Holocaust Memorial for Tsongas to come out and pose for outdoor photographs and television interviews. Tsongas aides let their candidate take too long inside the memorial, however, and he came out for the photographs long after the sun had set, thus losing the warm afternoon sunlight that would have made particularly compelling color newspaper photographs and television images.

The day before election day, the *Miami Herald* complained that it was so difficult getting schedule information from the Tsongas camp that the newspaper was having trouble "figuring out where Paul Tsongas was going to pop up next." The *Boston Globe* said that "some [Tsongas] aides have begun calling the campaign 'Noah's Ark,' since there seem to be two people assigned to each function." The *Boston Globe* went on to label the Tsongas campaign "Rolling Blunder" and worried that the organization was "hamstrung by chance and inexperience" and was so chaotic that it could cost Tsongas a nomination that he might otherwise win.[10]

As for the Clinton camp's negative campaigning, it had become so strong by the time of the Florida primary that the Tsongas forces felt compelled to answer back. This decision did not come easily. Tsongas had wanted to concentrate on pitching his own message calling for a pro-business economic policy and the American people working harder rather than asking for more government benefits.

In an interview with the *Miami Herald*, Paul Tsongas worried that going on the defensive and counterattacking Clinton could cost him the election. "I'm in a no-win situation," Tsongas said. "If I don't respond, I'm in the same situation as Michael Dukakis [in 1988]. If I do respond, I'm off my message."[11] Tsongas was referring to the fact that, in the 1988 campaign for president, Democratic candidate Michael Dukakis had been criticized for not responding to a torrent of negative advertising unleashed against him by his successful Republican opponent, George Bush.

Reluctantly, the Tsongas campaign began running a "defensive" television ad. It began with a picture of Tsongas and a superimposed printed quote from Bill Clinton: "I agree with Paul . . . we need a big investment strategy." The audio part of the ad left no doubt, however, that Clinton was not agreeing with Tsongas any more. An announcer said: "Last month, the candidates . . . agreed with Paul Tsongas. They praised his good ideas. But then the polls changed and so did the other candidates. Now they're attacking Paul Tsongas for his work, for his ideas, any attack to make him look bad." At this point in the ad, Tsongas's face was splattered with an unpleasant looking mixture of mud and garbage. The announcer went on: "But people who know Paul Tsongas know he tells it straight. Instead of gimmicks he's got answers to put the economy back on track. The old politics won't change things. Paul Tsongas will."[12]

As attack ads go, this one was somewhat mild and overly circumspect. The ad did not attack Clinton directly. In fact, Clinton's name was mentioned only in connection with the point that Clinton once said he agreed with Tsongas on economic issues. The Tsongas campaign then decided to go with something a good bit stronger. The next Tsongas commercial relied mainly on the audio to carry its message: "Some people will say anything to get elected president. Now Bill Clinton is distorting Paul Tsongas's record on Social Security, trying to scare people. . . . Isn't it time we sent a message that we've had enough negative campaigning?"[13] Continuing the attack, Todd Simmons, a Tsongas campaign spokesperson, charged that the Clinton literature "is reprehensible and just downright deceitful."[14]

The Sunday before election day, Bill Clinton was the subject of another apparent scandal. The *New York Times* charged that Clinton, while governor of Arkansas, had close financial ties to a friend whose business was regulated by the state. The *Times* said Bill and Hillary Clinton were partners in a land deal in the Ozarks which required little investment on the Clintons' part but from which they were to receive 50 percent of the profits. A failed savings and loan association, owned by a close friend of the Clintons' and subject to regulation by the State of Arkansas, had put up most of the money for the Clinton land deal.[15]

When asked about the Ozark land deal, Clinton said that he and his wife had lost money—more than $25,000—and for that reason it had not occurred to him to get out of the partnership because of conflict of interest as governor of Arkansas. Although the story received considerable play in Florida newspapers and on television, the financial arrangements apparently were too detailed and complex to spark the interest of the average Florida voter. Jeff Eller, Clinton's Florida campaign director, perhaps was right when he wishfully said he detected "no fallout" in Clinton's support in Florida as a result of the Ozark land deal.[16]

Super Tuesday election day dawned sunny, cool, and breezy in South Florida. The good weather guaranteed a good turnout at the polls. Election night found the two major candidates for the Democratic nomination far away from Florida. Bill Clinton was in Illinois, which was scheduled to hold its primary one week later. Paul Tsongas had flown home to Massachusetts, apparently preferring to spend his Super Tuesday election night in a state where a primary victory was assured.

The Clinton and Tsongas campaign organizations both held their election-night celebrations at hotels close to the Miami airport. That made it extra easy for out-of-state news personnel to fly in and cover the festivities. The Tsongas celebration was at a Howard Johnson's Hotel in Miami Beach, just a few miles down the expressway from the airport. The most notable thing about the Tsongas party was that many of the conversations were in Greek rather than English. Tsongas's fellow Greek Americans in the Miami area had turned out to support him, win or lose. In addition, someone had turned out an ample supply of delicious Greek pastries.

Unfortunately for the Tsongas campaigners, the Greek pastries were the only thing sweet about this particular election night. The many television sets scattered around the Tsongas suite at the Howard Johnson's Hotel reported miserable news. Bill Clinton was winning Florida with more than 50 percent of the vote. Tsongas was trailing fifteen to sixteen percentage points behind at the 35-percent level. Jerry Brown was finishing a distant third with about 13 percent. Tsongas, who at one point had thought he just might win it in Florida, did not even come in a close second.

The quiet bilingual conversations at the Tsongas election-night gathering stood in sharp contrast to the exuberant celebration at the Clinton party at the Miami Airport Hilton. Hundreds of Clinton supporters cheered wildly as each incoming election report indicated that Clinton was rolling to a blowout win in Florida. The bar at the hotel's Club Mystique was jammed with Clinton supporters arguing over just how decisive Clinton's victory had been. "I think it's all over with," speculated Bill Mauk, Clinton's Miami area campaign chairman. "We'll see for sure in Michigan and Illinois, but Tsongas's money will all start drying up." Hugh Rodham, the brother of Clinton's wife, Hillary Clinton, and an assistant public defender in Miami, expanded on the point. "Paul Tsongas put all his time and money in this race and he lost. They fell flat on their face on Super Tuesday. They wanted to make a stand in Florida and you can see what happened."[17]

Because Florida is more than just another southern state, Lieutenant Governor Buddy MacKay, Clinton's state chairman, saw Clinton's big victory in Florida as proof that Clinton could win anywhere in the United States, not just in the South. MacKay explained: "The condos in [Miami, Fort Lauderdale,] and Palm Beach are Northeastern U.S. We know that you've got the Middle West living on our West Coast. In Orlando, you've got a conglomeration of everything, and North Florida is still the South. [Clinton] won them all. This is kind of a pilot project on whether you can run all over America."[18]

Outside of Florida, the news from the other states that voted and caucused on Super Tuesday was exactly what everyone had expected. Tsongas won the primaries in Massachusetts and Rhode Island and led in the Delaware caucuses. That was all there was for Tsongas, however. Clinton swept the southern state Super Tuesday primaries by large margins. Texas, Oklahoma, Louisiana, Mississippi, and Tennessee all gave the Arkansas governor 60 to 70 percent of their votes. A Clinton victory in the Missouri caucuses provided even more icing for the Clinton Super Tuesday electoral cake.

Exit poll analysis of the southern state voting indicated that Clinton was indeed building a broad Democratic Party coalition behind his candidacy. More than 80 percent of the Black voters in the South supported Clinton. In Texas, Clinton received 57 percent of the Hispanic vote. He won two-thirds of the votes of southerners who have a labor union member living in their home. He gained an even split with Paul Tsongas in the well-publicized battle for the large number of transplanted northern Jewish voters living in South Florida. Only among well-educated and high-income voters, a relatively small proportion of the total electorate, did Clinton lose to Tsongas.

The only things Bill Clinton did not beat on Super Tuesday were the four major television networks and their exit polls. For example, ABC News hammered on the point that 25 percent of southern Democrats told exit pollsters they did not think Clinton had the honesty and integrity needed to serve as president.[19]

But one thing was crystal clear. The goal of the Southern Democratic state legislators who created Super Tuesday had been achieved. Bill Clinton, a moderate southern Democrat, had swept Super Tuesday in the South and thereby been propelled forward as the clear front-runner for the Democratic nomination for president. At last, Super Tuesday had worked!

As for the Republicans on Super Tuesday, their efforts were overshadowed by the considerably more exciting Democratic race. Pat Buchanan's campaign had hoped to do even better in the conservative South than it had done in New Hampshire, but the Georgia and South Carolina Republican primaries, both held prior to Super Tuesday, showed President Bush rather than Buchanan with increasing percentages of the vote.

"The President comes on stronger and stronger," Bush campaign chairman Robert Mosbacher told CNN after Bush received 67 percent and Buchanan only 26 percent of the vote in South Carolina. Furthermore, Mosbacher pointed out, President Bush is "winning them all." Mosbacher thereby emphasized the point that, as the Republican Super Tuesday campaigning was getting underway, Buchanan still had not won even one Republican primary election.[20]

Because Florida is more northern than the other southern states, Florida is less conservative than the other southern states, and for that reason the Buchanan campaign ended up avoiding Florida. Buchanan had one campaign event scheduled in Miami the weekend before Super Tuesday, but even that event was canceled and Buchanan made no late appearances in Florida whatsoever.

Wishing to exploit their obvious advantage and use a big win in Florida to discredit Buchanan completely, the Bush forces decided to campaign heavily in the state the weekend before election day. President Bush drew additional attention to his role as a Navy torpedo plane pilot during World War II by touring the National Museum of Naval Aviation at the Naval Air Station in Pensacola. Vice President Dan Quayle campaigned for Bush in Jacksonville. First Lady Barbara Bush toured Florida on her husband's behalf, attending a Little League baseball game in Boca Raton and then doing her customary shopping center routine at a mall in Orlando.

In addition to all the personal campaigning in Florida, the Bush forces sent out mass mailings that arrived in the mailboxes of registered Republicans the Monday before election day. The mailings were designed to direct voter frustrations away from President Bush and focus them on "liberals" in the Congress and the Democratic Party.

Exactly as there is a large Jewish vote in the Democratic presidential primary in Florida, there is a large Jewish vote in the Republican primary in Florida. Newspaper reporters speculated that most Republican Jews in Florida were "casting their lot with [President] Bush, fearful that challenger Patrick Buchanan's 'America First' rhetoric is a code word for anti-Semitism."[21]

Having written off Florida, Buchanan concentrated his time and efforts on Texas, Oklahoma, and the "Deep South" states of Louisiana and Mississippi. The Friday before election day found Buchanan posing with a flintlock rifle in front of the Alamo in San Antonio. At first Buchanan was wearing a Texas-style Stetson hat. Then he put on a coonskin cap. A French news agency decided that a picture of Buchanan in a coonskin cap with a flintlock rifle in front of the Alamo was just the thing to send back to its readers in Europe.[22]

Buchanan decided to discredit Bush with Texas voters by asking: "Just where does George Bush come from?" President Bush used Texas as his legal residence, but his address there was a hotel room. Having suggested that a hotel address does not really constitute living in Texas, Buchanan went on to describe Texas as "one of George Bush's 13 adopted home states." Buchanan concluded by saying that Bush "grew up in a little town near Amarillo called Kennebunkport. He can tie and rope a lobster with the best of them."[23]

Although Buchanan may have amused news personnel and voters alike with his "campaigning by quip," the Super Tuesday voting effectively ended any chance he might have had of denying President Bush the 1992 Republican nomination for president. Bush carried Florida with almost 70 percent of the vote, a 3-percent improvement over his 67 percent performance in South Carolina. In Louisiana and Mississippi, the two "Deep South" states where Buchanan had hoped to get some votes, Bush was doing just as well as he had done in Florida, getting close to 70 percent of the vote. Most damaging of all for Buchanan, George Bush won every Super Tuesday Republican primary, north and south, and ended up with an overwhelming delegate lead over Buchanan.

The 1992 Republican primaries were, for all intents and purposes, over. Pat Buchanan had been unable to improve or even maintain his strong showing in New Hampshire. Buchanan continued to campaign against President Bush throughout subsequent primaries and caucuses, but the news media paid ever diminishing attention to him. The 1992 Republican primaries had lasted only three weeks—from New Hampshire on February 18 to Super Tuesday on March 10.

12. Midwest Tuesday

One week after Super Tuesday, on March 17, 1992, two populous Midwest states, Illinois and Michigan, were slated to cast their presidential primary ballots. Illinois had occupied that mid-March primary date for a number of recent presidential elections. Michigan, however, was a newcomer where holding a primary was concerned. In 1988 it held caucuses.

Bill Clinton and his campaign advisers had long foreseen the crucial importance of the Illinois and Michigan primaries. The next event after the large number of southern primaries on Super Tuesday, Midwest Tuesday offered Clinton the chance to turn his expected southern victories on Super Tuesday into a virtual lock on the Democratic nomination. If Clinton could demonstrate he was popular in the Midwest just one week after sweeping the South, the nomination would be his.

To this end, Clinton had begun campaigning in Illinois as early as August of 1991. He selected a Chicagoan, David Wilhelm, as his national campaign manager. Wilhelm, who had run Richard Daley's recent campaign for reelection as mayor of Chicago, was obviously well-connected in Illinois Democratic politics. He would be a key link for Clinton to the famous Chicago Democratic Party "machine," reputed to be the most powerful political organization in the nation.

Clinton systematically constructed a powerful network of elected officials and ward politicians in Illinois supporting his candidacy. By the time there was less than one week to go before primary day, Clinton had a behemoth of a political organization in place. Virtually every prominent Democrat in Illinois had climbed on board the Clinton bandwagon.

A Clinton fund-raiser in the southern Illinois city of Carbondale amply illustrated the success of Clinton's organizational efforts. Held just a few days before primary election day, the fund-raiser featured a long list of prominent Illinois Democrats—members of Congress, party leaders, a former candidate for governor, and the Illinois state Democratic chairman—all of whom gave short speeches endorsing the Clinton candidacy. The parade of supporters was so long that Bill Clinton had to sit and wait almost two hours before getting to speak at the fund-raiser himself.

Clinton also was helped by the fact that southern Illinois is not all that far from Clinton's home state of Arkansas. Much of southern Illinois is closer to Little Rock, the Arkansas capital, than to Chicago. A number of speakers at the Carbondale fund-raiser made it clear they viewed Clinton as a "fellow southerner."

Six days before the Illinois voting, Bill Clinton and his wife, Hillary Clinton, campaigned at her high school alma mater in the Chicago suburbs. Hillary Clinton's Chicago roots thus were another Illinois asset that was ably exploited by the Clinton campaign.

Clearly the Clinton campaign was making Illinois its top priority on Midwest Tuesday. The goal appeared to be to beat Paul Tsongas so badly in Illinois that it would outweigh any strong showing Tsongas might make in Michigan.

For Paul Tsongas, Illinois and Michigan presented a do-or-die situation. After his poor showing in the South on Super Tuesday, Tsongas needed to demonstrate clearly that he could win at least one of these two Midwest states. If he did not win one of them, it would give credence to the charge that his New Hampshire victory was a "flash in the pan" and that he was a regional New England candidate and little more.

There was another reason Tsongas had to win somewhere on Midwest Tuesday. As was Bill Clinton, he was running a conventional campaign for president, which meant he had to maintain a high level of campaign expenditures. Tsongas was flying around the nation in a chartered airplane. Professional consultants and pollsters fed him useful but expensive-to-get information. He was renting offices in each important primary and caucus state and paying professional campaign personnel to manage them. Telephones, copy machines, fax machines— all these devices were being used by the Tsongas campaign and costing money. Tsongas needed a big victory, and soon, in order to keep the campaign contributions coming in that would keep his organization running.

Tsongas thus took an aggressive and challenging stance against Clinton as the Illinois and Michigan campaigns came down to the wire. Tsongas described Clinton as a slick politician who had character flaws that made him "unelectable." The Tsongas camp began running television ads that blamed Arkansas governor Clinton for the poor economy and the low educational levels in Arkansas. One of the ads showed two construction workers talking: "You heard the latest?" one of the construction workers asked, seeming to hint there had been another Clinton scandal. "What's Bill Clinton got to hide that's really big?"

"What's that?" the other construction worker replied.

"It's Arkansas," the first worker retorted. The ad then went on to list the low rankings in family income, worker safety, and school spending in Arkansas—and blamed them on Bill Clinton's governorship.

Tsongas also repeated his oft-stated complaints about Clinton's campaign tactics, particularly those used against him in Florida and other southern primaries. Tsongas said his positions on Social Security and support for Israel were badly misrepresented by Clinton, thus casting further doubts on Clinton's "character." Kitty Kurth, Tsongas's Illinois campaign director, described Clinton's tactics as "Willie Hortonesque," a reference to a particularly negative series of TV ads that George Bush had used against Michael Dukakis in the 1988 presidential election campaign.[1]

For his part, Bill Clinton continued to attack Tsongas as a pro-Wall Street candidate whose economic ideas were hostile to working people. He reminded voters of Tsongas's support for a major increase in gasoline taxes and for giving a capital gains tax cut to wealthy investors.

Clinton also was quick to defend himself against the Tsongas TV ad that attempted to blame Clinton for the lack of economic and social progress in Arkansas. Clinton acknowledged that Arkansas is a poor state, but he argued that economic and social ratings are not always a fair way to measure the job that a governor is doing.

Paul Tsongas was facing an overwhelming pro-Clinton organization in Illinois. In Michigan his problem was the state's demographics. Michigan has a large number of blue-collar workers, most of them members of labor unions. Despite putting on a United Auto Workers jacket and campaigning through the Hermes Automotive Manufacturing Company in Detroit, Tsongas found it difficult to sell his pro-business economic reforms to pro-labor auto workers.

Tsongas's message of self-sacrifice in the name of long-term economic growth appealed strongly, as it had in other states, to upscale professionals with good incomes. The problem was there were not a lot of people who met that description voting in the Michigan Democratic primary. Instead of taking the long view, Michigan's blue-collar workers and labor union members were mainly looking for short-term economic help.[2]

Another problem for Tsongas in Michigan was the Black vote. More than 14 percent of Michigan's voters are Black, and they are a particularly powerful bloc in Democratic primaries. Clinton received major endorsements from Black clergy in Michigan, particularly in the Detroit area. Tsongas, as had happened in other states, continued to have trouble finding issues and programs that appealed to minorities.

Bill Clinton worked hard at bringing blue-collar union members, many of whom had voted for Republicans Reagan and Bush in previous presidential elections, back into the Democratic fold. He tempered his message of helping working people in American society with the idea that the help also had to be extended to less fortunate groups, such as minorities and children growing up in poverty. Speaking at McComb County Community College, which is located in a suburb of Detroit, Clinton called on his audience to make a commitment to him as well as hear promises from him. Clinton said: "Somebody's got to come back to the so-called Reagan Democratic areas and say, 'Look, I'll give you your values back. . . . I'll help you build the middle class back.' But you have to say, 'O.K., let's do it with everybody in this country.'"[3]

An unexpected factor in the Illinois and Michigan primaries was former California governor Jerry Brown. Brown made very little effort in Illinois, but he campaigned hard in Michigan, emphasizing his pro-labor record when governor of California. Brown drew large and enthusiastic crowds when campaigning in labor union areas, crowds that were angry over the 9 percent unemployment rate in Michigan and recently announced General Motors Corporation layoffs. A number of local labor unions endorsed Brown.

Jerry Brown provided the major fireworks in the Midwest primaries when he blasted front-runner Bill Clinton during a one-hour debate on WLS-TV in Chicago. The debate was simultaneously broadcast in Michigan and throughout the nation on C-SPAN. Brown based his attack on a *Washington Post* story that raised the question of whether Clinton, as governor of Arkansas, had funneled business to his wife's law firm in Little Rock. The newspaper story noted that Hillary Clinton's law partnership had a number of Arkansas state agencies on its client list.

Brown unleashed his barrage after being asked a question about Clinton's "electability" against President Bush in the fall general election. "I think he's got a big electability problem," Brown said. It's a "scandal of major proportions. . . . He is funneling money to his wife's law firm for state business. . . . It's the kind of conflict of interest that's incompatible with the kind of public servant we expect."[4]

Brown pointed out that one of the law firm's biggest clients was a poultry processing firm that was a major polluter of Arkansas waterways. Brown then said that the charges concerning Hillary Clinton's law firm were simply the latest in a series of newspaper articles that raised real questions about Clinton's character and judgment. "There's a scandal a week here," Brown concluded.[5]

In his customary style, Bill Clinton answered Brown's charges with a countercharge and a firm denial. Pointing his finger at Brown, Clinton said: "Let me tell you something, Jerry. I don't care what you say about me, but you ought to be ashamed of yourself for jumping on my wife. You're not worthy to be on the same platform with [her]."

Clinton then attacked Brown directly: "I don't think you can take much of what he [Brown] says seriously. Jerry comes here with his family wealth and his $1,500 suit, making lying accusations about my wife. I never funneled any money to my wife's law firm. Never. Never. . . . I feel sorry for Jerry Brown. He reinvents himself every year or two."[6]

The *Washington Post* story about Hillary Clinton's law firm, and Jerry Brown using that story as a major campaign issue against Bill Clinton, illustrated an ironic development in the Clinton campaign for the 1992 Democratic nomination for president. Starting with Georgia and South Carolina, Clinton was winning primaries and eliminating Democratic opponents. The closer he came to sewing up the nomination, however, the more the news media released damaging stories about his public and personal life. By the time of the Illinois and Michigan primaries, it really seemed that Bill Clinton was running against the media rather than against any of his Democratic opponents. For Clinton, it was not a question of what Jerry Brown and Paul Tsongas were going to do to him next. It was a question of what the *New York Times* and the *Washington Post* were going to do to him next.

Clinton endeavored to turn the incredible series of press revelations about him into a campaign plus. When opposing candidates or questioners asked Clinton about the many charges and scandals surrounding his candidacy, he would argue that his ability to survive so many negative stories indicated that he had great strength and popularity as a potential candidate for president.

American politics marked something of a transition point when the *Washington Post* and Jerry Brown attacked Hillary Clinton on the grounds that she and her law firm may have benefited from Bill Clinton's position as governor of Arkansas. Previously, the career and conduct of a male politician's spouse had not been considered fair game for attack in a presidential election campaign, mainly because the wives of most presidential candidates did not have professional careers of their own. The attack on Hillary Clinton's profession and the way it might possibly relate to her husband's political office was plowing new ground in American political life.

Primary day in Illinois and Michigan, March 17, 1992, also happened to be St. Patrick's Day. The various candidates took advantage of this happy coincidence by marching in the St. Patrick's Day Parade on Chicago's South Side the Sunday before the election. The way the candidates participated in the parade symbolized the unique character of each of their distinctive campaigns for the Democratic nomination. Bill Clinton was completely surrounded by a large group of Chicago politicians, campaign boosters, and police officers. The crowd around Clinton was so thick that potential voters were unable to approach him to either shake his hand or ask questions. In one neighborhood a group of "boo birds" hooted at Clinton as he passed by.

Tsongas, on the other hand, walked alone in the parade, crossing from curbside to curbside to greet voters, shake hands, and quickly answer shouted questions. Tsongas appeared to really be enjoying the friendly reception he received along the parade route.

Jerry Brown also marched in the St. Patrick's Day Parade. He was greeted by very enthusiastic supporters as he went along, but they were few and far between.

Spirits in the Tsongas camp sank to a very low ebb the night before Midwest primary day. Paul Tsongas had hoped to possibly defeat Clinton in Michigan, but a *Detroit News* poll of likely Democratic voters put Clinton far in the lead with 49 percent, Tsongas in second place with 18 percent, and Brown a close third with 17 percent.[7] If Brown finished ahead of Tsongas in Michigan, which might just happen, the Tsongas campaign would be all but over.

Obviously Jerry Brown saw the results—and the implications—in the *Detroit News* poll. Campaigning at the Union Second Baptist Church in River Rouge, Michigan, an industrial city south of Detroit, Brown argued that it was his candidacy, and not the candidacy of Paul Tsongas, that would provide the alternative to the front-running Bill Clinton. Brown explained: "Three candidates have dropped and another one is about to drop out. It's coming down to us or Clinton."[8]

When the votes were finally tallied up in Illinois and Michigan on Midwest Tuesday, the worst fears of the Tsongas camp were realized. Bill Clinton won both primaries by wide margins. Worst of all, Jerry Brown finished second in Michigan, giving Tsongas a dismal third-place finish in a key midwestern industrial state. To any informed observer of the presidential nominating process in the United States, Bill Clinton now was the presumptive Democratic nominee. Tsongas had faced a "must-win" situation on Midwest Tuesday—and lost.

The day after Midwest Tuesday found Tsongas at home with his wife, Niki, in Lowell, Massachusetts. Also present was his longtime friend and campaign manager, Dennis Kanin. The question of whether to remain in the race for the Democratic nomination was discussed throughout the day. The devastating losses in the South on Super Tuesday and the double loss on Midwest Tuesday had eliminated all hope of eventual victory. Despite his "big wins" in New Hampshire and Maryland, Tsongas had to face the reality that he had not won one large state with a large number of convention delegates.

An additional problem was the state that lay ahead on the primary and caucus trail. New York, the second most populous state in the United States after California, would hold its primary on April 7, 1992. This was a state in which $300,000 to $500,000 would be required to run an adequate television advertising campaign. With his string of recent losses and his dismal future prospects, Tsongas had no hope of raising such a substantial amount of campaign money.

There was another problem, never discussed in the media but nonetheless a real problem for Tsongas. It was clear that Tsongas and Brown were now splitting the anti-Clinton vote, thereby making it impossible for either Tsongas or Brown to overtake Clinton. If Tsongas or Brown were to drop out of the race, the remaining candidate would have a better chance to beat Clinton, because the anti-Clinton vote would no longer be divided between two candidates. Brown, however, had frequently told the public and press that he was in the race until the very end. That left Tsongas no choice but to be the one to drop out of contention.

With that thought in mind, Tsongas gathered his most loyal supporters together at the Parker House Hotel in Boston on the Thursday after Midwest Tuesday. "It was clear that we did not have the resources necessary to fight the media war in New York," Tsongas said in his emotional farewell. "I would have been defined by others and would have been unable to defend myself. . . . If money is the mother's milk of politics, our mothers didn't show up."[9]

Tsongas was careful to suspend his campaign rather than withdraw completely. That permitted his 430 delegates to go ahead and attend the Democratic National Convention in New York in July. It also kept Tsongas eligible for federal matching funds to help pay off his campaign debts.

Tsongas told his supporters, many of whom urged him to stay in the race, that he had no desire to continue for the sole purpose of being a spoiler and weakening Bill Clinton's candidacy. "That is not what I'm about, that is not worthy," Tsongas said. "I did not survive my ordeal [with cancer] to be the agent of George Bush's reelection."

Tsongas said many times during his campaign that he ran for president because he wanted his victory over lymphatic cancer to mean something. "I feel deeply fulfilled," he said as his wife and children wiped tears from their eyes. "The obligation of my survival has been met."

Campaign aides to Tsongas hinted that personal reasons as well as money problems may have entered into the decision to quit. While doing late night television interviews the night of the Illinois and Michigan primaries, Tsongas slumped in his chair and complained about his heavy campaign schedule the next day, which allowed him only one hour of free time. "That won't do," Tsongas said. "I'm wiped out."

For all its surprise and excitement, the Tsongas candidacy was very brief. Tsongas's campaign first bloomed when he won the New Hampshire primary. The campaign died just four weeks later, with his Illinois and Michigan losses.

Democratic National Chairman Ronald Brown, who was officially neutral but appeared to support Clinton for the Democratic nomination, said Tsongas's announcement "means we are much closer to a conclusion of the process."[10] Ronald Brown made it very clear throughout the 1992 primary and caucus season that he wanted the Democratic nominee chosen quickly to reduce the divisions that would be created in the party by a long series of hard-fought primaries and caucuses.

The suspension of Tsongas's campaign was a giant step toward the Democratic nomination for Bill Clinton. As the New Hampshire winner, Tsongas was Clinton's only real competition. Clinton had wisely pursued the policy of first attacking and eliminating his most ferocious challenger—Paul Tsongas. Now that this first job was done, he could concentrate all his fire on his only remaining opponent—Jerry Brown.

Paul Tsongas had been the "bright surprise" of the 1992 Democratic primaries. The longest of long shots, he surprised everyone by emerging in New Hampshire as Bill Clinton's main opposition. The Clinton strategists had assumed that Bill Clinton would be the moderate Democratic candidate and would mainly be challenged by liberal, left-leaning Democratic candidates. With his hard-nosed economic policies, however, Paul Tsongas attacked Clinton from the right and forced him to move somewhat leftward on economic issues. As Tsongas won the votes of more and more upscale, professional, suburban Democrats, Clinton was forced to appeal to a constituency composed mainly of minorities and working-class White voters. With Tsongas at last out of the race, Clinton would be able to assume more of the moderate image that he had originally intended to project.

Paul Tsongas may have lost his bid for the 1992 Democratic presidential nomination, but he made a unique contribution to public understanding of international economics. Turning his back on the traditional Democratic economic philosophy that emphasizes government spending, Tsongas preached themes of government-supported economic development and fiscal responsibility. Most of all, Tsongas focused attention on the need for the United States to actively improve its competitive position in international trade. Long after the Tsongas candidacy ended, Democrats and others were still discussing and debating Tsongas's progressive economic ideas. A joke going around at the time was: "The Tsongas is over, but the melody lingers on."

The exciting Democratic races on Midwest Tuesday completely obliterated what little interest remained in Pat Buchanan's dying campaign against George Bush. Buchanan made an aggressive effort in Michigan, hoping to exploit widespread displeasure with the weak national economy in a state with a large number of blue-collar workers. Right up until election day, however, public opinion polls showed President Bush outstripping Buchanan by a wide margin. Bush was so far ahead that he spent the Sunday before election day relaxing at the Camp David presidential retreat in Maryland rather than campaigning for more votes in Illinois and Michigan.

Election day produced the expected Bush landslide. Whatever glimmer of hope of winning Pat Buchanan might have had after his Super Tuesday losses was completely extinguished by the size of his losses in Illinois and Michigan. The Buchanan campaign now was of interest only to Pat Buchanan and an ever-shrinking band of archconservative Republican supporters.

On the Democratic side, the Illinois and Michigan primaries were real elections. The three remaining Democratic candidates—Clinton, Tsongas, and Brown—campaigned hard in both states. The national media paid close attention, and the air was filled with radio and television commercials for the candidates. Illinois and Michigan Democrats thus had the honor of using their ballots to make an important decision—the final elimination of Paul Tsongas from the race.

On the Republican side, the Illinois and Michigan primaries were meaningless and a waste of time. Pat Buchanan went doggedly on campaigning, but Republican voters had nothing to do except go to the polls and cast an automatic vote for George Bush. It was not a real election in any sense of the word.

13. CONNECTICUT AND VERMONT

The withdrawal of Paul Tsongas from the 1992 race for the Democratic presidential nomination left Jerry Brown as the only candidate still opposing Bill Clinton. As Tsongas said "Tsayonara," Clinton strategists faced an important decision. Should Clinton focus the remainder of his primary and caucus campaign on President Bush and ignore Jerry Brown? Or should Clinton train his formidable campaign artillery on Brown and work to eliminate him from contention as thoroughly as he had eliminated Paul Tsongas?

Brown, after all, was an enigma. In one of the most amazing turnarounds in American political history, Brown had gone from the bottom of the heap of Democratic presidential candidates to the only remaining Clinton challenger. A laughingstock after his fifth-place finish in New Hampshire, Brown now was in a position to exploit the many negatives the press had generated about Clinton and perhaps snatch the Democratic nomination away from him.

Brown's biggest problem, however, was that he was such an unconventional candidate. Saddled with an image in many voters' minds that screamed "Governor Moonbeam" and "flake," Brown was running a very unorthodox campaign. His main message was that all American politics is corrupt and only a complete overhaul of election campaign financing would fix things. His insistence on limiting campaign contributions to $100 meant that he would never really have enough money to seriously challenge Clinton, particularly in large states like New York, Pennsylvania, Ohio, New Jersey, and California, all of which would be holding primaries in the next two months. Perhaps most unusual about Brown, he was advocating a 13 percent flat tax proposal that most voters could not understand and which, if adopted, might have unpredictable effects on the national economy.

Despite his unusual persona and campaign style, Brown now found himself the ABC candidate—Anyone But Clinton. He had been the ABC candidate sixteen years earlier when he challenged former Georgia governor Jimmy Carter in the 1976 Democratic primaries. As the Anyone But Carter candidate, Brown won the California primary but failed in his effort to deny Carter the nomination.

"The person Bill Clinton has to fear the most is Jerry Brown," said Sherry Bebitch Jeffe, a California political analyst. "Why in the world should Jerry Brown drop out? Jerry might have a chance of winning California."[1]

As it turned out, Clinton was not able to ignore Brown, even if he had wanted to. For one thing, now that Clinton was an almost certain bet for the Democratic nomination, he began to receive even closer scrutiny from the news media. The other problem was that Brown, far from stepping quietly aside, decided to go after Clinton hammer and tongs.

The first round in the one-on-one contest between Clinton and Brown was fought in Connecticut, which held its Democratic primary on March 24, 1992, one week after the Midwest Tuesday primaries in Illinois and Michigan. In a surprising rebuff for Clinton, Connecticut Democrats went for Jerry Brown in a close vote. Brown received 38 percent of the vote compared to 35 percent for Clinton. Paul Tsongas, who had dropped out of the race but still had his name on the ballot, received 20 percent.

Jerry Brown jumped happily into the role of Clinton's main competitor. "The media picked Bill Clinton," he said. "The people of Connecticut rose up and said, 'Forget it.'"[2]

Clinton's analysis of what Connecticut voters were saying agreed with Brown's. "They don't want this race to be over and neither do I," said Clinton, although he tried to maintain his winning momentum by calling the Connecticut results a "small setback."[3]

As usual, the exit polls conducted by the news media generated much worse news about Bill Clinton than did the actual election results. According to the *New York Times*, Clinton received the support of six out of ten Black voters in Connnecticut but only about one out of three of the White voters. Worse still, Clinton did not receive strong support from blue-collar workers, one of the most important constituent groups in the Democratic voting coalition. Only three in ten blue-collar workers backed Clinton while four in ten went for Jerry Brown.

The *New York Times* exit polls contained other ominous signs for the Clinton campaign. More than half of Connecticut Democratic voters said they wanted to see someone besides Clinton and Brown enter the race. Those same voters split fifty-fifty over whether Clinton had the honesty and integrity to be president.

Although Tsongas received 20 percent of the vote in Connecticut, his dropping out of the race worked to Brown's benefit. According to the *New York Times*, four in ten of those who voted for Jerry Brown said they would have voted for Paul Tsongas if he were still an active candidate.[4]

One week after the Connecticut primary, on Tuesday, March 31, 1992, Jerry Brown scored a second straight victory over Bill Clinton in the Vermont presidential caucuses. This time, however, it was a runaway victory for Brown, in contrast to his close win in Connecticut. Brown was first in Vermont with 46 percent of the vote, uncommitted votes totaled 25 percent for second place, Clinton was a dismal third with 17 percent, and campaign dropout Paul Tsongas received 9 percent.

At first Brown allowed himself the luxury of an overstatement by saying that he had made a strong showing in Vermont against "what has been the front-runner." Later on, his analysis was more realistic. "I'm very pleased, but this is a very tight race. Governor Clinton is ahead in delegates, and we've still got to fight."[5] Brown was referring to the Arkansas governor's big lead in the Democratic National Convention delegate count. After the Vermont caucuses, Bill Clinton had 1,018 of the 2,145 delegates needed for nomination while Brown had only 159, a better than six-to-one ratio in favor of Clinton.[6]

The real significance of the Connecticut primary and the Vermont caucuses was the tremendous sendoff they gave Brown for the New York primary, scheduled one week after Vermont on Tuesday, April 7, 1992. New York is one of the most heavily populated states in the nation, second in population and delegate count only to California. Brown sailed into the New York fight with two solid wins under his belt. Clinton came in having lost his last two encounters with Democratic voters. If Jerry Brown could turn his Connecticut and Vermont wins into a victory in New York, the Clinton campaign would be badly wounded, perhaps fatally so.

14. NEW YORK

The 1992 New York Democratic presidential primary was not really an election. It was more like a trial, and the man on trial was Bill Clinton.

With two weeks to go before the New York voting, a series of stories began playing in the national news media that cast doubt on Clinton's judgment and honesty. The public had hardly absorbed one damaging report about Clinton before the next one broke. Adding to the problem was the fact that there are three tabloid newspapers in New York City with several million daily readers, and each new negative story about Clinton was turned into overstated tabloid-style headlines and displayed on the newstands for all to see.

Clinton's troubles began when the press learned he recently had played a few rounds of golf at the Little Rock Country Club, an all-White private club in Arkansas's capital city. This would have been damaging news at any point in the presidential election, but it was particularly bad given that one in five voters in the New York Democratic primary is Black and one in three voters is Jewish. Clinton tried to mend this badly broken fence by hosting a breakfast with Black members of the New York news media and touring an exhibition in New York City about discrimination against Blacks and Jews.

Then the *New York Times* published a story charging that Clinton, while serving as governor of Arkansas, altered a proposed ethics law so that it would exempt the Arkansas governor from ethical standards imposed on the state legislature. Once again Clinton had to call an early morning press conference, defend himself against the charges, and provide the press with a thick stack of documents that supposedly refuted the charges. In this case, Clinton claimed he exempted himself from the Arkansas ethics law because that was the only way to get the state legislature to pass the bill.

The *New York Times* also charged that Clinton exempted his wife, Hillary Clinton, from the proposed ethics law. Hillary Clinton, an attorney, was associated with a law firm that did business with the state of Arkansas. The *Times* said that a senior partner in the law firm, Webb Hubbell, advised Clinton on how to change the ethics law so it would not include the governor's wife.

Next, trapped while answering questions during a New York television debate, Clinton admitted that, while a student at Oxford University in the 1960s, he smoked marijuana. More incriminating than that simple admission, however, was the revelation of how Clinton had been sidestepping the question in the past.

For years Clinton responded to all queries about whether he had smoked marijuana by saying he had "never violated the laws of my country." On the New York TV show he was asked if he had violated state or international laws, and that brought forth the honest answer that he had violated the law while overseas. "When I was in England," Clinton said, "I experimented with marijuana a time or two, and I didn't like it and didn't inhale and never tried it again."

Questioned at length by reporters after the TV debate ended, Clinton said he had not disclosed his smoking of marijuana earlier "because nobody's ever asked me that question point blank. . . . I've said I've never broken the drug laws of my country, and that is the absolute truth."[1]

Newspaper columnists and editorial writers jumped all over Clinton, not because he admitted using marijuana, which was pervasive among young people at the time of his youth, but because his disclosure confirmed Clinton's reputation for avoiding straight answers to politically embarrassing questions. It appeared to be more of the evasiveness and manipulation that had earned Clinton the derogatory campaign nickname of "Slick Willie."

The weekend before New York's primary day, the Associated Press ran yet another story concerning Bill Clinton and draft dodging. Apparently Clinton had actually received a draft induction notice from the United States Army while studying at Oxford in 1969, but he had carefully hidden the existence of that draft notice from the news media. Here again, the problem was not the existence of the induction notice as much as Clinton's not mentioning it during all the previous discussion of his draft status.

A Clinton campaign aide told the news media the draft notice had been sent in error and that Clinton's draft board allowed him to complete his spring term at Oxford. There was no immediate explanation, however, of why Clinton had not revealed any of these facts to the press and public until forced to do so.

The constant hammering Clinton received from the news media in New York began to affect the way voters were treating him on the campaign trail. Suddenly it was "open season" on Bill Clinton where nasty questions and comments were concerned. Clinton approached a commuter on the Staten Island Ferry and tried to shake his hand. With a large press entourage looking and listening, this particular New Yorker loudly upbraided Clinton for playing golf at a Whites-only country club and then walked angrily away.

A few days later, as Clinton campaigned down a New York City street, a man stuck a bullhorn out the window and bellowed the words, "Racist! Racist!" Another citizen approached Clinton waving a golf club over his head and yelled: "Go back to your honky country club."[2]

Then there was the morning Bill Clinton was scheduled to give a speech at New York's Harlem Hospital. He was forced to break off his remarks after a group of hecklers, led by New Alliance Party presidential candidate Lenora Fulani, made so much noise he could not be heard. Fulani, who had made many previous tries for political office, told Clinton: "I want to talk about the issue of democracy." Clinton was drowned out when Fulani and her supporters began loudly chanting: "We want democracy."[3]

One afternoon Bill Clinton stepped up to the microphone to address a rally in downtown New York City. He looked over the people in the crowd, many of whom were carrying signs that were clearly hostile to his candidacy. Clinton stepped back and, without knowing that a TV camcorder was picking up every word he said, complained bitterly to a campaign aide: "What are you doing to me? There are as many people here against me as there are for me." The incident was played for the entire nation to see on the CBS TV Evening News.[4]

Bill Clinton's harshest encounter with the public occurred at a fund-raiser at New York's fashionable Laura Belle Club. Bob Rafsky, an AIDS activist, staged a confrontation with Clinton on behalf of ACT UP, the AIDS Coalition to Unleash Power. ACT UP was critical of Clinton, claiming that no state money had been spent on AIDS in Arkansas until 1991. Rafsky accused Clinton of "dying of ambition," a remark that caused Clinton to point an accusing finger at Rafsky and let loose a blizzard of angry words. Clinton shouted: "I'm sick and tired of all these people who don't know me, know nothin' about my life, know nothin' about the battles that I've fought, know nothin' about the life I've lived, makin' those snotty-nose remarks about how I haven't done anything in my life and it's all driven by ambition. That's bull."[5]

Knight-Ridder Newspapers took this outburst as a sign that Bill Clinton might be "cracking under the stress of the presidential campaign." In a nationally syndicated story, Knight-Ridder summed up Clinton's problems this way: "In New Hampshire, Clinton won the blue ribbon for grace under pressure. But after two months of relentless media scrutiny, a punishing round-the-clock schedule and a humiliating loss in Connecticut to an opponent he never took seriously, Clinton looks frayed at the edges." Knight-Ridder did hold out the possibility, however, that Clinton intentionally blew up at the AIDS activist in a "calculated jab to show that he's tough, combative and not so slick after all."[6]

Added to Clinton's problems with the news media and hostile New York voters was an all-out attack by Jerry Brown on Clinton's character and performance as governor of Arkansas. Brown told reporters that Clinton had been a "right-to-work, union-busting, scab-inviting, wage-depressing, environmental disaster" governor.[7]

A Brown television ad playing in New York contrasted Brown's achievements as governor of California with Clinton's achievements. The ad portrayed Brown as a governor who had accepted no pay increases, cut state taxes, created new jobs, and appointed large numbers of women and minorities to state offices. "Governor Clinton's Arkansas?" the ad continued. "A right-to-work state—ranks dead last in worker safety, its wages among the lowest in the country. And while Bill Clinton plays golf at a restricted all-white club, Arkansas remains one of only two states with no civil rights act."

The Brown ad concluded with a not-so-veiled reference to Bill Clinton's "Slick Willie" nickname: "Now that's slick, but we want real change."[8]

Jerry Brown's attacks on Bill Clinton, coupled with his negative TV ads, produced a reaction from Ronald Brown, the national chairman of the Democratic Party. During a newspaper interview, Ron Brown charged that Jerry Brown had "crossed the line in terms of inappropriate attacks" on Clinton. Ron Brown said he had wanted to remain neutral in the Democratic presidential nomination campaign but had to speak out because of Jerry Brown's "scorched earth policy" of all-out verbal assaults on Clinton's character.

The *New York Times* described Ron Brown's outspoken criticism of Jerry Brown as "most remarkable," implying that it was inappropriate for the national chairman of a political party to intervene in a hotly contested presidential primary contest under any circumstances. The *Times* then reminded its readers that the Democratic party chairman had "long urged party leaders to settle on a nominee early in the process so that the designated candidate would have more time to prepare for a general election fight in the fall."[9] Clearly, Ron Brown had concluded that Bill Clinton was going to be the Democratic presidential nominee in 1992, and he did not want Clinton's image further tarnished by Jerry Brown's attacks.

As usual, Clinton was as ready to give as to get on the negative campaigning scene. He opened fire on Jerry Brown's 13 percent flat tax proposal, charging that it would benefit the rich and harm the poor. As an example, Clinton said the flat tax plan would put money in Clinton's own pocket—and probably Jerry Brown's pocket as well—while raising taxes for low income individuals who can least afford to pay them. Clinton said: "My wife and I have released our tax returns. You can look at them. We'd make a lot of money on Jerry Brown's plan, because we don't consume that much of our income and 13 percent is a lot less than we normally pay. I bet Jerry Brown would make a lot of money on his tax plan. He ought to release his tax returns and we can see."[10]

As New York's primary election day got closer, Clinton turned up the heat on Brown where the flat tax was concerned. At a noontime rally on Wall Street, in the heart of the New York financial district, Clinton labeled the flat tax proposal "the most reactionary proposal ever made in a presidential campaign in my lifetime or yours."[11]

Clinton was joined in his attack on Brown's flat tax proposal by Senator Patrick Moynihan of New York. Moynihan pointed out that the Brown tax plan would eliminate Social Security taxes and replace them with a 13 percent income tax and a 13 percent national sales tax. Moynihan said such a scheme would "put a silver bullet through the heart of Social Security."[12]

Suddenly it seemed that every economist and business newspaper columnist in the country was evaluating Brown's flat tax proposal and writing about it. Almost all of them found the plan lacking in some important respect, and many dismissed it as too risky a venture because no one could really tell for sure what the effects of the plan would be. The Clinton campaign picked up a quote from a harsh evaluation of the Brown tax plan that ran in the Long Island newspaper *Newsday* and used it in a TV spot. "Jerry Brown says he wants change," the Clinton advertisement said, "but *Newsday* says his tax changes would, quote, 'stick it to the very people he claims to help.'"[13]

More damaging to Jerry Brown than his tax plan was his decision to announce that he was considering Black civil rights leader Jesse Jackson as his candidate for vice president. Brown's mentioning of Jackson as his possible running mate produced an immediate outcry from Jewish leaders in New York City, many of whom considered Jackson to be anti-Semitic and an opponent of Israel. Jackson had been on uneasy terms with New York's Jewish community ever since he referred to New York City as "Hymietown" during his unsuccessful campaign for the 1984 Democratic presidential nomination.

Brown found out just how angry New York Jews were when he gave a speech to the Jewish Community Relations Council. "You disqualify yourself from support from the Jewish community," shouted Dov Hikind, a Brooklyn city council member. Hikind was so confrontive with Brown that he had to be brusquely escorted away from the meeting before Brown could go on.

Then Charlotte Jacobson, past national president of Hadassah, a Jewish women's organization, criticized the proposed alignment with Jackson. "We are certainly not opposed to a Black vice president," she said. "We think you have not chosen wisely." Brown tried to convince his audience of the wisdom of his vice-presidential choice, but he had to speak over a constant chorus of hisses, jeers, and boos.

Brown further antagonized Jewish voters in New York when, speaking at a Wall Street rally, he called on his supporters to "drive the money lenders out of the temple of power." Jewish leaders interpreted the remark as anti-Semitic because the term "money lenders" comes from the Old Testament and refers to ancient Hebrews. "No Jew can fail to understand the implication of that phrase," said Harold Shulman, president of a local chapter of B'nai B'rith, an organization dedicated to fighting religious and racial discrimination.[14]

Suddenly the news media were having just as much fun attacking Jerry Brown as they had been attacking Bill Clinton. The Friday before primary election day, CNN launched an attack on the one truly unique thing about Jerry Brown—his 800-number for fund raising. A CNN reporter had called Brown's 800-number pretending to want to make a contribution and claimed the operator had offered tips on how to get around Brown's $100 limit on contributions. According to CNN, the operator said: "There's ways around it. . . . I mean like, if you have like family members, I'm not supposed to tell you that, but, you know, and each of them gives or something, but like $100 per person."

Jerry Brown denounced the CNN report as a "complete canard." Having made his $100 contribution limit a central part of his campaign, Brown felt compelled to stoutly defend its honesty. "My whole campaign, my integrity, the vision that I'm standing for is to invite people with small donations to join an effort to take back their country," Brown said. "And this kind of effort to stigmatize that, I think is really unconscionable. . . . There is nothing in this operation other than a commitment to build a large insurgent movement that can challenge the corrupt status quo."[15]

The weekend before New York's primary election day, the *Los Angeles Times* charged that, while governor of California, Brown rewarded with judgeships the kind of big-money political contributors he was condemning in his campaign for the presidency. The newspaper said that one-fifth of the lawyers Brown appointed as judges had made contributions to his various election campaigns.[16]

The news media attacks and voter contempt for both Clinton and Brown as they campaigned in New York soon became a major aspect of the election. The *Los Angeles Times* described New York as "this unforgiving city."[17] A *Philadelphia Daily News* columnist referred to "New York's mean streets" and described the city as "the Meat Grinder of the Universe."[18] Cox News Service, in summing up the latest media allegations, described the campaign as sliding "toward political disorder."[19]

It was at this point that the Clinton campaign managers made one of the most important decisions of the 1992 presidential primary elections. Clinton agreed to debate Jerry Brown on local New York City television, and he began accepting invitations to appear on television "talk shows." The debates and the talk show appearances were necessary, a Clinton adviser said, so that Clinton could present himself "directly to the voters and around the tabloids."[20]

It had become clear that the newspaper and television reporters were constantly feeding negative images of Bill Clinton to their reading and viewing audiences. If Clinton went directly to the voters in television debates and on talk shows, however, the audience would see him as he really is rather than seeing the negative images provided by reporters as they wrote newspaper stories or commented during television news clips.

This technique of going directly to the voters on live television worked very successfully for Clinton. He began by appearing with television talk show host Phil Donahue. When Donahue began asking Clinton questions about his personal life and his business affairs, the audience booed Donahue and told him to confine his questions to political issues. It was obvious that the studio audience was going to ask much easier questions than news reporters would ask and thereby enable Clinton to present a more favorable image to the public.

The Clinton forces then agreed to have a debate with Jerry Brown on the Donahue show, but with Phil Donahue out of sight off stage rather than directing the questioning. In this atmosphere, with the candidates responding directly to the public without hostile press interpretation, both Clinton and Brown were able to make good impressions. Their debate on the *Phil Donahue Show* was one of the high points of the New York presidential primary in terms of the civility with which the two candidates treated each other and the importance of the political issues they discussed.

The Clinton campaign decided to go one step further and try to make a campaign asset out of the brutal treatment Clinton was receiving in the New York news media. Clinton press assistants began suggesting that it was a real candidate plus that Clinton could take such heavy hitting in the media and still come back for more. The Clinton campaign produced and ran a television commercial boasting that Bill Clinton "stood up to the tabloids."[21]

Three days before primary election day in New York, aides to Paul Tsongas announced that the former Massachusetts senator would get back into the race for the Democratic nomination for president if two things happened. First, Tsongas, whose name was still on the New York ballot even though he was no longer an active candidate, would have to get at least 15 percent of the vote. Second, Clinton would have to lose New York to Jerry Brown.

Then a "Draft Tsongas" committee began airing radio and cable television advertisements urging New York Democrats to vote for Tsongas. The ads were narrated by television actor E. G. Marshall and said: "As we all know, Paul Tsongas suspended his campaign due to lack of funds. But he's still on the ballot here in New York. We need to bring Paul Tsongas back into this race and keep his message alive."[22]

No one could say for sure what was really going on, but it appeared that the battering both Clinton and Brown were receiving at the hands of the news media in New York had convinced Tsongas that, if Clinton stumbled badly in the New York primary, Tsongas might have a chance to reenter the contest and win the nomination. Thus, as New York Democrats went to the polls on primary day 1992, there were once again three candidates asking for their votes—Bill Clinton, Jerry Brown, and Paul Tsongas.

Despite all the assaults from the New York press and all the heckling from New York audiences, Bill Clinton handily won the New York primary with 41 percent of the vote. Amazingly, Paul Tsongas finished second with 29 percent, and Jerry Brown third with 26 percent. Clearly, Tsongas's hints that he might get back into the race had wiped out any chance Brown might have had of beating Clinton in New York.

Unfortunately for Tsongas supporters, the New York primary had met only one of Tsongas's requirements for reentering the contest. True, Tsongas had received more than 15 percent of the vote, but Brown had not defeated Clinton. A few days after the New York results were known, Paul Tsongas reaffirmed his decision to stay out of the race.

That meant that Bill Clinton was going to be the 1992 Democratic nominee. Although 59 percent of New York Democrats had not voted for him, Clinton had decisively defeated Jerry Brown and thereby sewed up the Democratic nomination. The outcome was no longer in doubt. Clinton had disposed of Brown in New York just as he had disposed of Tsongas in Illinois and Michigan. Democratic National Chairman Ron Brown made it all but official when he told CNN: "With over 1,300 delegates, Clinton has it all but locked up."[23]

The exit polls in New York sent the now familiar message of high voter dissatisfaction with how the presidential primaries were turning out. According to NBC, almost two-thirds of New York Democrats, 66 percent, said they wanted some other candidate to enter the race. Almost half, 46 percent, said they doubted that Bill Clinton had the integrity to serve as president.[24]

Amazingly, 70 percent of New York Democrats told Voter Research and Surveys they agreed with Jerry Brown that big campaign contributions have too much influence over the American political system. Unfortunately for Brown, however, only 39 percent saw him as level-headed and practical enough to be president.

Although a moderate White southerner, Clinton continued to do well among northern minority groups. He received 55 percent of the Jewish vote in New York and 52 percent of the Black vote. The White Catholic vote split more or less evenly among Clinton, Tsongas, and Brown.

Bruised and banged up as he was after his New York experience, Bill Clinton bragged about the fact that he had taken on the very worst New York had to offer and had survived. One Clinton aide described it all in Western horse-opera terms: "Hey, getting out of Dodge alive is a triumph." Another aide was more enthusiastic and thereby more truthful: "We're unstoppable. This was a grand slam."[25]

The national news media were quick to note a grim irony in the New York results. Bill Clinton came in first in the primary and thereby won the Democratic nomination for president, but at the same time his standing in the eyes of the American public was dropping fast. David Broder of the *Washington Post* summed up this somewhat unprecedented situation: "What's unusual about this year is that the more Clinton wins, the larger the question marks loom over his candidacy. It's usually the other way around: victory stifles the skeptics. Clinton seems to accumulate as many doubters as delegates."[26]

Syndicated columnists Rowland Evans and Robert Novak were even harsher in their analysis of the effect of the New York mudbath on Clinton's candidacy: "It was New York that erased the perception of Clinton as a magnificent campaigner who happened to be burdened with questionable character. In New York, character problems so handicapped him that Clinton turned into a miserable campaigner. His belated admission, following evasion, that he had tried marijuana as a youth but did not 'inhale' made him an American laughingstock."[27]

The *Washington Post National Weekly Edition* joined in the news media rush to present Bill Clinton as a winning candidate with severe character and credibility flaws. It headlined its wrap-up story about Clinton and the New York Democratic primary this way: "A Question of Character: Despite His Success, Clinton Remains Defined by Doubts."[28]

To the Clinton camp, it now had become obvious that the news media were using the exit polls to reverse the results of the primary elections. A complete readjustment in campaign style was called for. Clinton's goal would no longer be just to win primary elections. He would have to spend more time making sure he came out looking good in the media's exit polls. "Dammit," Clinton complained the morning after the New York voting. "We won that primary, and they took it away from us." The big story, Clinton fumed, was not his winning a big victory but that 55 percent of the voters thought he could not be trusted. "From now on," Clinton said, "we run for the exit polls."[29]

15. WISCONSIN, MINNESOTA,
AND KANSAS

Although it was difficult to notice, three other states were holding Democratic presidential primaries the same day that New York was voting. If there was one thing the states of Wisconsin, Minnesota, and Kansas learned in 1992, it was that it is next to impossible to get news media attention for your presidential primary if a major state such as New York is voting the same day.

The saddest case was Wisconsin, whose presidential primary is one of the oldest and most famous in the nation. Back when fewer than ten states held presidential primaries, midsize Wisconsin was one of the high spots on a short but exciting primary trail. The Badger State gained its greatest primary fame in 1960 when Democrat John F. Kennedy defeated Hubert H. Humphrey, despite the fact that Kennedy was from faraway Massachusetts and Humphrey was from next-door Minnesota. Kennedy's upset of Humphrey in Wisconsin in 1960 was the break Kennedy needed to establish his credentials as a national rather than a regional candidate for president.

For a few days in 1992, it appeared that Jerry Brown might have a chance of coming into Wisconsin and seriously challenging Bill Clinton. Wisconsin is known as a progressive state, one that takes readily to new ideas and calls for governmental reform. To many observers, Brown's emphasis on clean government and open politics, and his frequent condemnation of the nefarious influence of big money in Washington, was a campaign tactic that just might catch on in Wisconsin.

As was his consistent habit, Brown worked the college and university campuses. He drew several thousand students to a rally at the University of Wisconsin in Madison. A few days later, he used a bullhorn to address a large outdoor crowd at the University of Wisconsin in Milwaukee.

Another Brown asset was Wisconsin's open primary, which meant that Republicans who liked Brown's anti-establishment rhetoric could "cross over" and vote for him in the Democratic primary. Wisconsin also lacked sizable numbers of Black and Hispanic voters, two groups which had been a big part of Bill Clinton's past primary victories.

A closer look at the Brown organization in Wisconsin, however, revealed the customary weaknesses. There was a Brown headquarters, but it did not even have a telephone. The telephone number given for the Brown effort in Wisconsin was the home telephone of Doug Belknap, a psychologist who had never before worked in an election campaign. When asked why he alone appeared to be the Brown organization in Wisconsin, Belknap replied: "I got involved with Jerry Brown because I think this campaign is psychotherapy on a national cultural scale."[1]

When the votes were counted, Jerry Brown did do much better against Bill Clinton in Wisconsin than he did in New York. Clinton won with 38 percent of the vote, but Brown was a close second with 35 percent. In the end it meant nothing, however, because the big news of the day was that Clinton had so easily defeated Brown in New York. Wisconsin, at one time one of the most important dates on the presidential primary calendar, was reduced in 1992 to near meaninglessness.

The other two states holding primaries on New York's primary day, Minnesota and Kansas, received virtually no candidate and news media attention whatsoever. Minnesota was particularly uninteresting because its Democratic primary was "non-binding" and did not influence the selection of Minnesota's delegates to the Democratic National Convention. Bill Clinton narrowly won the Gopher State "beauty contest" with 31.1 percent of the vote compared to 30.6 percent for Jerry Brown and 21.3 percent for Paul Tsongas.

Kansas provided yet another example of what happens to a smaller state when it votes the same day as a big state. Neither Bill Clinton nor Jerry Brown could find even a half day to break away from the big show in New York and do some campaigning in Kansas. The candidates did not run any advertisements on television, and no polls were published by either the local or the national media. The only sign of any campaign activity whatsoever in Kansas was a one-day fly-through by Hillary Clinton on behalf of her husband. The candidates did not even have surrogates—prominent Kansas Democrats who were backing their respective bids for the presidency—out making news for them.

Ironically, although Bill Clinton never campaigned there, he scored his biggest win of the day in Kansas. In fact, Kansas was the only one of the four states voting on April 7, 1992, that gave Clinton a majority of the vote. Kansas went for Clinton with 51 percent of the vote compared to 15 percent for Tsongas and 13 percent for Brown. Some Democrats argued that Clinton showed real strength as a presidential candidate by winning big in a moderate state like Kansas, a state that reflected the national electorate more accurately than liberal states like New York, Wisconsin, and Minnesota.[2]

It also was difficult to notice on April 7, 1992, that there still was a campaign for the Republican nomination going on. Late in March, conservative commentator Patrick Buchanan announced that he was renewing his presidential campaign, only from now on he would be attacking the Democratic establishment in Congress as well as President Bush.

Buchanan acknowledged that only "celestial intervention" could keep George Bush from getting the Republican nomination, but he said Congress was "a swamp that must be drained" and therefore he would devote the remainder of the campaign to that task. "It is, friends, time to clean house, to throw the rascals out, to err on the side of challengers rather than incumbents," Buchanan said. "Now if your congressman is clean as a hound's tooth and doing a great job, keep him in. But when in doubt, throw them out."[3]

Buchanan said he would take his revitalized presidential campaign into the Wisconsin and Minnesota primaries. He would not be campaigning in the New York Republican primary because, due to the complexity and early filing deadlines in New York, he had not been able to get his name on the ballot there.

President Bush responded to Buchanan's reactivated campaign by ignoring it. The national news media very much ignored it, particularly after the fireworks started going off in the New York Democratic primary. On election day, Bush defeated Buchanan in Minnesota by 70 percent to 24 percent and in Wisconsin by 78 percent to 17 percent. For Buchanan, it was the final convulsion in a presidential campaign that had begun dying many weeks earlier.

Three weeks later, on May 2, 1992, George Bush completely locked up the Republican nomination. At the Maine Republican state convention, held in the capital city of Augusta, Bush won all of the state's twenty-two delegates to the national convention. That gave Bush 1,114 delegates, nine more than the 1,105 needed for a mathematical majority. A smiling John McKernan, Maine's Republican governor, proudly told the cheering state convention: "Maine is putting George Bush over the top."[4]

16. The Rise of Ross Perot

On February 20, 1992, a Texas billionaire named Ross Perot made a guest appearance on a popular television show, CNN's *Live with Larry King*. It was just two days after the New Hampshire primary, in which Paul Tsongas had beaten Bill Clinton in the Democratic race and Pat Buchanan had polled a surprising 37 percent of the vote against President Bush.

At the end of his interview with Larry King, Perot said he would run for president as an independent if people throughout the nation would volunteer to work for him and, by the petition process, put his name on the ballot in all fifty states. To many viewers, Perot's somewhat offhanded proposal sounded like a solemn pledge. If volunteers would collect enough signatures to put Perot's name on the ballot in every state in the Union, Perot would make a serious and committed campaign for the White House.

Furthermore, Perot let it be known that he would be willing to use up to $100 million of his immense personal fortune to finance his presidential campaign. The problem that had plagued most independent campaigns for president in the past—lack of money—simply would not be a problem with Ross Perot as the candidate. His personal fortune totaled more than $3.3 billion. His annual income probably exceeded $300 million.

Within minutes of Perot's surprise proposal on the Larry King show, the telephone lines at his computer services firm in Dallas were jammed with incoming calls. So many people were calling to volunteer for Perot for president that no one at Perot's corporate headquarters could get a telephone line to call out. It was instantly obvious to both Perot and the news media that there were large numbers of Americans who did not like the field of candidates, both Democratic and Republican, that had been presented in New Hampshire. They wanted another choice—and Perot had sounded like he was willing to be that other choice.

On March 13, 1992, taking a page from the Jerry Brown campaign book, Ross Perot set up an 800-number to track his support and begin organizing the campaign to put his name on the ballot in all fifty states. More than six thousand calls came in the first day the 800-number was on line. As word spread that volunteers could telephone Perot headquarters for free, the volume of calls went up dramatically. In just one thirty-second period a record eighteen thousand calls were placed. In a subsequent twenty-four-hour period the Perot 800-number was dialed 500,000 times.

By late March the Perot campaign had volunteer organizations working in every state. All across the nation, vacant offices and empty stores were opened up, cleaned up, and turned into local "Perot for President" headquarters. Thousands of Americans suddenly were carrying petitions to put Perot on the ballot, and millions of Americans were signing those petitions. On March 23, 1992, barely more than a month after Perot's appearance on the Larry King show, Tennessee became the first state to put Ross Perot's name on its November presidential election ballot.

Perot's meteoric rise in popularity was aided by the "front-loaded" nature of the Democratic and Republican presidential primaries. By mid-March it was obvious that George Bush was going to demolish Pat Buchanan and be the Republican nominee. By early April, following Bill Clinton's defeat of Jerry Brown in New York, it was clear that Clinton was going to be the Democratic nominee. As public and news media interest in the Democratic and Republican primaries progressively decreased, interest in the Perot campaign progressively increased. Perot was perfectly positioned to fill the news vacuum created when the Republican and Democratic presidential primary contests ended early.

On April 9, 1992, two days after the New York primary, a *Time*/CNN poll revealed that 21 percent of the voters were now supporting Ross Perot for president.[1] In only six weeks Perot had established himself as a major contender, able to give the candidates of the two established political parties a real run for their money. From early

April onward, Perot's name was included in every major public opinion poll on who was going to win the presidential election. By early May the trend was clear. Bush and Clinton were dropping in the polls, and Perot was rising at an ever more rapid rate.[2]

Perhaps the most amazing thing about the Perot candidacy was that most of it was being done for free. Instead of buying expensive paid advertisements to win party primaries, as Bush and Clinton were having to do, Perot was pursuing his candidacy mainly on free television. He appeared on a long series of radio and television talk shows, answering questions from the public and giving vague, general answers on policy issues. So dazzled were the media by Perot that NBC's *Today* show made him the featured guest for an entire morning. Perot was rising fast in the polls, his independent campaign for president was taking off, and he was not having to spend very much money to accomplish all this.

Suddenly large numbers of reporters and commentators were flying to Dallas and interviewing Perot in person. The most popular show on television, CBS's *60 Minutes*, interviewed Perot in his Dallas office, as did longtime interviewer/commentator David Frost. During April and May, newspapers and magazines across the nation published major feature articles on Perot. His life and his business accomplishments were suddenly available to any American willing to take the time to read about them.[3]

These early stories about Perot were surprisingly uncritical. Perot's ability to recruit staggeringly large numbers of volunteers and almost instantly become a presidential contender produced a "gee whiz" attitude among most of the nation's news personnel. In the exciting early days of his candidacy, Ross Perot was spared the relentless scrutiny which most candidates for president routinely undergo.

To be fair to the news media, there was much to admire and praise about Ross Perot. A native of Texarkana, Texas, he earned money delivering newspapers as a youth. Early on he demonstrated his penchant for hard work and goal-attainment by becoming an Eagle Scout. After graduating from the Naval Academy and briefly serving as an officer in the Navy, Perot went to work for International Business Machines (IBM), soon becoming one of the computer giant's top salespersons.

In 1962 Perot borrowed $1,000 from his wife and founded Electronic Data Services (EDS). He left IBM after he failed to convince his bosses that there was just as much money in showing customers how to use computers as in selling them computers. With its emphasis on ideas and services rather than just computer hardware, EDS was an instant financial success. Six years later, when Perot began selling EDS stock on the stock market, the company was valued at over $375 million.

Perot became a financial celebrity in 1984 when General Motors bought Electronic Data Services for $2.5 billion. Perot's personal share of the sale was $1.4 billion. Because of all the publicity over how much money he made from a single financial transaction, Ross Perot suddenly became a well-known member of the super rich, that relatively small number of individuals who count their wealth in billions rather than millions.

Perot subsequently founded another computer services firm, Perot Systems, and invested heavily in commercial and residential real estate in Atlanta, Dallas, and Kansas City. It was the Perot Systems headquarters in Dallas that provided the telephone lines and the office space that enabled the Perot campaign for president to get operating so swiftly.

In addition to being a successful businessperson, Perot supported a number of political causes. He had long made it a personal project to use his vast fortune to try to free any United States prisoners of war that might still be imprisoned in Vietnam. In what appeared to be a highly valorous action, Perot claimed he had helped two of his employees escape from illegal imprisonment in an Iranian jail. A full-length book about Perot's exploits in Iran, *On the Wings of Eagles*, had become a national bestseller and was turned into an NBC television "docudrama" seen by an estimated 25 million viewers.[4]

Ross Perot presented himself to the American people in the spring of 1992 as a man of action and determination. His independence and honesty, already proven in the business world, would enable him to break the stranglehold of "politics as usual" on American government. He would, in his own words, "take out the trash and clean out the barn." He claimed to be a Mr. Fix-It who could get the stalled machinery of democracy running smoothly again.

By mid-May the *Time*/CNN poll found nearly one-third of American voters (33 percent) supporting Ross Perot for president.[5] He already had passed Bill Clinton in the polls and was pulling even with President Bush. The political map of the 1992 presidential election had been altered completely by the Perot candidacy. The presidential primaries were not even over yet, but it was very clear there was going to be a three-way race for president. The third man in the race, independent candidate Ross Perot, had a more than reasonable chance of winning it.[6]

17. THE IRRELEVANT
PRIMARIES I: OREGON

After the New York primary, the question of who was going to be the Democratic nominee was answered for all to see. Bill Clinton, the governor of Arkansas, was going to be the Democratic standard-bearer in 1992. Despite that fact, Clinton still had to run in a long series of primaries, many of them in some of the most populous states in the United States. The one Democratic candidate left in the race against Clinton, former California governor Jerry Brown, could not mathematically catch the front-runner, but Clinton could not lock up a majority of the convention delegates until the last primary day, when populous states such as California, New Jersey, and Ohio were scheduled to vote.

In an analysis column the day after the New York primary, Tom Baxter of Cox News Service described this process as a "suicide-assistance machine." Baxter explained: "In slow doses, the suicide machine has managed to mete out the worst of both worlds for the Democrats. It has guaranteed that no one but Bill Clinton can win the Democratic nomination before the party's national convention this summer. Yet it makes it impossible for Clinton to sew the nomination up before the last primary day of the year, ensuring that he will be stalked . . . by Jerry Brown . . . right to the end."[1]

Walter F. Mondale, the Democratic nominee who lost to Ronald Reagan in the 1984 presidential election, agreed that Clinton's position following the New York primary was a "nightmare." Mondale said: "[Jerry] Brown is a battering ram, not a nominee, but he may be able to make the nomination worthless. Clinton is still our likely candidate, but all we're doing is beating him up, not giving him time to rest, polish his program and raise money. Here we go again. There's got to be a lot of joy in the White House tonight."[2]

The fact that Clinton was assuredly the Democratic nominee but would have to keep on campaigning for two months was particularly disturbing in view of the low opinion so many voters had of him. The one thing that made the entire situation somewhat tolerable was that the prospective Republican nominee, incumbent president George Bush, was almost as unpopular as Clinton. Pennsylvania's Democratic governor, Robert P. Casey, summed up the situation: "[George] Bush is trying to hand us the election, and we're trying to hand it back."[3]

There was perhaps only one thing more bothersome and boring than having to run in a series of meaningless primaries. That was having to vote in them. Republicans and Democrats alike, in states such as Pennsylvania, Indiana, North Carolina, Oregon, and California, were going to have to troop to the polls and dutifully cast their ballots in primary elections that no longer would have any effect on who was nominated.

As might be expected in such a situation, the news media only paid routine attention to this long series of meaningless primaries. The number of reporters and television camerapersons traveling with the candidates rapidly dwindled. Many of them were off covering Ross Perot and his surging independent campaign for president.

Generally speaking, only the election-day results of the various primaries received major news media attention. Even then the reporters were more likely to concentrate on the exit polls than on the actual election results. In the exit polls large majorities of voters continued to state that they did not particularly like either Clinton or Bush. Many said they would have voted for Ross Perot if his name had been on the primary ballot in their state.

Take the case of Pennsylvania, one of the most populous states in the nation but one which had the misfortune of scheduling its primary for April 28, 1992, three weeks after New York. Although Bill Clinton and Jerry Brown both campaigned in Pennsylvania, the primary generated little or no enthusiasm among the Quaker State electorate. "[Clinton] will win here," said Dennis Casey, a Pittsburgh political consultant, "but only 14 people will vote." Ed Mitchell, a Democratic consultant from Scranton, echoed much the same sentiment: "Everyone will hold their nose and vote for [Clinton]."[4] Both of these analyses proved to be correct. Clinton defeated Jerry Brown in Pennsylvania by better than a two-to-one margin, but turnout was low and voters expressed little enthusiasm for the Clinton candidacy.[5]

Another case in point was the Oregon primary, at one time one of the most famous and most important presidential primaries. Oregon is special because it holds its primary at the end of May, two weeks before the California primary, which always is held on the first Tuesday in June. Traditionally candidates campaign hard in Oregon in hopes of getting a victory that will give them an edge in the California voting two weeks later.

Bill Clinton set the tone for the meaninglessness of the Oregon primary when, one week before primary day, he appointed a vice presidential search committee. The news media reported this action routinely, not one reporter or commentator bothering to suggest that it was presumptious of Clinton to appoint a vice presidential search team while the presidential primaries were still taking place.

As had become his habit, Jerry Brown campaigned through Oregon as if he were still a viable candidate. The Sunday before election day, Brown made a typical airport arrival in Salem, the capital of Oregon. Only about twenty-five people turned out on the McNary Airport tarmac to greet him and hear his remarks. The next day, however, Brown drew a crowd of more than fifteen hundred supporters to a noontime rally in downtown Portland's Pioneer Courthouse Square.

Amazingly, although Brown had no possible chance of winning the Democratic nomination, his campaign for president now appeared to have plenty of money to spend. It was a complete contrast with Brown's situation back at the time of the New Hampshire and Colorado primaries, when he appeared to have virtually no funds. The 800-number for soliciting donations, and the government matching funds that were thereby generated, clearly had worked very well for Brown. He spoke in Portland from an expensive wooden platform. His words were carried to the audience by an expensive outdoor sound system. Supporters were given professionally printed cardboard signs to wave. Behind the speaker's platform, volunteers sold professionally designed "Brown for President" T-shirts and sweatshirts, all of which contained the campaign slogan "Take Back America" and the 800-number. T-shirt and sweatshirt sales were going briskly.

At first glance, an observer might conclude that Jerry Brown had expanded his appeal from the college and university set to the general population. Pioneer Courthouse Square was filled with people of all ages. Below the stately dome and marble pillars of Portland's old courthouse, a large crowd had filled and overflowed a circular outdoor amphitheater of step-style seats. On the lower floors of the office build-ings that surrounded the square, office workers had opened the win-dows and were spending their lunch hour listening to Brown's speech. By the time Brown began talking, listeners surrounded the speaker's platform on all four sides. The crowd size and the crowd enthusiasm for a really good political rally were all there.

Alas for Brown, it did not take long to figure out that Pioneer Courthouse Square is located just a few blocks from Portland State Uni-versity, an urban university with a diverse student body, particularly in terms of age. The major part of the audience was made up of Portland State students and faculty who had walked over to see and hear Brown perform. The backbone of his support was still the college and univer-sity crowd.

There was something else taking away from Jerry Brown's other-wise successful Portland rally. There was no press platform loaded with reporters from the major newspapers from throughout the United States. Also, there were no network television reporters and camera operators. At the back row of the outdoor amphitheater, which also was the top row, two lone television reporters and two lone camera operators filmed highlights of the Brown rally for two local Portland television stations. In the final stages of its existence, the Brown cam-paign had ceased to be of any national significance. It now was strictly a local event, and a minor local event at that.

Following a spirited introduction by movie actor Martin Sheen, Brown gave a talk to his Portland supporters that is best described as "walking the left side of the street." In a compelling and urgent tone, Brown touched on every cause that had inspired the liberal sensibilities of college youth for the past thirty years. He spoke glowingly of the AIDS Hospice in Portland and of a group that was protesting the Trojan nuclear power plant in nearby Rainier, Oregon. He made his customary attack on the influence of big money in politics, and he said the Democrats were just as bad as the Republicans where this kind of finan-cial corruption was concerned.[6]

Brown charged that every job in the United States was under pres-sure from the competition of cheap labor in Mexico, and he said that was the reason he opposed "fast track" free trade with Mexico. In his one humorous aside, he suggested shipping both the Republican pres-ident and the Democratic Congress to Mexico. "Once they are down there," Brown speculated, "we will get much more work from them for much less money."

Brown attacked both the Democrats and the Republicans on the abortion issue, charging that neither party was really pro-choice because "a Democratic Senate willingly confirmed anti-abortion Republican Supreme Court nominees." After noting that "the only major housing program of the Bush Administration is building more prisons," Brown pointed out that, as governor of California, he had created "more jobs than Bush [as president] and Clinton [as governor of Arkansas] combined."

In the foreign policy field, Brown raised the question of whether the recently dissolved Soviet Union had ever been a real problem for the United States. He hinted that the Communist threat might have been cooked up more for the purpose of stimulating military arms manufacturing than providing for needed national security. "Was the Red threat overstated? I think it was! If we could find $1 trillion to fight the phony threat of Communism, why can't we find $1 trillion to help poor Americans in Appalachia and in our cities?"

Brown said it was he, not Bill Clinton, who was the real "agent of change" in the Democratic Party. He called on the crowd to join him in helping to "change the dead habits of the Democratic Party." He concluded his talk by reminding everyone to call his 800-number and make a donation.

There was a noticeable contrast between the Jerry Brown who had campaigned in Colorado in early March and the Jerry Brown who was campaigning in Oregon in late May. Early in the primaries Brown had sounded "progressive" rather than "liberal," concentrating his talks on new ideas such as generating electricity with wind power and building high-speed intercity passenger trains. By the time Brown got to Oregon, however, his speeches and statements to the press overflowed with the standard liberal, left-wing rhetoric of the 1960s and 1970s.

As Brown was nearing the end of his talk, a light rain began to fall, thereby upholding Oregon's reputation for wet weather. As he spoke his final words, the rain was coming down hard, and the crowd hurried rapidly away from Pioneer Courthouse Square. Soon only the most dedicated Brown supporters remained, packing up and cleaning up while being pelted by a cold rain.

Bill Clinton was campaigning in Oregon, too, but in a completely different atmosphere. Because he was now certain to be the Democratic nominee for president, large crowds turned out to meet Clinton and see what he was like. Unlike Brown, who traveled with only a small entourage of campaign workers, Clinton had a veritable army of people campaigning with him. Police patrols cleared his way through automobile traffic when he was driven from place to place. A large contingent of security guards stayed close to him and closely watched those who shook his hand and asked him questions. Clinton maintained the atmosphere of a serious and important candidate, even if the primary elections he was running in were not taken seriously by the national press.

One did not have to watch Bill Clinton in Oregon very long to realize that he was adopting some of the techniques of his defeated opponents. At the same time Jerry Brown was speaking in Pioneer Courthouse Square in Portland, Clinton was addressing an outdoor crowd of three thousand students and faculty at the University of Oregon in Eugene. Apparently the Clinton camp had learned what Brown always knew—that college and university campuses are an easy place to generate a large crowd at very low cost.

Clinton also was running television advertisements in Oregon which talked about his "Economic Plan" for restoring the national economy, a campaign technique that had been used most effectively by Paul Tsongas, particularly in the New Hampshire primary. If viewers wanted a copy of the Clinton Economic Plan, all they had to do was dial Clinton's new 800-number and ask for it. Also, Clinton supporters now could use an 800-number to make a financial contribution to the Clinton campaign, a direct steal of Jerry Brown's most innovative campaign technique.

Another change in Oregon was the nature and style of Clinton's television advertisements. They were no longer comparative, that is, negative, in character. Clinton's one remaining opponent, Jerry Brown, was never mentioned in them. The ads were designed to present Clinton in as positive a light as possible. The theme of the Oregon ads was that Bill Clinton was a talented young man who very much wanted to be president so that he could "do things for America."

Election night of the Oregon Democratic primary found the Clinton faithful gathered together at the Bridgeport Brew Pub, a brewery-style bar in the northwest section of downtown Portland. Bill Clinton was not in Portland, of course, having already moved on to one of the states that had a primary ahead of it, not behind it, as now was the case in Oregon. Still, it was a surprisingly small group drinking and chatting at the Brew Pub in view of the fact that Clinton was the all-but-guaranteed Democratic presidential nominee. No more than fifty people were on hand, and not one well-known Democratic officeholder in Portland or Oregon took the trouble to be present.

To be fair, the professional basketball team from Oregon, the Portland Trailblazers, was playing an important play-off game on television that evening. Presidential politics also is important, however, and one had to think that at least one or two of Portland's and Oregon's important Democrats could have taken the time to be at Clinton's Oregon victory party.

As always, television sets were scattered around the Bridgeport Brew Pub so the Clinton faithful could watch the election returns come in. Good news was not long in coming. Clinton got off to an early lead over Brown in Oregon that never faded. When the ballots were all counted, Clinton defeated Brown in Oregon by 45.3 percent to 31.4 percent.

Since the election returns quickly became boring, there was not much to do at the Clinton victory party except listen to a musical group composed of three women playing and singing modern folk songs. If that got tiring, one could look at a large map of the United States with all the states carried by Bill Clinton in the primaries colored in. By the time of the Oregon primary, Clinton's many primary victories looked most impressive when presented on a brightly colored map.

Most people, however, were trying to talk with and listen to Paddy McGuire, the Oregon state director of the Clinton for President Committee. As the evening went by and Clinton's Oregon victory over Jerry Brown became more and more of a "done deal," Paddy became the center of media and social attention. When not doing short television interviews for local Portland television stations, Paddy made himself available to newspaper reporters and anyone else who wanted to talk about what was going on in the Clinton campaign for president.

Paddy McGuire looked to be not very much over thirty years old. He clearly was an "organization" and "career" Democrat, having previously served as the paid state director of the Oregon Democratic Party. As a "professional" Democrat, Paddy was exactly the sort of person one would expect to find running Bill Clinton's campaign in Oregon.

"The Clinton campaign is in a very unusual but very important period," Paddy explained. "Clinton is now using free media, such as campaign rallies and radio and television talk shows, to avoid the filter of the national press. It is the national press that is digging up all the stories that put Clinton in a bad light. Our goal here in Oregon is to let people see Bill Clinton as he really is. We have worked to create situations where people can talk directly to Bill Clinton and ask him questions. Our belief is that when people see and meet the real Bill Clinton, whether in person or on television, they come away liking him and forget the negative images that are constantly presented by the news media."

Paddy McGuire then put the Oregon Democratic primary in its proper perspective. "The Oregon campaign was not about right now. Everyone knew that Bill Clinton was going to win Oregon and has already won the Democratic nomination. This campaign was about the race against President Bush. Oregon will be a critical state for Clinton in the November general election, and he was campaigning in the primary mainly looking for votes for the fall.

"That was why we had Clinton speak yesterday at the University of Oregon in Eugene," McGuire continued. "We know that right now that is Jerry Brown country, but we want those Brown voters to remember Bill Clinton in November when their major choice will be between George Bush and Bill Clinton. When it's Bush or Clinton, we think most of the Brown vote will go to Bill Clinton."

When asked about Ross Perot's candidacy, McGuire acknowledged there was a problem and a challenge. "Our job between now and November," he said, "is to convince people that Bill Clinton, and not Ross Perot, is the credible alternative to George Bush."

Paddy McGuire described himself as a "paid political professional." He was asked how he, as a politically informed Oregonian, felt about the fact that the Oregon primary was scheduled too late to have any effect on who gets the Democratic nomination for president. "To tell the truth," McGuire replied, "the Oregon Democratic primary has not mattered since 1972, when Oregon voted for George McGovern and greatly helped him defeat Hubert H. Humphrey for that year's Democratic nomination. There was a movement to change the Oregon primary to a date in March, and we probably would have changed if other Pacific Coast states had joined us."[7]

The most enlightening part of Paddy McGuire's comments was his statement that Bill Clinton was using free media to avoid the negative filter of the national press. Traditionally in American politics, presidential candidates and their images had been presented to the public by newspaper reporters writing stories and television news editors selecting the topics for "reports" on the evening network news. Under this old system, the newspaper reporters and television news editors had a great deal of control over what was selected for presentation to the public. The reporter "chose" the story he would write on any particular day, and often as not that story could be a very negative one about the candidate. In the same way, television news editors picked the subjects to be discussed and the questions to be asked on the evening network news. Sometimes the subject matter and the questions selected put the candidate in a positive light, but in many cases they were negative and presented the candidate to the public in a bad light.

In deciding to go around the newspaper reporters and the television news editors and take his persona and his ideas directly to the public, Bill Clinton was simply taking advantage of the major changes that had occurred in communications in the United States during the

1980s. In that ten-year period, the number of households subscribing to cable television expanded from 15 million to more than 50 million. As cable access expanded, so did the number of people who watched twenty-four-hour-a-day cable news rather than half-hour nightly network news programs. For real afficionados of politics, C-SPAN provided a cable channel where political events could be watched from beginning to end with virtually no editing or commentary by media personnel.

In such a world, voters can use radio and television talk shows and lengthy live presentations on CNN and C-SPAN to gather their own information about candidates and draw their own conclusions about their worth or nonworth. In fact, it can be argued that most voters prefer to look at presidential candidates directly and make up their own minds rather than accept the more critical and negative views presented by the traditional news media.

David Matthews, president of the Kettering Foundation, argued that voters no longer trust the media to give them an accurate picture of political candidates and political events. He said: "People simply do not believe what the media often believes [sic] about themselves, that they are neutral observers who have no real role in the action. . . . They [the people] believe the media has a real bias, that it is essentially a negative bias and that that bias shuts out other voices or perspectives on the problem."[8]

It was this voter sentiment—that the media might be distorting his image—that Bill Clinton was trying to reach as he made his way through the phony phase, the irrelevant final portion of the 1992 Democratic primaries. From *Larry King Live* to the *Phil Donahue Show* to the *Oprah Winfrey Show*, Clinton worked to present his face, his voice, his ideas, and his programs directly to the American people. Since the news media insisted on presenting a negative view of Bill Clinton to the American people through conventional news channels, he had no choice but to bypass conventional news channels and take his case directly to the American people, both on the political stump in the remaining primary states and on live radio and television.

Subsequent to the Oregon primary, Clinton made an appearance on a television talk show that considerably brightened his image with the American people, particularly young people. On June 3, 1992, Clinton tied a flowered necktie around his neck, donned a pair of dark sunglasses, grabbed a tenor saxophone, and played a jazzy version of "Heartbreak Hotel" on *The Arsenio Hall Show*. A photograph of Clinton playing the saxophone with "shades" on was printed the next morning in virtually every newspaper in the country.

So, getting as much live and free TV as possible was the strategy the Clinton campaign was applying at the time of the Oregon primary. As the Oregon primary came to an end, however, that strategy was not working too well, at least not yet. Media-sponsored exit polls conducted the day of the Oregon primary showed that, among Democrats, 45 percent favored Ross Perot for president and only 42 percent supported Bill Clinton. Up to 13 percent of Oregon Democratic primary voters actually wrote in Perot's name.

Despite his attempts in Oregon to go around the media and present himself directly to the voters, Bill Clinton found himself running a dismal third in national public opinion polls. An NBC News/*Wall Street Journal* poll, published the day after the Oregon primary, put Bush in the lead with 35 percent, Perot second with 30 percent, and Clinton last with just 27 percent.[9]

18. The Irrelevant
Primaries II: California

For decades, the California primary was the big finish to the presidential primary season. Always scheduled for the first Tuesday in June, it was both the last primary and the biggest primary in terms of the numbers of delegates at stake. If there was a close race, so the traditional thinking went, it would be settled once and for all by the big final shoot-out in the Golden State.

During the 1970s and 1980s, however, the California presidential primary became "the primary that doesn't count."[1] As the number of states holding presidential primaries rapidly increased, presidential nominating fights were won and lost long before the primary election calendar ever got close to California with its late voting date in early June.

California voters ended up with two very unsatisfactory and basically meaningless choices. On the one hand, they could cast a symbolic protest vote for candidates who no longer had a chance of winning. California Democrats did just that when they chose Jerry Brown over Jimmy Carter in 1976 and picked Gary Hart over Walter Mondale in 1984. On the other hand, Californians could dutifully vote to confirm what their fellow party members in other states had already decided. Thus California Democrats supported George McGovern over Hubert H. Humphrey in 1972, and California Republicans lined up behind Ronald Reagan over George Bush in 1980.

The last time the California primary actually decided which candidate received a major party nomination for president was in 1964, when Barry Goldwater, a conservative United States senator from Arizona, narrowly defeated Nelson Rockefeller, the liberal governor of New York, in the California Republican voting. California Republicans have a "winner-take-all" rule where delegates to the party national convention are concerned, so Goldwater received all of California's large pot of Republican delegates. If Rockefeller had won and gained all those Golden State delegates, he would have been the Republican nominee in 1964 rather than Goldwater.

In the Democratic races in 1968 and 1972, the California primary could have been the deciding factor but, in the end, had no effect. In 1968 Robert Kennedy won the California primary and looked as though he might catch up with Hubert Humphrey and win the nomination at the Democratic Convention. Kennedy was assassinated the night of his California primary victory, however, and Humphrey ended up with the 1968 Democratic nomination by default.

Four years later, in 1972, it was Hubert Humphrey who was trying to catch a front-runner by staging an upset in the California primary. Humphrey's big effort fell short, however. George McGovern won California, 44 percent to 39 percent, and thereby guaranteed himself the 1972 Democratic nomination.

Similarly to Oregon, therefore, California has not been a factor in presidential nominating politics since 1972. The situation is particularly strange in view of the fact that California is the most populous state in the United States and should be the biggest player, not a nonplayer, in who receives the Republican and Democratic nominations for president.

How big is California? Because of recent population increases as recorded by the 1990 U.S. Census, California is now home to one out of every eight Americans. In 1992 the Golden State was slated to cast 18 percent, or almost one out of every five, of the delegate votes needed to win the nomination at both the Democratic and Republican National Conventions.[2]

Early in 1990 a major effort was made to move California's presidential primary date from the first Tuesday in June to the first Tuesday in March. Only the presidential primary would have been held on the new, earlier date. Primary elections for state and local offices still would have been held in June.

After a bill providing for such a date change for the presidential primary passed the lower house of the California state legislature, California Democrats persuaded the Democratic National Committee in

Washington to "open up" the first Tuesday in March for state presidential primaries. "California felt very strongly [it] wanted to be a player in the process," said Alice Travis, a member of the Democratic National Committee from California. "Coming last made it somewhat irrelevant."[3]

Previously national Democratic rules permitted new presidential primaries to be scheduled only on or after the second Tuesday in March, the date now known as Super Tuesday. California Democrats did not want to hold their primary on the same day all of those southern states, particularly Florida and Texas, were voting, so they used their political muscle on the Democratic National Committee to open up a date one week earlier.

Ironically, California ended up not moving its 1992 presidential primaries from the first Tuesday in June to the first Tuesday in March. The California state constitution provides that political issues can be initiated onto the ballot whenever any state election is held, and most authorities agreed that would include a stand-alone presidential primary held in early March. Californians are notorious for loading their state election ballot by way of petition drives. Given that the turnout for presidential primaries is usually very low compared to general elections, the California state legislature decided it did not want major questions of state policy being voted on in the same election as the early presidential primary. The low turnout of voters might produce weird results, unrepresentative of the California electorate as a whole, if citizen initiatives were voted on in a separate presidential primary.

In retrospect, it can now be seen that California's effort to change its primary date had a big effect on the 1992 presidential nominating season, even though California itself did not change dates. By getting the Democratic National Committee to open up the first Tuesday in March for presidential primaries, California made Junior Tuesday possible. Although California did not schedule its primary for the first Tuesday in March, four other states—Colorado, Maryland, Georgia, and Utah—did. As pointed out in Chapter 10, Junior Tuesday was the big innovation of the 1992 presidential primary season and, thanks to Georgia grabbing a Junior Tuesday primary date, became a major factor in Bill Clinton's winning the 1992 Democratic nomination for president.

Before it became clear that California was not going to move its presidential primary to the first Tuesday in March, political commentators had a field day speculating on how such a major change would affect the nominating system. Syndicated columnist George Will argued that an early California primary would, in most cases, be a de facto national primary. Winning such a large state so early in the process would be tantamount to winning the nomination. Will wrote: "A primary in a socially, ethnically and economically diverse state where [one-eighth] of the nation lives will be a semi-national primary. If other states, such as Texas, feel impelled to move up their primaries, we will have, de facto, a national primary. That will be a mechanism capable of making a quick, decisive, continental mistake."

Will also was concerned that an early California primary would overly benefit candidates with national reputations and lots of money to spend. "California, with seven major media markets, is a maw that devours political money. The more the nominating process is 'front-end loaded' with huge delegate prizes won early in states that require millions to be spent (and hence millions to be raised long before the process begins), the more the process favors candidates who are national figures already. It especially favors those who have leverage with large givers."[4]

Syndicated columnists Rowland Evans and Robert Novak speculated that an early California primary would mainly benefit Jesse Jackson, the Black civil rights leader who had unsuccessfully run for the Democratic nomination for president in both 1984 and 1988. If California votes early, Evans and Novak wrote, Jackson would be the lone Black candidate in a crowded field of White opponents. With California's large minority population, consisting mainly of Blacks and Hispanics, Jackson could very well be a big plurality winner in California. With the momentum gained from winning in the nation's most populous state, Evans and Novak concluded, Jackson might then be the plurality winner on Super Tuesday, when large numbers of southern states with high percentages of Black voters hold their presidential primaries. If Jackson won both California and Super Tuesday, his drive for the Democratic nomination in 1992 might prove unstoppable.[5]

As it turned out, California did not change its primary date, and Jesse Jackson decided not to be a candidate in 1992. That did not stop the speculation, however, about "what might have been" if California had voted early. R. W. Apple Jr. of the *New York Times*, writing after it had become known that Bill Clinton was going to be the 1992 Democratic nominee, opined that the 1992 Democratic race might have turned out completely differently if there had been an early primary in the Golden State. The biggest effect, obviously, would have been on former California governor Jerry Brown, who would have been running as a favorite son in his home state early in the race. Brown probably would have finished first or second, and thereby would have had his candidacy taken seriously.

Apple also speculated that an early California primary might have helped Tom Harkin: "An all-out liberal candidate like Senator Tom Harkin of Iowa might have done better among Democrats [in California] than he did with a more conservative electorate in New Hampshire. . . ." Most important, Apple pointed out, a populous state like California voting so early in the primary calendar might have lured different candidates into the 1992 Democratic race for president. "Some Democrats who did not run might have run."[6]

But California in 1992 was the big primary that wasn't. Because Jerry Brown refused to acknowledge defeat and give up the race for the Democratic nomination, Bill Clinton was forced to bring his presidential caravan to California and go through the motions of serious campaigning. As he had done in Oregon, Clinton used the California primary to do as much personal campaigning as possible and thereby counteract the negative image of him that had been generated by the news media. The emphasis was on speaking to and answering questions from the voters and off speaking to and answering questions from news reporters.

California was not the only state voting on June 2, 1992. For unknown reasons, five other states made the illogical and irrational decision to hold their presidential primaries at a time when there was little likelihood their voters could have any effect whatsoever on determining the party nominees. Two of the states were small in population, Montana and New Mexico, one was middle-sized, Alabama, and two were large, New Jersey and Ohio.

Because it was his home state and his best chance for winning a few more delegates, Jerry Brown quite naturally concentrated all his efforts in California. Bill Clinton, on the other hand, decided to campaign in all six states at the same time. The early polls showed Clinton well ahead of Brown in California, therefore Clinton decided to build support for the November general election by giving speeches and meeting the voters in all the states that were slated to vote on the first Tuesday in June. As would be expected, Clinton paid particular attention to New Jersey and Ohio, two states that he would very much need to carry if he were going to defeat George Bush and Ross Perot in November.

As had happened in Oregon, Clinton and Brown were completely overshadowed in California by the rapidly rising star of independent candidate Ross Perot. Five days before election day, the *New York Times* described Clinton as "trapped in a script of someone else's making." Instead of being allowed to discuss his own candidacy and his own program for solving America's ills, Clinton was constantly being questioned by news personnel and voters about his lagging poll ratings and the growing threat of Perot to his candidacy.

At one point Clinton became so frustrated he told reporters he was going "to stop answering foolish questions about polls." Within hours, however, during a live television interview, he was asked about a new poll that showed him running third behind Bush and Perot in Ohio. Clinton was going to have to discuss Ross Perot whether he wanted to or not.[7]

David S. Broder, the leading political analyst for the *Washington Post*, came to California to observe the primary campaigning there. In the end, he was more impressed by the grassroots efforts of the Perot people than by what Clinton or Brown was doing. Broder wrote: "The ubiquitous Perot petition-collection card tables are everywhere in California, manned by men and women who tell you they either have given up on Republicans and Democrats or have abandoned their apathy in hopes Perot may be 'different than those politicians.' In the week before the primary, they were camped on the steps of the state capitol, signing up tourists and even, they said, some state employees."[8]

California pollster Mervin Field agreed that the Perot boom had taken all the spark out of the California Democratic primary. "What has happened," Field said, "is that the boom for Perot has pre-empted public attention and enervated the other campaigns. Except for [Perot], the public doesn't see the ballot box as a means of doing anything about whatever it is that ails us. There's just so much political space in people's heads, and for the moment at least, Perot fills it."[9]

Bill Clinton made it a point to reach out to one constituency while campaigning in the California primary. A glittering fund-raiser was held for Clinton at the Palace Theater in Hollywood. The audience was mainly male, and many of the men stood arm-in-arm with their male friends and lovers. Clinton used the occasion to openly appeal for gay and lesbian support for his presidential candidacy.

Clinton spoke for twenty-five minutes at the rally, and his words were warmly received. He pledged, if elected president, to end the ban on homosexuals serving in the United States military. He also said he would support national legislation protecting the civil rights of gays and lesbians, and he promised to work for increased AIDS research spending.

The national press covered Clinton's "gay rights" fund-raiser and described it as a significant event. *USA Today* noted: "And for the first time in the memory of [gay and lesbian] activists, the presumptive nominee of a major political party openly appealed for homosexual support." The national newspaper also pointed out that "homosexual voters represent a significant block [sic] in important states like California. . . ."[10]

Clinton had originally intended to spend the weekend before the California presidential primary campaigning in Ohio and New Jersey as well as California. That previous Thursday, however, telephone polling indicated the race was tightening in California, with Clinton now barely one percentage point ahead of Jerry Brown. Clinton immediately canceled his planned trip to Ohio and New Jersey and spent all of the final weekend before election day campaigning hard in California.

When the votes were counted, however, Clinton scored his expected victory in California. He received 48 percent of the vote compared to Brown's 40 percent. Elsewhere, Clinton's victories were even more impressive. In New Mexico it was Clinton 53 percent, Brown 17 percent. In New Jersey Clinton took 59 percent compared to Brown's 20 percent. Ohio turned out to be really good for Clinton. He defeated Brown there 61 percent to 19 percent.

California thus was the great "could have been" of the 1992 presidential primary season. If the California state legislature had gotten itself together, worked out the problem of citizen initiatives, and given California an early primary date, California could have been the biggest factor in deciding who was going to be the Democratic nominee for president. As it was, California stayed with its late primary date and thereby became just another "after the fact" Bill Clinton victory.

The 1992 Democratic and Republican presidential primaries at last were over. Well, not quite. One week later, on June 9, 1992, North Dakota held a nonbinding "beauty contest." On the Republican side, only President Bush and comedian Pat Paulsen were on the ballot. Bush won easily.

On the Democratic side, no major candidate, including Bill Clinton, bothered to put his name on the North Dakota primary ballot. Substantial numbers of voters, however, decided to take a pencil to the polls and write the names of either Clinton or Perot on their ballots. On the final, absolutely last, truly end-of-the-line primary day, Ross Perot defeated Bill Clinton in North Dakota on write-in votes, 28 percent to 13 percent.[11]

19. Toward a Model Calendar of State Presidential Primaries and Caucuses

Although no one ever would have guessed it from what the news media were saying about them, George Bush and Bill Clinton were two of the biggest winners in United States presidential primary history.

President Bush won every one of his thirty-eight Republican primary contests. His major opponent, conservative commentator Pat Buchanan, was a media sensation following his strong showing in New Hampshire but was completely out of the running just three weeks later. Bush's string of primary victories matched the records of Richard Nixon and Ronald Reagan, who in 1972 and 1984 went undefeated prior to winning landslide reelection victories.

Bill Clinton's record was almost as good as President Bush's. The Arkansas governor won twenty-eight of thirty-five Democratic primaries, doing particularly well in states with large populations and large numbers of minority voters. Although Clinton began by losing New Hampshire to Paul Tsongas, he quickly recovered and dispatched Tsongas on Super Tuesday in the South and Midwest Tuesday in Illinois and Michigan. Jerry Brown temporarily threatened Clinton after a narrow primary win in Connecticut and a big caucus victory in Vermont, but Clinton rallied his forces one more time and finished Brown off in New York.

How could two men be such big statistical winners and yet appear to so much of the American public to be losers? The more George Bush won primaries, the further his approval ratings fell in national polls. As Clinton marched from victory to victory, he became increasingly loaded down with character questions concerning marital infidelity, military draft avoidance, and failure to give honest answers to probing questions.

The biggest part of the problem was the front-loading of the primary process and its effect on the news media, particularly television. The major result of front-loading is early closure, candidates wrapping up the nomination very early in the primary process. Once Bush and Clinton had sewed up their party nominations, the news media in general and television in particular lost interest in them.

Statistics compiled by the Center for Media and Public Affairs dramatically demonstrated the extent to which television news lost interest in Bush and Clinton, and the entire presidential primary process, the minute Bush and Clinton were the undisputed front-runners. "Bush and Clinton were featured in 366 network news stories on ABC, CBS and NBC from the first of the year until the April 7 New York primary, where Clinton's status as Bush's general election opponent was essentially established. From then through May 25, each of them made the air only 80 times."[1]

Another part of the problem was the manner in which the television networks and major national newspapers used exit polls. The exit pollsters repeatedly asked one question to voters in both political parties: "Do you wish someone else was running for president?" The effect of this question was to diminish the impact of Bush's and Clinton's many primary victories. The voters kept voting for the two men, but the networks and newspapers used exit polls to point up that many voters were not happy with their choices. As the primary season developed, of course, Ross Perot stepped in and presented himself as the "someone else" the exit pollsters had continually been asking about.

In looking over the presidential nominating system in the United States as it had developed to 1992, the following ten realities stood out:

1. The presidential nominating system in the United States, particularly the calendar of state primaries and precinct caucuses, is in a constant state of change.
2. Precinct caucuses can have an impact on the presidential nominating system only if clear-cut results (winners and losers) are available the same day the caucuses take place.
3. Precinct caucuses receive minimal candidate and news media atten-

tion if they are held on the same day as a presidential primary in a different state.

4. Precinct caucuses can have a major impact on the presidential nominating process only if they occur very early in the process (the first two weeks after the first primary).

5. Over the past twenty years, the voters and the news media in the United States have come to accept presidential primaries as the principal means by which major party candidates for president are determined.

6. Primaries in states with small and medium-sized populations will receive minimal candidate and news media attention if a populous state is holding a primary on the same day.

7. Regional primary days such as Super Tuesday do not work because candidate and news media attention concentrates on the large-population states in the region to the neglect of those with small and medium-sized populations.

8. Generally speaking, the nominee is determined on the first day a large-population state (or a number of large-population states) holds a presidential primary. In recent years this has been on Super Tuesday when Florida and Texas vote.

9. At present, the primary and caucus calendar is more than sixteen weeks long. In recent years it has taken only six to eight weeks for the nominee to be decided and all opposition finally eliminated. Caucuses and primaries that occur after the nominee is decided receive minimal news media and voter attention.

10. If states continue to front-load the primary-caucus calendar (move primaries and caucuses to ever-earlier dates), a de facto national presidential primary will have been created with only a small number of states participating.

Clearly the most disturbing aspect of the front-loading and early closure in the present presidential primary system is the large number of states that conduct late primaries and thereby have no impact on the nominating process. Included on this "left out" list are such populous states as Pennsylvania, Indiana, North Carolina, Oregon, Kentucky, New Jersey, Ohio, and California. A high degree of frustration develops among voters from those states, many of whom would like to vote in a meaningful presidential primary but rarely get the chance to do so.

Presidential primaries thus can be divided into three groups: those that are *relevant*, those that are *somewhat relevant*, and those that are totally *irrelevant*. Table 19.1 places each of the fifty states into its appropriate group for 1992.

TABLE 19.1
Relevance of State Presidential Primaries and Caucuses in the
1992 Campaign for the Democratic Nomination

RELEVANT

A state is deemed RELEVANT if it conducts a primary or a caucus that receives considerable attention from candidates and the news media and has a major effect on determining who receives the party nomination for president.

Iowa*	South Carolina	Texas
New Hampshire	Florida	Massachusetts
Maine*	Louisiana	Illinois
South Dakota	Mississippi	Michigan
Colorado	Missouri*	Connecticut
Georgia	Oklahoma	Vermont*
Maryland	Rhode Island	New York
	Tennessee	

* caucus states

SOMEWHAT RELEVANT

A state is deemed SOMEWHAT RELEVANT if it conducts a primary or caucus that, although receiving little attention from candidates and the news media, has a minor effect on determining who receives the party nomination for president.

Utah	Arizona*	Hawaii*
Minnesota*	Wyoming*	Kansas
Idaho*	Nevada*	Wisconsin
	Delaware*	

* caucus states

IRRELEVANT

A state is deemed IRRELEVANT if it conducts its primary or caucus after the nominee has already been determined in early state primaries and caucuses. Caucuses also fall into the IRRELEVANT category when they fail to produce an identifiable "winner" the same day the caucus is held.

Washington*	Nebraska	Alabama
North Dakota*	West Virginia	California
Alaska*	Oregon	Montana
Virginia*	Washington	New Jersey
Pennsylvania	Kentucky	New Mexico
Indiana	Arkansas	Ohio
North Carolina		North Dakota

* caucus states

The nominating system currently in use in the United States might best be described as a *manipulated sequential* primary and caucus system. It is manipulated because candidates and their supporters set up primaries and caucuses—and change the dates of primaries and caucuses—to benefit particular candidates. It is sequential because the primaries and caucuses are held one after the other over a period of more than four months.

There have been many proposals over the years for improving the manipulated sequential primary and caucus system. One of the most popular ideas is the regional primary—having all the states in a particular region of the nation hold their primaries and caucuses on the same day. A sincere but unsuccessful attempt was made to create a regional primary in New England in the mid-1970s. In the mid-1980s the southern and border states got together and successfully created Super Tuesday, the southern regional primary day which, thanks mainly to Florida and Texas, has dominated the nominating system ever since.

The main argument for the regional primary is that it cuts travel costs for both the candidates and the news media personnel covering the candidates. It also is argued that the increased excitement of having all the states in a particular region vote at the same time will increase voter turnout. As noted above, however, the main drawback of regional primaries is that they are dominated by the large-population states in the region. There is also the problem of which region will get to vote first. As with the current situation involving Iowa and New Hampshire, the region that gets to vote first will have a disproportionate say in who gains early momentum in the nomination race.[2]

Another improvement often suggested for the current nominating system is to create a national presidential primary in which all registered voters in a political party throughout the entire nation cast their presidential primary ballots on the same day. The major effect of this proposal would be to favor well-financed candidates with national reputations and the sort of moderate, middle-of-the-road political views that would appeal to a broad constituency of voters across the country.

The national primary has been criticized because it would eliminate from presidential nomination competition the "outsider" candidate who has just enough reputation and just enough money to get things started in the Iowa caucuses or the New Hampshire primary. There would be no opportunity for "out-of-nowhere" candidacies such as Jimmy Carter's in 1976, George Bush's in 1980, Gary Hart's in 1984, and Paul Tsongas's in 1992.

In addition, political scientists fear that the national primary would weaken the two-party system. People would start to register to vote in the political party that looked as if it was going to have the most exciting national primary, or they might start to register in large numbers in the political party that was winning the White House most of the time. Strong supporters of the two-party system prefer that voters choose their party affiliation on the basis of party principles and programs, not which party's national presidential primary they want to vote in this year.[3]

An ideal solution for reforming the presidential nominating process would be to preserve the current sequential system but reform it in such a way that the system is more orderly and balanced and less subject to manipulative control by presidential candidates and their supporters.

The state legislatures of the fifty states, acting in concert, are the major group in the United States that has the power and authority to correct the many drawbacks in the current presidential nominating system. Within each state, it is the state legislature that sets the date and the detailed rules for that state's presidential primary or caucus.

Under the present situation, where each state sets its primary or caucus date with minimal consideration for what other states are doing, it is in a state's interest to "beat out" other states by getting an earlier, and thus more influential, date on the presidential primary and caucus schedule.

If state legislatures will start acting together rather than separately in setting primary and caucus dates, the most important goal will be to schedule presidential primaries and caucuses in such a way that *the voters of each state participate in the most meaningful and effective way possible in the presidential nominating process.*

One way to accomplish this goal would be to adopt a Model Calendar of State Presidential Primaries and Caucuses. This model calendar should be structured to accomplish the following goals:

1. *Shrinking the present lengthy primary and caucus season into a more workable period of time.* The 1992 nominating season began with the Iowa caucuses on February 10 and did not end until five states, the most populous of which were Ohio, New Jersey and California, held their primaries on June 2. The 1992 primaries and caucuses thus stretched out over sixteen weeks, almost one-third of a calendar year.

This long nominating season is grueling and exhausting for the candidates. It also is so long that average voters start to get bored and lose interest in the process. Most important, highly qualified party candidates for the presidency are discouraged from running because of the major time commitment required. Governors of populous states, and influential United States senators, find it particularly difficult to make the lengthy campaign for a presidential nomination while at the same time discharging their official duties as governors and senators.

Ideally, the presidential caucus and primary season should be limited to eight weeks, half the length of the present sixteen-week schedule.

2. *Creating a nominating system that does not overly favor or neglect any particular state or any particular region of the country.* The present primary and caucus system tends to favor states that vote early and penalize states that vote late. New Hampshire has long enjoyed a favorable position, and states such as South Dakota and Colorado have recently increased their clout by adopting early primary dates.

The one region that has benefited the most from the present caucus and primary calendar has been the South, with its large number of early primaries on Super Tuesday. Lately this southern bloc has been breaking up. Maryland and Georgia moved their primary dates ahead of Super Tuesday for the 1992 presidential election. Other major southern states that did not vote on Super Tuesday in 1992 included South Carolina, North Carolina, Kentucky, Arkansas, and Alabama.

A Model Calendar of State Presidential Primaries and Caucuses should have a number of states voting or caucusing on each primary and caucus date. The states voting or caucusing on a particular date should be from all parts of the nation rather than favoring one region or another.

Does this mean New Hampshire will have to give up its position as the first presidential primary, and Iowa will have to give up holding the first presidential caucuses? No. These particular states hold traditional positions of importance in the process, positions that are widely accepted by the American public. New Hampshire and Iowa should not be forced to relinquish their present primary and caucus dates against their will.[4]

3. *Allowing two weeks between primary and caucus dates.* Under the present lengthy and haphazard primary and caucus schedule, often there is as little as two days from one important primary and caucus date to another. In the spring of 1992, for instance, New Hampshire held its primary on February 18. Five days later Maine held its caucuses. Two days after that South Dakota had a primary. One week later eight more states, including Maryland and Georgia, staged their primaries and caucuses.

This crowded schedule is unfair to candidates and voters alike. Candidates campaign hard up to one primary or caucus date and then have to rush on to the next set of primaries and caucuses. No time is given to rest after an important primary or caucus day, catch one's breath, and carefully and rationally plan campaign strategies for the next series of primaries and caucuses.

The same kind of pressure is applied to the voters. The citizens of one particular state often have little time to consider what happened on the previous caucus and primary day before they are voting in a primary or attending a caucus themselves.

An ideal nominating system would concentrate primaries and caucuses on particular days, preferably Tuesdays for the sake of tradition, and leave at least two weeks before the next day of caucuses and primaries takes place.

The Model Calendar of State Presidential Primaries and Caucuses in Table 19.2 is the type of model calendar the state legislatures should be thinking about if they want to join together and rationalize the presidential nominating system in the United States. Except for Iowa and New Hampshire, which are left in their current early positions, this model calendar concentrates the state caucuses and primaries on only five dates. These five primary and caucus dates are all two weeks apart; therefore, the entire caucus and primary season lasts only slightly more than eight weeks.

The most important characteristic of this model calendar is that it concentrates the largest-population states, with the largest numbers of delegate votes, on the last of the five primary and caucus days. With so many delegate votes at stake on the final day of the caucus and primary season, no candidate will be able to "lock up" a party nomination for president prior to the last primary and caucus day. Thus, voters in states voting on the last primary and caucus day will be more likely to be participating in a meaningful primary or caucus.

This model therefore is *back-loading* the presidential nominating system with the larger-population states. Smaller- and medium-sized-population states, which will be voting and caucusing on the four earlier primary and caucus days, will make the "first cut." They will narrow the presidential field in each party from five or six major contenders to two or three. The larger-population states will make the "final cut," choosing between the last two or three surviving candidates on the fifth, final primary and caucus day.

It is vitally important that America's state legislatures, acting together with a spirit of cooperation and goodwill, begin to tackle the problem of creating a more reasonable and workable nominating system. The National Conference of State Legislatures, the national organization based in Denver, Colorado, that represents the fifty state legislatures and shares information among them, would be the logical group to undertake this important task.

TABLE 19.2
A Model Calendar of State Presidential
Primaries and Caucuses (Democratic Party)*

Iowa Caucus—Monday, February 12, 1996

State	Delegates**	Type	1992 Date
Iowa	49	Caucus	2-10-92

New Hampshire Primary—Tuesday, February 20, 1996

State	Delegates	Type	1992 Date
New Hampshire	18	Primary	2-18-92

Total Delegates IA and NH = 67   Cumulative Total = 67

First Day—Tuesday, March 5, 1996

State	Delegates	Type	1992 Date
Guam	3	Caucus	5-3-92
Virgin Islands	3	Caucus	3-28-92
American Samoa	3	Caucus	3-3-92
Dems. Abroad	7	Caucus	3-7-92
Alaska	13	Caucus	4-2-92
Wyoming	13	Caucus	3-7-92
Delaware	14	Caucus	3-10-92
North Dakota	14	Caucus	3-5-92
South Dakota	15	Primary	2-25-92
Montana	16	Primary	6-2-92
District of Columbia	17	Primary	5-5-92
Nevada	17	Caucus	3-8-92
Arkansas	36	Primary	5-26-92
South Carolina	43	Primary	3-7-92

Total Delegates First Day = 214   Cumulative Total = 281

Second Day—Tuesday, March 19, 1996

State	Delegates	Type	1992 Date
Vermont	14	Caucus	3-31-92
Idaho	18	Caucus	3-3-92
Hawaii	20	Caucus	3-10-92
Rhode Island	22	Primary	3-10-92
Utah	23	Primary	3-3-92
New Mexico	25	Primary	6-2-92
Nebraska	25	Primary	5-12-92
Kansas	36	Primary	4-7-92
Mississippi	39	Primary	3-10-92
Oklahoma	45	Primary	3-10-92

Total Delegates Second Day = 267   Cumulative Total = 548

* The number of Republican delegates for each state would be smaller but in
  roughly the same proportions as the number of Democratic delegates.
** Number of delegates to the 1992 Democratic National Convention.

(continued)

TABLE 19.2 *(continued)*

Third Day—Tuesday, April 2, 1996

State	Delegates	Type	1992 Date
Maine	23	Caucus	2-23-92
West Virginia	31	Primary	5-12-92
Arizona	41	Caucus	3-7-92
Colorado	47	Primary	3-3-92
Puerto Rico	51	Primary	4-5-92
Kentucky	52	Primary	5-26-92
Alabama	55	Primary	6-2-92
Louisiana	60	Primary	3-10-92
Tennessee	68	Primary	3-10-92
Indiana	77	Primary	5-5-92

Total Delegates Third Day = 505   Cumulative Total = 1053

Fourth Day—Tuesday, April 16, 1996

State	Delegates	Type	1992 Date
Oregon	47	Primary	5-19-92
Connecticut	53	Primary	3-24-92
Maryland	67	Primary	3-3-92
Washington	71	Caucus	3-3-92
Georgia	76	Primary	3-3-92
Missouri	77	Caucus	3-10-92
Virginia	78	Caucus	4-11-92
Minnesota	78	Caucus	3-3-92
Wisconsin	82	Primary	4-7-92
North Carolina	84	Primary	5-5-92

Total Delegates Fourth Day = 713   Cumulative Total = 1766

Fifth Day—Tuesday, April 30, 1996

State	Delegates	Type	1992 Date
Massachusetts	94	Primary	3-10-92
New Jersey	105	Primary	6-2-92
Michigan	131	Primary	3-17-92
Florida	148	Primary	3-10-92
Ohio	151	Primary	5-5-92
Illinois	164	Primary	3-17-92
Pennsylvania	169	Primary	4-28-92
Texas	196	Primary	3-10-92
New York	244	Primary	4-7-92
California	348	Primary	6-2-92

Total Delegates Fifth Day = 1750   Cumulative Total = 3516

20. Perot Surges—and Sags

On June 3, 1992, the day after the California primary, a *Time*/CNN Poll revealed that Ross Perot was the first choice of 37 percent of American voters.[1] The Texas billionaire was narrowly ahead of George Bush and well ahead of Bill Clinton.

Polls in individual states were even more astounding. Perot was ahead of both Bush and Clinton by five percentage points or more in six western states, two of which, California and Texas, were two of the most populous states in the nation. The other four Perot states were Washington, Oregon, Colorado, and Montana. If Perot's obvious strength in the West were to spread to the East and the South, the independent candidate would have a real chance of winning the White House.[2]

On the same day these gratifying poll results were announced, the Perot campaign greatly increased its aura of political effectiveness. Two of the best-known political managers in America, Ed Rollins and Hamilton Jordan, signed on as advisors to Perot. Ed Rollins was a Republican who had directed Ronald Reagan's overwhelmingly successful 1984 reelection campaign. Hamilton Jordan was a Democrat who had managed Jimmy Carter's efforts in both 1976 and 1980. Rollins and Jordan were given the job of turning Perot's heretofore volunteer effort into a professional organization capable of winning the November general election.

Not that the Perot volunteers needed that much help. In state after state across the nation, Perot rallies were being held at which thousands of petition signatures were being turned in to state election officials. In most cases Perot's supporters were able to gather more than two times, sometimes three and four times, the number of signatures required.

Exactly as the dates and rules of presidential primaries and caucuses are determined by state law, the number of signatures required to put an independent candidate's name on the general election ballot is set by state law. As with primaries and caucuses, there is incredible variety among states. For example, Wisconsin requires only two thousand signatures, but, over on the other side of Lake Michigan, the state of Michigan requires 25,646 signatures.

Throughout May and June of 1992, each day's newspaper brought another report of another state in which Perot's army of volunteers had greatly oversubscribed the number of signatures required to put Perot on the ballot. Perot's home state of Texas was typical. On May 12, 1992, Perot was present when supporters delivered to the state capitol in Austin ninety big boxes brimming over with petitions containing 225,000 signatures, more than four times the 54,275 that Texas state law requires.

One of the biggest days for the fast-rolling Perot bandwagon was Friday, May 29, 1992. Drawing on his extensive business experience with computers and electronic communications, Perot linked together petition rallies in six states by satellite television. Perot was in Orlando, presiding over the turning in of his Florida petitions, but both his image and his voice were carried to similar gatherings in Boise, Idaho; Cheyenne, Wyoming; Columbus, Ohio; Montgomery, Alabama; and Topeka, Kansas. In all six states, there was the now routine petition overkill. Perot's volunteer army was advancing on fifty fronts, and triumphing everywhere it appeared.

In each state, Perot and his backers did whatever state law required. In Bill Clinton's home state of Arkansas, on May 30, 1992, about forty-five hundred Perot supporters gathered at a nominating convention in downtown Little Rock, the state capital. A party convention is one of the requirements for putting an independent candidate on the Arkansas ballot. Perot was on hand to give an acceptance speech, and country singer Willie Nelson, an ardent Perot fan, stopped by to lend his support. At the end of the festivities, Perot signed an acceptance of candidacy form that was turned in to the Arkansas secretary of state's office.

The Perot campaign in Colorado began in the middle of April, when Perot for President campaign offices opened up in Denver, Colorado Springs, Grand Junction, and most of the other major cities in the state. Saturday, May 9, 1992, was selected as the opening day for the statewide petition drive. On that one day, Perot's organizers claimed they gathered the five thousand signatures needed to put the Texas billionaire on the Colorado ballot. They did not stop there, of course. "We want to show that the polls are indeed correct, that he is the No. 1 candidate," said Diane Rees, a Perot organizer from Denver.[3]

On Friday, June 19, 1992, more than seven thousand Coloradans gathered in Denver's Civic Center Park for the turning-in ceremony for Perot's Colorado petition signatures. As of that date, it was by far the largest crowd that had gathered in Colorado for any event in connection with the 1992 presidential election campaign.

Civic Center Park is one of those rare treasures in urban America—a truly beautiful park located right in the middle of a busy downtown. At the eastern end of the park, on a gently rising hill, sits the Colorado state capitol, a marble edifice with the customary pillars at the entrances and topped by a gold-plated capitol dome. At the western end of the park is the Denver City Hall, a more modest marble structure that perfectly complements the state capitol. In between the two buildings is a four-block area of green grass, monuments, statues, and park benches. To the west, the snowcapped peaks of the Rocky Mountains are readily visible on clear days.

On the southern edge of Civic Center Park sits a large Greek-style marble amphitheater. Although an outdoor facility, the amphitheater is decorated with pillared porticos. It was in this amphitheater on a beautiful sunny morning that the Perot faithful of Colorado gathered to turn in their petition signatures.

The event was organized similar to a Republican or Democratic state political party convention. At the bottom of the amphitheater, seated just in front of the stage, sat the hardworking core of Perot's Colorado army. The volunteers were seated together according to the county they were from, and each county had a homemade sign on a high stick giving the county's name.

The crowd filled the remainder of the amphitheater and overflowed into the pillared portico area. Some of the younger and hardier types climbed the pillars and sat on the portico tops to get a better view. The crowd was so large that several thousand people were forced to sit on the lawn or stand on the broad sidewalk leading up to the amphitheater. These latecomers, and there were a lot of them, could hear what was going on over a loudspeaker system but could not see any of the activity on the amphitheater stage.

The atmosphere was that of a carnival. On both sides of the sidewalk leading up to the amphitheater, large covered booths had been erected. In these booths, well-groomed and well-dressed Perot volunteers sold Perot T-shirts, Perot sweatshirts, Perot bumper stickers, Perot hats, and Perot pins. Amazingly, none of these materials had been provided from the Perot campaign headquarters in Dallas, Texas. Perot's Colorado volunteers had personally arranged for these materials to be manufactured just for the campaign in Colorado.

Early comers to the Perot rally in Denver were treated to an hour of band music and other entertainment. Then, at 11 A.M., the ritualistic turning-in of the petititons began. As the name of one of Colorado's sixty-three counties was read off, the county's Perot volunteers would bring down to the front of the stage the boxes from that county filled with petition signatures. The boxes piled ever higher as the master of ceremonies plowed through the long list of county names. When it was all over, the signatures of 139,000 Colorado voters sat in boxes on the stage, more than twenty-seven times the five thousand signatures required.

Then it was time to give prizes to the two counties that had gathered the highest percentage of signatures compared to the county's population. One was Boulder County, which is located about twenty miles northwest of Denver and is the site of the University of Colorado's main campus. It is well known that Boulder County is one of the more liberal and heavily Democratic counties in the state. The other prize went to Pitkin County, which has as its county seat the internationally known ski resort of Aspen. With its many upscale and intensely fashionable year-round residents, Pitkin County rivals Boulder County as one of the more liberal and Democratic counties in Colorado.

The fact that two of Colorado's more Democratic counties gathered the highest percentages of petition signatures for Ross Perot suggested that, at least in Colorado, the Perot campaign was mainly stealing votes from Democrat Bill Clinton rather than Republican George Bush.

Shortly after noon, just at the time when downtown Denver office workers could walk over and listen to him if they wanted to, Ross Perot took the stage at the amphitheater to give a political speech. He was introduced to the crowd by Admiral James Stockdale, a recently retired Naval officer who was being considered as a possible vice-presidential running mate for Perot.

Perot's speech to his Colorado supporters got off to a rocky start. He began by praising Admiral Stockdale for being one of the few American military men with the courage to oppose the use of United States military forces in the recent Persian Gulf War. As Perot made the statement, an audible gasp went through the crowd. Colorado was a state with a large number of military installations and a long record of supporting United States military intervention overseas. Colorado obviously was not a good place for anyone, not even Ross Perot talking to Ross Perot supporters, to criticize the Gulf War.

The remainder of Perot's speech in Denver was typical of what he had been saying everywhere up to this point in his independent presidential campaign. He spent much of the time talking about the job his volunteers were doing rather than talking about himself. It was their spirit and their efforts and their belief in building a better future for America that was driving the campaign. Perot made it clear in Denver that, no matter what might happen in the future, no one could ever take away from his Colorado volunteers the achievement represented by those 139,000 petition signatures.

In his speech, Perot was long on criticisms of both the Democratic and Republican parties and short on giving any specific proposals for correcting the many problems he saw in the United States. He carefully presented himself to his Colorado supporters as a man of action, but he just as carefully gave no details as to what his future actions might be.

Perot was not impressive as a speaker. His voice had a colorful Texas twang, but he failed to give much verbal or physical emphasis to his various points as he presented them to his audience. He suffered badly by comparison to Bill Clinton and George Bush, both of whom were experienced political speakers who knew how to effectively hit the high points in a political speech. After the intense excitement of the large crowd being on hand and the dramatic turning-in of the petition signatures, Perot's Denver speech was something of a letdown.

There was a stunning climax to the Denver rally, however. As Perot left the amphitheater to walk to a limousine that would drive him to the Colorado secretary of state's office, cheering supporters lined both sides of his path. Newspaper photographers and television camcorder operators scurried to find advantageous positions from which to get one last photograph or one last videoclip. In their desire to see Perot, his more ardent supporters overran police barricades and hurried in groups to the next place they thought he might be. Clearly, Perot had gained the celebrity and public popularity that goes with being a major contender for the presidency of the United States.

As the Perot campaign surged forward, however, one of the great traditions of American presidential campaigns began to assert itself. The minute Ross Perot took the lead over George Bush and Bill Clinton in the public opinion polls, the news media got over its "gee whiz" attitude toward his candidacy and began subjecting him to the close scrutiny that all front-runners receive. The press attack on Perot began

slowly and then gained speed as more and more reporters started looking for a "ticket to page 1" by finding something negative on Ross Perot.

In late May *Newsweek* suggested that Perot's campaign for president was anything but an "honest draft." Apparently the Texas billionaire had been considering a run for the presidency ever since the summer of 1991, and he told friends at the time he was holding back only
because of concern for his family. Then, in January of 1992, Perot com-
missioned an expensive and exhaustive state-by-state poll which
showed that an independent candidate could, indeed, win. Perot himself was not mentioned by name in the poll. "That was no idle statement
Perot made on *Larry King,*" a Perot adviser told *Newsweek*. "He'd been
laying the groundwork for some time."[4]

Then the *Washington Post* revealed that, far from being a Washington "outsider" uncorrupted by the tainted politics practiced on the
banks of the Potomac River, Perot had a long history of making contacts
and wielding influence in Washington's corridors of power. He apparently had a long series of dealings with both the Nixon and Reagan
administrations. Peter M. Flanigan, at one time an aide to President
Nixon, described Perot as "the ultimate insider. . . . He knows his way
around the corridors of power almost better than anybody I know."[5]

The first really revealing negative story about Perot concerned his
record as a young naval officer following his graduation from the
United States Naval Academy in Annapolis. Assigned to a destroyer
division, Perot supposedly was so appalled by the bad language and
immoral behavior of his fellow shipmates that he wrote a letter request-
ing an early discharge from the Navy. Then a reporter found a 1955
letter from Perot's commanding officer, Captain G. H. Miller, which
described Perot as "emotionally maladjusted for a regular Navy
career."[6]

Suddenly there was a rash of stories that raised concerns about
Perot's psychological fitness to be president. Supposedly he was overly
aggressive and self-seeking in his business dealings. It was charged
that he pursued his effort to free the POWs and MIAs in Vietnam to the
point of obsession. "When you listen to him for the first hour he sounds
like a normal person on the topic," said a former Senate intelligence
staffer. "By the third hour you begin to wonder if the man is crazy."[7]

Then there were a number of stories that Perot had hired private
investigators to spy on business and political enemies. In one well-doc-
umented case, Perot retained a former FBI agent who carried out an
eighteen-month investigation of a Perot rival in the computer processing business. The investigator not only spied for Perot but endeavored
to get government officials to prosecute the executives of the rival com-

pany for bribery and fraud crimes the investigator said he had discovered.[8]

Another private investigator hired by Perot supposedly searched for negative information about President Bush, First Lady Barbara Bush, and the Bush children and grandchildren. Soon editorial writers and editorial cartoonists were caricaturing the Texas billionaire as "Inspector Perot."[9]

Then a major national news magazine presented Perot to its readers as a man who was self-centered and determined to have his own way, even if it meant sidestepping the law. *Time* charged that Perot hired a construction crew to blow up an environmentally protected section of coral reef near his vacation home in Bermuda so that he could more easily dock his sixty-eight-foot luxury cabin cruiser.[10]

President Bush's campaign surrogates joined the news media in the all-out assault on the character and stability of Ross Perot. In late May Bob Michel, the Republican leader in the United States House of Representatives, endeavored to exploit the fact that Perot had given very few details on what he would do if elected president. Perot "doesn't have a clue as to how to solve even one major issue," Michel told reporters at the GOP's Capitol Hill Club in Washington. "It is frightening because a large number of good Americans, people who genuinely love this country, desperately want to believe Ross has the answers."[11]

In mid-June, Bush's vice president, Dan Quayle, fired the major Bush campaign barrage against Perot. Quayle labeled the independent candidate a "temperamental tycoon who has contempt for the Constitution of the United States." Quayle's attack had been coordinated with the president's top campaign advisers, who were now pursuing a strategy of portraying Perot as "too risky a choice" for the American people.[12] Earlier, presidential Press Secretary Marlin Fitzwater labeled Perot a "dangerous and destructive personality," suggesting that voters should wonder "what kind of monster are we buying here?" The entire effort was designed to present an image of Perot as a "Dictator-in-Waiting."[13]

The Clinton forces took an occasional swipe at Ross Perot. Speaking to community leaders in Louisville, Kentucky, Democratic Party Chairman Ron Brown said he was glad the press was now taking a closer look at Perot. "I think the press is now feeling a little guilty that he has gotten a free ride. My own judgment is he's a little dictator."[14] By and large, however, the Clinton camp was more than willing to let Bush and Perot battle it out and stay back in the shadows. Running third in national public opinion polls, Clinton apparently decided it was the better strategy to let George Bush have the risky and unpleasant job of trying to politically bloody-up Ross Perot.

As the news media and Bush campaign attack on Perot proceeded apace, problems began to surface within the Perot campaign itself. The *Denver Post* ran a major story that Perot's volunteer supporters in Colorado were upset because operatives from the Texas headquarters were taking over the grassroots operation in Denver and forcing the local volunteers out.[15] Gannett News Service revealed that Perot was requiring his potential presidential electors to sign notarized loyalty oaths and submit undated resignations, something that a number of his would-be electoral college electors refused to do.[16]

As might be expected, the news media assault on Ross Perot and his independent campaign for president began to have an effect on the public opinion polls. All through June and into July, Perot's standing in the polls steadily dropped. According to the *Time*/CNN poll, Perot went from 37 percent support on June 3-4 to only 26 percent support on July 8-9.[17] Although it was George Bush who had vigorously joined the news media attack on Perot, it was Bill Clinton who gained in popularity as Perot slipped. As America prepared itself to watch the Democratic National Convention, Perot had fallen back enough and Clinton had risen enough that all three candidates were in a virtual dead heat in the polls.

21. The Evolving
National Conventions

At one time political party national conventions were a significant part of the presidential selection process. Before the recent rise in the number of presidential primaries, national conventions actually decided who was going to be the party nominee in the November general election.[1] By 1992, however, the national conventions served only to advertise the presidential candidates who had been selected many months before in the primaries.

Now it is more correct to refer to the national conventions as "ratifying" conventions rather than "nominating" conventions. They "ratify" the primary results by presenting the winning candidate and his or her vice-presidential running mate to the American people. The national conventions have not really "nominated" anyone since 1952.[2]

In that year, at the Republican convention, World War II military hero Dwight D. Eisenhower overtook Senator Robert Taft of Ohio, who had been leading in the delegate count when the convention began. At the 1952 Democratic conclave, Illinois governor Adlai Stevenson and Tennessee senator Estes Kefauver came into the convention more or less evenly matched. Skillful political work at the convention itself, particularly by Chicago political leader Jacob Arvey, enabled Stevenson to wrest the nomination from Kefauver.

A typical "ratifying" convention took place in 1960 in the Democratic Party when John F. Kennedy won all six of the presidential primaries he entered and lined up the support of Democratic political leaders in large cities in the Northeast and Midwest. As the convention began, it was already well known that Kennedy had five votes more than he needed to win the nomination. People who listened to the convention on the radio or watched it on television were mainly interested in whether or not the Kennedy juggernaut could be stopped. It could not, and the convention rapidly proceeded to the foregone conclusion that Kennedy was going to be the 1960 Democratic nominee.

A landmark in the evolution of national conventions was the 1968 Democratic National Convention in Chicago. Lyndon Johnson, the incumbent president, decided not to run for reelection because of the unpopularity of the Vietnam War, which had greatly escalated during his administration. The incumbent vice president, former Minnesota senator Hubert H. Humphrey, had Johnson's enthusiastic support and therefore came into the convention with more than enough delegates to win the nomination.

As did Johnson, Humphrey supported United States involvement in the war in Vietnam. In an effort to dramatize their opposition to the war, protesters took to the streets of Chicago and soon were engaged in violent confrontations with the city police. Television cameras caught much of the action as Chicago police officers dressed in riot gear used nightsticks, police dogs, and tear gas to push back advancing war protesters. Some of the protesters responded by throwing rocks and trying to hit the police over the head with plastic bags filled with human urine. The tumult and mayhem was beamed into the living rooms of America along with the regular convention proceedings.[3] Both political parties learned a valuable lesson. If not carefully controlled and regulated, national conventions can be a negative rather than a positive advertisement for the political party.

The major result of the 1968 Democratic National Convention was a series of attempts by the Democratic Party to reform the delegate selection process so that more women, minorities, and young people were chosen. These new rules were so complex and difficult to operate—particularly where state party caucuses and state party conventions were concerned—that large numbers of states opted for presidential primaries instead. In 1968 only seventeen states held presidential primaries, but by 1976 the number had grown to thirty. In 1968 less than half of the delegates were selected in primaries, but by 1976 almost three-fourths of the delegates were thus chosen.[4]

The more the national Democratic Party worked to "reform" the national convention, the more problems the convention seemed to make for the party. In 1972 a significant number of delegates were youthful anti-Vietnam War protesters who delighted in making liberal statements on television and to the press. Middle-class Democrats watching at home gazed with amazement at these flower children wearing purple sunglasses and draped in love beads who were expressing such unorthodox and unconventional ideas.[5]

Another catastrophe at the Democratic convention took place in 1980, when incumbent president Jimmy Carter sought to project an image of party unity by shaking the hand of the man he had easily defeated in the primaries, Massachusetts senator Ted Kennedy. Just at the moment Carter put out his hand, Kennedy turned to move away and, with the television cameras picking up the entire comedy, Carter chased Kennedy across the speaker's platform with his hand outstretched. Instead of demonstrating his unity with Kennedy, Carter succeeded only in showing that Kennedy had little or no respect for him.[6]

After each of these convention fiascos, the Democrats went on to lose the general election to the Republicans. The message was clear. Political parties were going to have to work hard to keep their national conventions under control and thereby make certain they presented only positive images of party unity to the American public. Party members who wanted to advance controversial ideas or protest current party policies were no longer welcome.

As the importance of national conventions to the nominating process progressively diminished, so did the television coverage. Back in the late 1940s and 1950s, when conventions actually nominated the candidates for president, all three major television networks provided live coverage from the opening gavel to the closing gavel. Coverage would begin in the early morning and not stop until the day's business was completed, even if that came well after midnight.

By the late 1960s two clear trends were taking place. On the one hand, the political parties began scheduling the major events of the convention to take place in the early evening when they would attract the largest possible television audience. This was easy to do because everyone already knew who the nominee was going to be and therefore the events were now rituals rather than confrontations between competing candidates. At the same time, naturally, the television networks began limiting their coverage to these convention highlights that were scheduled in prime viewing time.

By the 1980s the two political parties and the television networks had adopted the following informal prime time schedule. Monday night a leading party spokesperson gives the keynote address. Tuesday night additional speeches are made, often centering on a theme or idea the party wants to emphasize. Wednesday night is highlighted by the nominating speeches and the balloting for president. On Thursday night, the final night of the convention, the party nominee gives his or her acceptance speech. For 1992, the three major networks said they believed they could adequately cover a national convention with just one hour of prime time broadcasting on each of the convention's four nights.

Although party national conventions have declined in importance and now merit greatly reduced network television coverage, there is still something to be said in their favor. They serve as a weeklong glittering advertisement for the political party. Not only do the party candidates for president and vice president get a great deal of television exposure, but so do the rising young stars of the political party who are selected to give keynote addresses and nominating speeches. It also is good for party members from all over the country to gather together once every four years and devote a week to thinking about and talking about where their party stands on the major issues of the time and where their party should be going in the future.

Realistically, however, it no longer is accurate to refer to the national conventions as "party conventions." Their major function now is to serve the electoral interests of the man or woman who wins the party's presidential nomination in the primaries. Thus they really are "presidential candidate conventions," or perhaps even "presidential candidate coronations." Whatever they are called, all other issues and interests are subverted to the great goal of giving the party presidential candidate as rousing a sendoff as possible into the November general elections.

22. BILL CLINTON'S CONVENTION

From the very beginning, the 1992 Democratic National Convention was designed to be as dissent-proof and ruckus-free as possible. Every effort was made to see that any decision that might cause controversy at the convention was made and disposed of long before the convention began.

Take the party platform, often a major source of debate and discord at previous Democratic conventions. The Resolutions Committee, the select group of convention delegates assigned the task of drawing up the party platform, held its meetings and its public hearings in June. The committee's recommended party platform was adopted on June 27, 1992, a full two weeks before the delegates began arriving in New York City for the convention itself. That greatly reduced the likelihood of the Resolutions Committee's deliberations turning into a public brawl over divisive issues within the party.

The party platform recommended by the committee was a masterpiece of moderation. It almost perfectly reflected Bill Clinton's and the Democratic Leadership Council's philosophy that the Democrats had projected too left-wing and liberal an image in the past and now must take the middle ground. The platform particularly emphasized economic development and support for the business community. "Liberalism," said Al From, the executive director of the Democratic Leadership Council, "lost favor when we quit being a party of prosperity and growth."[1]

To highlight this new position of support for national economic development, the 1992 Democratic platform relied heavily on words such as "entrepreneurial economy," "new enterprise," "personal responsibility," and "hard work." From now on, private-sector economic growth was to be as important a part of Democratic ideology as government spending—or, as Bill Clinton preferred to call it, "government investment." But government should not try to do too much. The platform attacked "entrenched bureaucracies" and "big government theory." It called for a national government that would be "more decentralized, more flexible and more accountable."

On social issues, the platform included a long list of liberal programs, such as expanded child care, universal health insurance, equal pay for women, and civil rights protection for gays and lesbians. But there were consoling concepts for conservative Democrats as well. The platform stated that "people who bring children into this world have a responsibility to care for them, to give them values, motivation and discipline." It praised the American people for "the religious faith they follow, the ethics they practice, the values they instill, the pride they take in their work."[2]

An incident prior to the Democratic convention illustrated that, forced to choose between the liberal path or the centrist path, Bill Clinton would always choose the centrist. Speaking to a meeting of the National Rainbow Coalition, a group organized by Black civil rights leader Jesse Jackson to further minority group causes, Clinton denounced as "racist" remarks by rap singer Sister Souljah who, in an earlier interview, had appeared to advocate killing White people. In making such a provocative statement, particularly in the presence of a well-known Black leader such as Jackson, Clinton was emphasizing his independence from the more left-wing groups in the Democratic Party, militant Blacks included, that in the past had frightened middle-class Democrats into voting Republican.[3]

This sort of dedication to the middle of the road led the *Washington Post* to conclude that the 1992 Democratic platform accomplished Clinton's moderate and centrist goals perfectly. It was "putting liberal words to conservative music," rhapsodized the *Post*.[4] No matter how it was described, the technique worked. There were a few complaints here and there, but by and large the platform was quietly accepted by both the liberal and moderate wings of the party. The platform recommended to the convention by the Resolutions Committee was adopted on the convention floor with minimal debate and little dissent. A possible source of divisiveness and discord in the party—the party platform—had been skillfully shoved into the background by Bill Clinton and his political managers.

Then there was the question of the vice presidency. There was a time when party presidential nominees waited until after they were officially nominated at the convention on a roll call vote before announcing their vice-presidential selection. Even when candidates had gained the delegate votes needed for nomination long before the convention officially began, it was still general policy not to announce the name of the vice-presidential running mate until the convention was officially in session.

Apparently Bill Clinton did not want even the question of his vice-presidential choice to add mystery or possible controversy to the 1992 Democratic convention. On Thursday, July 9, 1992, three days before the convention was to begin, Clinton announced the name of his running mate to the press and the American people. His choice was Senator Al Gore Jr. of Tennessee.

Clinton got the most publicity possible out of the announcement. He made it on the grassy lawn of the governor's mansion in Little Rock, Arkansas, under a bright noonday sun. Both Clinton and his family and Gore and his family were present. The two candidates, with their wives and children arrayed behind them, emphasized their commitment to family values as they described their plans for the campaign ahead.

The selection of Al Gore immediately caused raised eyebrows among political commentators. Traditionally presidential nominees use the vice-presidential spot to "balance the ticket." They select a nominee from a different geographical area or a different philosophical branch of the party from their own. In the case of Clinton and Gore, however, both were southerners and both were moderates. Gore, in fact, was a longtime fellow member with Clinton on the centrist Democratic Leadership Council.

If there had been any doubt that Bill Clinton considered the South absolutely essential to his winning the White House in November, the selection of Al Gore as his running mate ended that doubt once and for all. Tennessee and Arkansas are located so close together in the South that they share a common border. Because Clinton and Gore were both young White southerners, and because "bubba" is southern slang for a conservative White southern male, comedians and commentators immediately began referring to Clinton and Gore as the "Double Bubba" ticket.

Gore added a great deal more to the 1992 Democratic ticket than just being a moderate White southerner. Unlike Clinton, who avoided serving in the military during the Vietnam War, Gore was a Vietnam veteran with a strong record of support for defense issues in the

Congress. Furthermore, Gore was an outspoken environmentalist, a trait expected to win votes for the ticket in the West. Perhaps most important of all, Gore's wife, Tipper Gore, recently had led a drive to force record companies to put warning labels on records, tapes, compact discs, and videos that contain foul and violent language. It was believed that Tipper Gore's efforts, which sought to warn parents when they were buying musical recordings for their children that contained offensive language, would add to the moderate image being projected by the Clinton-Gore ticket.[5]

The Clinton-Gore ticket offered generational unity as well as geographical and philosophical unity. Clinton was forty-six years old and Gore forty-four. If elected, they would be the youngest pair of running mates to win the White House in the nation's history. Clearly Clinton was fashioning a "Baby Boomer" ticket designed particularly to appeal to the large numbers of Americans born in the "Baby Boom" following the end of World War II. "Throughout American history, each generation has passed on leadership to the next," Gore said at the announcement ceremony. "That time has come again, the time for a new generation of leadership for the United States of America."[6]

Criticism of Clinton's selection of Gore for his running mate was minimal. Civil rights leader Jesse Jackson suggested Clinton and Gore were too much alike to create a really strong ticket. "It takes two wings to fly," Jackson said, "and here you have two of the same wing." A more typical comment came from Democratic strategist Duane Garrett, who evaluated Clinton's choice of Gore this way: "We're going to fight George Bush in his strongest base—the South—make the Border States contestable areas and use Gore's strength in the West."[7]

With the platform quietly adopted and the vice-presidential selection out of the way, there was very little left to possibly go wrong at the 1992 Democratic convention. To keep the delegates safe from New York City's infamous muggers and holdup men, an army of twenty-four hundred police officers plus antiterrorist teams and Secret Service agents patrolled Madison Square Garden. Just before the delegates hit town, New York's Democratic mayor, David Dinkins, ordered the pimps, prostitutes, homeless persons, and drug dealers hustled away from the neighborhoods surrounding the convention hall. That was to keep them from bothering the delegates and, more importantly, to keep them from giving New York City a bad image on national TV.

To guarantee that no unfavorable words would be said about Bill Clinton from the speaker's platform, the convention managers applied a very simple rule: If you haven't endorsed Bill Clinton for president, you can't give a speech. The threat of losing fifteen minutes on national television was enough to get almost every important Democrat in the country to jump on the Clinton bandwagon. One conspicuous holdout was Bob Casey, the Democratic governor of Pennsylvania, who refused to endorse Clinton because of the Arkansas governor's position on abortion. An outspoken opponent of abortion, Casey was not allowed even five minutes of convention speaking time to present the pro-life viewpoint.[8]

Another holdout from endorsing Clinton was former California governor Jerry Brown, who had been Clinton's most enduring and most critical opponent in the presidential primaries. When it was announced at the convention that only those who endorsed Clinton could address the convention, the Brown delegates began wearing adhesive tape on their mouths to symbolize the idea that Brown and his followers had been "silenced." For a moment, it appeared there might be something approaching excitement at the 1992 Democratic convention, particularly if Jerry Brown decided to gather up his delegates and lead a dramatic march out of the convention hall.

In the end Brown got himself the right to address the convention by having his campaign manager, Jodie Evans, put his name in nomination. He thus gave a speech to the convention that was technically a speech in support of his own candidacy. Although Brown continued to refuse to endorse Clinton, he did not attack Clinton in his speech. Instead, he portrayed the Democratic Party as the bulwark against Republican greed and called on the Democrats to be true to the people who "pay the bills, fight our wars, but never get invited to the reception."[9]

The Clinton forces worked so hard at removing all possible tension and controversy from the convention that they were attacked for making it dull. "Harmony, though, is boring," wrote Sandy Grady of the *Philadelphia Daily News*. "Clinton's peace-at-any-price convention will rivet even fewer TV viewers to this bloodless, obsequious love-in. With no conflict or drama, the audience will zap to a sitcom."[10]

Harsher criticism came from Roone Arledge, president of ABC News, who said there was little that could be done to make the conventions worth watching. "They're irrelevant," Arledge said. "Nothing of significance happens at them. Almost every decision of importance happens out of sight. I don't think we should try to pretend that conventions are what they used to be." Having said that, Arledge announced that ABC would not even broadcast the roll call, when political leaders enthusiastically plug their home states as they cast their state's delegate votes.[11]

Nationally syndicated columnist Jeff Greenfield concluded that the only value of national conventions was their ability to elicit nostalgic feelings from older television viewers. "Conventions look like what most of us believe politics is supposed to look like. The banners, the bunting, the buttons, the packed halls, the funny hats, all evoke a time when conventions really were gatherings of disparate political tribes, when politicians behaved without the self-consciousness that they might at any moment be on national television. . . . The convention, in sum, is a theme park for political junkies."[12]

According to the *New York Times*, Bill Clinton's managers did entertain a number of ideas for making the 1992 Democratic convention more entertaining and thereby more effective for the party. One idea was to have "Wake Up America" night, on which the nearly five thousand delegates would rise from their seats waving ringing alarm clocks. Another was to involve TV viewers in the convention by letting them telephone in their opinions to instant polls on key national issues. Perhaps the best idea was to have Bill Clinton nominated on Tuesday night rather than Thursday night so that he would have more time to be a part of the proceedings and present himself to the American people on television.

In the end, Clinton and his advisers rejected all these ideas for spicing up the show. One participant in these convention-improvement discussions made the following point. "The Clinton group, having come from a very rough primary season, are very cautious about doing anything wrong, taking chances that might lose him ground."[13]

One innovation the Clinton forces did institute was to have three keynote speakers instead of one on Monday night. The assumption was that three short speeches would make better television than one long speech. The three keynoters were Senator Bill Bradley of New Jersey, Governor Zell Miller of Georgia, and former Representative Barbara Jordan of Texas. Being selected as one of the keynote speakers undoubtedly was part of Zell Miller's reward for moving the 1992 Georgia Democratic primary to an earlier date and thereby greatly helping Clinton win the nomination.

Faced with a convention that mainly was going to be speeches by leading Democrats, the television networks decided to cover the convention by having their reporters and anchorpersons do live interviews. For instance, Senator Jay Rockefeller of West Virginia gave a major speech on Tuesday night, but NBC News chose to use that time period to do live interviews with former President Jimmy Carter and civil rights leader Jesse Jackson. Tuesday night was supposed to be the night the Democratic Party showcased the many new women officeholders and women candidates in the party, but NBC News had anchorperson Tom Brokaw analyzing the new role of women in the party instead of putting the women on television when they addressed the convention.

There is a good reason why the television networks do their own interviews rather than carry live speeches. When a convention speech is covered on TV, the speaker determines the subjects to be discussed. The subjects selected by the speaker may not be subjects interesting to the general public and thereby able to attract a large viewing audience. If the network has its own reporter or anchorperson do an interview, however, the network news editors can directly control the subject matter being discussed. The reporter's questions to the interviewee will concern the subjects that the editors feel are interesting and will attract and keep viewers.

On Wednesday night it was time for the nominating speeches and the pro forma roll call vote that would officially make Bill Clinton the 1992 Democratic nominee. New York governor Mario Cuomo gave the nominating speech for Clinton, and in this case the networks carried the entire speech live. Cuomo was the very embodiment of the northeastern, ethnic, urban, labor union wing of the Democratic Party. This was the wing of the party that had been completely left out when two moderate White southerners, Bill Clinton and Al Gore, became the 1992 Democratic ticket. Cuomo's ringing nomination speech for Clinton was designed to give the Clinton-Gore ticket credibility with this important northeastern group of voters.

Bill Clinton watched the roll call vote for the nomination for president on television in the basement of Macy's department store close by Madison Square Garden. With him were the "Arkansas Travelers," a group of friends and supporters from his home state who had traveled around the country with him to work in his campaign. There was a band playing, and Clinton spent much of the evening dancing with his wife, Hillary Clinton. The television networks had cameras present, and warm scenes of Bill Clinton surrounded by close friends and dancing with his wife were broadcast to the American public along with the roll call vote.

As the roll call vote gave Clinton a majority, he and Hillary and their teenage daughter, Chelsea, walked hand in hand down the streets of New York toward the convention hall. The television coverage alternated between the wild celebration on the convention floor and the Clinton family entering Madison Square Garden. As confetti rained from the ceiling and a band played, Bill Clinton walked onto the convention floor and was immediately engulfed by the cheering, whooping delegates. The crowd chanted "We want Bill" as Clinton climbed part way up the steps leading to the speaker's podium.

Nominee Clinton was very careful not to go all the way up to the speaker's podium. Party rules called for him to give his official acceptance speech the following night, not this night. Only a few words, spoken through a small microphone at the base of the speaker's podium, would be acceptable. "The rules preclude my acceptance tonight," Clinton told the delegates and the television audience, "but tomorrow night, I will be the Comeback Kid."[14]

The roll call vote coupled with the Clinton family's walk through the streets of New York to Madison Square Garden was the highspot of the 1992 Democratic National Convention. It was the kind of warm, fuzzy, inspirational television event that campaign managers dream about. The television images of Bill and Hillary Clinton dancing happily together in Macy's basement put the lie to the idea that their marriage was in trouble. Bill Clinton's long walk toward the convention hall perfectly symbolized the long trail he had fought his way up to get to this moment of success—becoming the 1992 Democratic nominee. His appearance on the convention floor, surrounded by celebrating Democrats as far as the eye could see, was compelling visual proof that he was now, without doubt, the Democratic Party's choice for president.

The magical, unforgettable television moments the night Bill Clinton was nominated were no accident. A pair of successful Hollywood television producers, Harry Thomason and Linda Bloodworth-Thomason, carefully scripted and stage-managed every last detail. The Thomasons had a home in Little Rock and were longtime friends of the Clintons. At the time they did the "choreography" for Bill Clinton's nomination night, they were the creators, writers, and directors of three of the most successful shows on network television—*Designing Women*, *Evening Shade*, and *Hearts Afire*. Their involvement perfectly symbolized the extent to which the national conventions have become "Hollywood" events rather than "political" events.[15]

The following night Clinton returned to the speaker's podium in Madison Square Garden and gave his acceptance speech. There was little new material in the speech. It mainly hammered on themes that Clinton had used repeatedly throughout the presidential primaries—the need for "change" and the need for a president who would take care of "the forgotten middle class."

It was a good speech but not a brilliant one. That may have been just as well. Early that Thursday morning, the last day of Clinton's convention had been upstaged by a totally unexpected event. Ross Perot, the independent candidate for president in 1992, announced that he was withdrawing from the race. He cited the rejuvenated state of the

Democratic Party under Bill Clinton as one of the main reasons he was quitting.

Bill Clinton had a practically perfect convention week. No major disputes or arguments marred the image of party unity generated by the convention. Real television magic occurred on the night he was nominated. On the final day of the convention, one of his two opponents dropped out of the presidential contest and gave Clinton the credit for causing him to leave. Best of all, public opinion polls taken the weekend after the convention showed Clinton, now in a two-way rather than a three-way race, running a solid twenty percentage points ahead of George Bush.[16]

23. Why Perot Pulled Out

Ross Perot's sudden withdrawal from the 1992 presidential race produced a veritable wave of newspaper stories and magazine articles. It clearly was one of the most widely reported and thoroughly analyzed decisions not to run for president in American political history.[1]

Newspaper columnists and TV commentators alike rejected Perot's claim that he quit because the Democrats had revitalized themselves. Most analysts argued that Perot pulled the plug on his campaign because he could not handle the competitive give-and-take of electoral politics. (A man used to running everything his own way, Perot was uncomfortable with having to sit back and let professional campaign consultants make the big decisions.) He also detested having to undergo the close scrutiny of the press, and he did not like taking a pounding from his opponents, particularly President Bush.

Perot had pledged to his legions of volunteer supporters that, in his efforts to galvanize the government into action, he would "take out the trash and clean out the barn." In the end, however, it appeared he was willing to "take out the trash" only if his reputation remained unsullied. He would "clean out the barn" only if he did not have to get his hands soiled.

Ross Perot "is not temperamentally qualified to come out as a first-timer and take on this brutal system," said James Squires, Perot's campaign press secretary. "I think he would have made a good president, but he was not a good politician or a good candidate." Squires concluded that it was extensive criticism of Perot by the news media that drove him out of the race: "The glare of the media has never been anything like this in American political history."[2]

Ed Rollins, the Republican political consultant who joined the Perot campaign in June, saw arguments over paid advertising as a major factor in the demise of the Perot effort. "To win, which would be to do it our way, was not what he was about," Rollins said of Perot. "He didn't see himself as being like anyone else, and he wouldn't use the tools everyone else used. When we tried to explain those tools and explain you couldn't get there without them, well, he just couldn't go forward."[3]

Apparently Perot objected to the high cost of paid campaign advertising and questioned whether it was really needed. He turned thumbs down on a $2 million to $3 million direct mail campaign designed to thank and energize his petition-signers. He tended to toss junk mail in the trash basket, he told his staff, and he felt even his most ardent supporters would do the same thing with his thank you notes.

Perot also rejected urgent pleas for a $7 million initial advertising campaign designed to define his image and begin presenting his ideas for governmental action to the voters. Rollins and other media advisers believed such a paid advertising campaign was essential because the news media, with its critical stories about Perot, was beginning to question his character and past accomplishments and thereby cost him votes. In his own paid television commercials, Rollins pointed out, Perot would have complete control over the images and ideas about him that were being presented to the public.

Some test television ads were presented to Perot for approval. They showed scenes of charged-up volunteers singing the praises of Perot at his intensely upbeat rallies in the various state capitals. Rollins felt the ads were excellent, as good as political advertising ever gets. Perot rejected the ads because, in his personal opinion, they looked too political.

Rollins recalled one meeting where the staff showed Perot the raw videotape of his state rallies and asked him what kind of television ads he, candidate Perot, would like to see made. Instead of answering the question, Perot talked about how much he enjoyed being on free television—on television talk shows and early morning television news programs. Instead of helping his staff design the paid commercials, Perot simply asked: "Why should I pay $100,000 to shoot a single ad, when I can get as much free time on talk shows as I want?"[4]

The first sign of real trouble in the Perot camp came in mid-July when Perot dismissed Hal Riney, the most experienced advertising man working in his campaign. Riney, who produced the television ads that Perot had been consistently rejecting, was the San Francisco advertising genius who created Ronald Reagan's famous "Morning in America" campaign for the 1984 presidential election. The press interpreted the firing of Riney as direct proof that Perot was micromanaging his campaign himself and maintaining a too-tight personal grasp on decision-making and strategy.

Then there was the problem of Perot's platform. The policy planning team which the Texas billionaire had brought together came up with a proposal to cut $500 billion from the federal budget. To make the plan work, taxes would have to be raised and all government programs cut back an average of 10 percent. This budget-cutting proposal was the kind of "clean out the barn" action Perot had been promising his supporters. It also was much more specific than the budget-cutting plans George Bush and Bill Clinton had been presenting. Politically, however, the Perot budget was a nightmare. It was very clear that Perot would be roundly criticized by conservatives for raising taxes and by liberals for cutting government spending programs so drastically.[5]

In the end, the Perot campaign failed because Perot himself could not decide who he was and what kind of campaign he was going to run. "We could never get to, 'Okay, let's go,'" said Sal Russo, a Perot campaign worker hired by Ed Rollins. "It was mind-boggling how many half-roasted plans were being pulled from the ovens: Maybe they'd have a convention at the Rose Bowl, maybe 2,000 separate meetings of volunteers, maybe gatherings of Hollywood supporters. We were getting panicked. We were watching this thing crumble."[6]

The end came when Ed Rollins wrote a desperate memo to Perot urging the Texas billionaire to choose from one of three options. He could run a real campaign with professional staff and paid advertising—and possibly win. He could continue the current noncampaign of volunteer rallies and free TV—and certainly lose. Or he could call it quits.

When Perot notified Ed Rollins that he had rejected option one—running a real campaign—Rollins resigned. This was interpreted by the press as a real blow to the Perot campaign, given the high respect the news media had for Rollins as a skilled political operator. Rollins gave a very simple explanation for abandoning the Perot effort. "The reality is that the kind of campaign that I wanted to run and the kind of campaign that Perot wanted to run just weren't compatible."[7]

One day after Rollins resigned, to almost everyone's surprise, Perot chose the third option in Rollins's memo and got out of the race. Perot held the press conference at which he announced his decision to quit in Dallas. For a man who had decided he did not like the news media, signing off the campaign down in Texas was a good decision. Because the Democratic National Convention was still in session, all of the nation's top political reporters, the sort that would ask the most penetrating and damaging questions, were still in New York.

Molly Ivins, the political columnist for the *Fort Worth Star-Telegram*, wrote an apt epitaph for the Perot campaign. In her opinion, Ross Perot illustrated why it is important to have professional politicians, rather than amateurs, governing the nation. "Politics looks easy from the outside," Ivins wrote. "That's why guys like Perot think they can do it and do it without all the consultants and fol-de-rol and shuckin' and jivin' you have to do to get elected. He's learned better. . . .

"When you run for public office, you don't get to decide what other people think of you," Ivins continued. "Watching someone without political skills try to run for public office sure as hell increased my respect for political skills, including artful evasion, always so preferable to the outright lie.

"Myself, I always kind of liked Ross Perot," Ivins concluded. "But by the time he announced he wouldn't run, he sure had convinced me he shouldn't."[8]

In the end, Ed Rollins gave George Bush and his all-out media attack on Ross Perot the credit for befuddling Perot and getting him to throw in the towel. Three weeks before Perot quit, Rollins predicted that the negative campaign launched by the Republicans would be so intense "they can take us out" unless Perot could find some way to fight back.[9] Perot never did find a way to respond to the Republican attack, and shortly thereafter his stumbling campaign was over.[10]

The Bush forces made such short work of Ross Perot and his independent campaign for president that political observers were left with the following question. Would Bill Clinton do any better at standing up to the negative barrages from the Bush camp than Ross Perot did?

24. THE REPUBLICAN CONVENTION

The Republican National Convention got underway in late August of 1992 under a cloud of statistical gloom. As the delegates filed into their seats in the Houston Astrodome, the *New York Times*/CBS News poll gave Democratic nominee Bill Clinton a seventeen-percentage-point lead over George Bush, the incumbent Republican president.[1] The *Washington Post*/ABC News poll revealed that Bush had suffered the greatest drop in popularity of any American president, his approval rating having fallen fifty-seven points since the conclusion of the Persian Gulf War in the spring of 1991. Worst of all for Bush, the *Washington Post*/ABC News poll said he had the highest disapproval rating ever of any incumbent president going into the final ten weeks of a reelection campaign.[2]

If the 1992 Democratic National Convention mainly symbolized the Democratic Party moving from the far left to the middle of the political spectrum, the 1992 Republican National Convention mainly represented the Republican Party sticking to and affirming its position on the right. Speaker after speaker at the Republican convention took a conservative stance, endorsing such favorite right-wing causes as lower taxes, less government bureaucracy, reduced government regulation of business, and tougher law enforcement to fight urban crime.

Even further to the right was the 1992 Republican platform. Unlike Bill Clinton, who exercised tight control over the Democratic platform and saw to it that a moderate document was produced, George Bush gave the conservative drafters of the Republican platform almost a free hand. The result was a document that suggested tax cuts far in excess of anything President Bush had ever promised, proposed that a physical barrier be built along the entire border with Mexico in order to keep out illegal immigrants, called for rigid restrictions on abortion, and launched a strident attack on public broadcasting for being porno-graphic and politically liberal.

On Monday night, August 17, 1992, Pat Buchanan, President Bush's only significant opponent in the Republican presidential pri-maries, gave a major address to the convention. Buchanan began his talk by endorsing Bush, stating that "the right place to be now . . . is right beside George Bush."[3] After congratulating Bush on winning the primaries, Buchanan said he wanted to remove any doubts that he was supporting the President. "The primaries are over," the conservative columnist said to loud applause, "and the Buchanan Brigades are enlisted—all the way to a great comeback victory in November."

Buchanan then went on to give one of the most scathing speeches in party convention history. He called the Democratic convention in New York "that giant masquerade ball at Madison Square Garden—where 20,000 radicals and liberals came dressed up as moderates and centrists—in the greatest single exhibition of cross-dressing in American political history." Buchanan also attacked Democratic nominee Bill Clin-ton's wife Hillary Clinton, accusing her of practicing radical feminism for comparing "marriage as an institution to slavery . . . and life on an Indian reservation."[4]

Buchanan then condemned Bill Clinton for being a Vietnam War draft dodger and a supporter of gay rights. He tagged Demo-cratic vice-presidential nominee Al Gore as an environmental extrem-ist. He described both Bill and Hillary Clinton as hiding a radical-liberal reform program behind the word "change." Buchanan declared: "The agenda that Clinton & Clinton would impose on America—abortion on demand, a litmus test for the Supreme Court, homosexual rights, discrimination against religious schools, women in combat units—that's change, all right, but not the kind of change America needs."[5]

Buchanan worked hard to portray the 1992 presidential election as the political equivalent of the battle between good and evil. "There is a religious war going on in our country for the soul of America," he told the delegates, and "George Bush is on our side."[6]

Famous for his humorous digs and jabs at political opponents, Buchanan turned some of his rapier-like wit in the Democratic presi-dential nominee's direction. "Bill Clinton's foreign policy experience," he said to widespread laughter, "is limited to having breakfast at the International House of Pancakes."[7]

As always happens at national conventions, signs in the audience expressed party sentiments in their baldest and most unsubtle form. The most notable and noted was a large hand-painted sign referring to Bill Clinton's alleged marital infidelities. It read: "If Hillary Can't Trust Him, How Can We?"[8] Less prominent were "stick on" buttons that said: "Smile if you have had an affair with Bill Clinton."[9] For those Republicans concerned about increased government spending under the Democrats, a large sign read: "Bill and Al's New Covenant: You Send It; They Spend It!"[10]

As would be expected, the major attraction at the 1992 Republican convention was George Bush himself. The incumbent president generated a number of positive moments and positive images that went out to the nation over network television. The Monday afternoon before the convention began, George Bush addressed a crowd of seven thousand or so Republican partisans jammed into an auditorium adjacent to the convention hall. It was a perfect timed-for-TV rally with the President walking into the arena just as the three major television networks were beginning their evening news programs on the East Coast.

Bush clearly was buoyed by the overflowing enthusiasm of so many supporters. "It starts right now," he said. "You know me. In politics, I've always done better when I fight back, when I'm behind. . . . I'm going to roll up my sleeves and do what's right for the American people, and I don't care what the polls say."[11]

Equally positive was the press and public reaction to a Monday evening convention speech by former President Ronald Reagan. In the talk, Reagan warmly endorsed the man who had served eight years as his vice president. "The presidency is serious business," Reagan said. "We cannot afford to take a chance. We need a man . . . who has been at the table with Gorbachev and Yeltsin. A man whose performance as commander-in-chief of the bravest and most effective fighting force in history left the world in awe, and the people of Kuwait free of foreign tyranny."

Reagan concluded by telling the delegates he had come to Houston to "warmly, genuinely, wholeheartedly . . . support the reelection of George Bush as president of the United States. . . . His is a steady hand on the tiller through the choppy waters of the 90s, which is exactly what we need."[12]

This theme of George Bush's great foreign policy skills was picked up by the keynote speaker, Senator Phil Gramm of Texas, who addressed the convention on Tuesday evening. Gramm gave both Bush and Reagan the credit for the recent breakup of the Soviet Union and the end of the Cold War. "It was Ronald Reagan who put the Kremlin in the crosshairs," Gramm told the delegates, "but it was George Bush who pulled the trigger." Gramm concluded with the thought that the Republicans "must never allow the Democrats to disarm America again."[13]

If there was television magic at the 1992 Republican convention, it came on Wednesday night, August 19, 1992. Those delegates who had brought their children with them to Houston were encouraged to bring their offspring to the Astrodome to see Bush formally nominated. Throughout the evening, as speaker after speaker lauded the importance of the American family, television cameras focused on the many children seated with their parents throughout the convention hall. From babes-in-arms to teenagers, the youngest Republicans were visible in the living rooms of America. In addition to providing entertaining and "warm fuzzy" television images, the presence of so many children left no doubt that "family values" was going to be a major Republican issue in the 1992 presidential election.

The highspot came when the President's wife, Barbara Bush, gathered on the convention podium with the couple's twenty-two children and grandchildren. Wearing a red suit and her trademark pearl necklace, Barbara Bush drew large ovations from the delegates for her repeated tributes to her husband. "Tonight you will nominate George Bush to lead our nation into the future," the First Lady said. "With all my heart—and I know him best—you have made a superb choice."[14]

The crowd went extra wild when, as Barbara Bush finished her talk, the President walked out on the podium and kissed her, after which the two of them embraced their many grandchildren. It was one of those warm and emotional television moments that political TV consultants work so hard to deliver.

Once the official roll call of the delegates was completed, and George Bush was officially the Republican nominee, over 180,000 red, white, and blue biodegradable balloons cascaded down from the top of the Astrodome. The television networks described it as the largest balloon drop in history, a full 120,000 more balloons than the 60,000 the Democrats had used when Bill Clinton was nominated in Madison Square Garden.

As the Republicans' convention week progressed, the news media placed more and more emphasis on George Bush's acceptance speech, arguing that it would be the embattled president's best opportunity to defend his first term in the White House and lay out his programs for the coming four years. On Thursday night, August 20, 1992, Bush took the podium and made the best effort he could to revive his sagging candidacy.

The President began by citing his foreign policy accomplishments and claiming that the collapse of communism during his time in the White House was not an accident. "Some want to rewrite history, want to skip over the struggle, claim the outcome was inevitable," Bush said. "And while the U.S. postwar strategy was largely bipartisan, the fact remains that the liberal, McGovern wing of the other party—including my opponent—consistently made the wrong choices."[15]

In his speech President Bush tried to answer the Democratic Party's frequent charge that he spent too much time on foreign policy. He explained: "I seized those opportunities for our kids and our grandkids, and I make no apologies for that."

The President emphasized his successful leadership in the Persian Gulf War and then made fun of Bill Clinton's qualifications to be the nation's highest military decision-maker. "What about the leader of the Arkansas National Guard, the man who hopes to be commander-in-chief? Well, while I bit the bullet, he bit his nails."

Moving on to economic issues, President Bush promised a new round of across-the-board tax cuts to put more money in taxpayers' pockets and thereby help stimulate the economy. The proposed tax cuts would not increase the budget deficit, he said, because they would be tied to specific reductions in government spending. As for his Democratic opponent's economic policies, Bush accused Clinton of raising taxes and fees "128 times" while governor of Arkansas. The President predicted that electing Clinton to the White House would send government spending soaring.

President Bush sought to blame the nation's economic ills on the U.S. Congress, where the Democratic Party had enjoyed majority control of both the House and the Senate for a number of years. He accused the Congress of failing to pass his economic growth package, thereby costing the nation 500,000 new jobs. Electing Clinton, he said, would create "a rubber-check Congress and a rubber-stamp president."

Bush said that the 1992 presidential election would offer "a sharp choice" between "different agendas, different directions, and yes, a choice about the character of the man you want to lead this nation." The president concluded that he and the Democrats had distinctly different visions of how to restore the nation's economy. "Their [vision] is to look inward and protect what we already have," Bush said. "Ours is to look forward—to open new markets, prepare our people to compete, to restore the social fabric, to save and invest so we can win."

Bush's acceptance speech, although not considered a "great" speech, received generally favorable comment in the news media and from political analysts. To most observers, the speech made it clear that the Republicans were going to develop the "trust" issue as the best way of winning George Bush four more years in the White House. "Here is my question for the American people," Bush said in his acceptance speech. "Who do you trust in this election?"

In the effort to convince voters that George Bush was more trustworthy than Bill Clinton, the Republicans had made it clear that they intended to emphasize two major issues: foreign policy and family values. "Trust taps into the two things Bush has going the most for him," said Tom Smith, a University of Chicago survey researcher. Those two things are "foreign policy experience and Clinton's character."[16]

Although no one came right out and said it, the "trust" issue was partly emphasized to take advantage of the large amount of publicity concerning Clinton's alleged marital infidelities. As an anonymous Republican strategist told the *Washington Post*: "Our purpose is to define George Bush and the Republican Party as the proponent of fundamental social norms in terms of the family, in terms of sexual behavior and in terms of reward for work. Conversely, we intend to define Clinton and the Democrats as advocates of individual fulfillment, without regard to generally held values and beliefs."[17]

How good a job did the 1992 Republican convention do of supporting George Bush's candidacy for president? There was a wide variety of opinions. The more liberal elements in the news media saw the convention as so "right wing" that it was harming the President's chances for reelection. Although Patrick Buchanan's speech was only one of many at the four-days-long Republican convention, much of the news media seized on his speech as symbolizing the mood of the convention, which some described as "exclusive" and "meanspirited."

A typical analysis of Buchanan's speech was presented by political columnist Molly Ivins writing in *Newsweek*. She described the Republican convention as "sour, mean, and dull" and took particular exception to Buchanan's call for a "religious war" for "the soul of America." She wrote: "Religious warfare. . . . Gad, think of the fun we can have—mass slaughter in the name of God, killing for Christ, pogroms, heretic hunts. We, too, can at long last enjoy the charming ambience of Northern Ireland and Lebanon."[18]

Jonathan Alter, a senior editor at *Newsweek*, argued that Pat Buchanan's speech was so far to the right that it could possibly cost George Bush the presidential election. "Encouraging [Buchanan] and the religious right is not working on the American public this time,"

Alter said. "If Bush loses, history will show that Buchanan's speech was a major factor in the defeat. His speech was a disaster."[19]

In retrospect, the news media later acknowledged that they may have played up the role of the "far right" at the Republican convention more than was fair. There had been lots of "far left" elements present at the Democratic convention, but the press had overlooked them and gone out of its way to hang a "moderate" label on the Democrats' confab. The *Washington Post* dutifully acknowledged this sentiment that the Republicans may have received unequal treatment: "Some analysts have criticized coverage of the Republican convention as harsher than the media's treatment of the Democratic convention."[20]

Of course the real determinant of whether the 1992 Republican convention was a success or not would be George Bush's standing in the public opinion polls once the convention was over. But even this normally reliable barometer of success and failure failed in this instance. The polls taken the first few weeks after the convention varied all over the block. For example, a Harris Poll conducted the last week in August showed Bill Clinton with only a five-point lead over President Bush, quite a comedown from the seventeen-point lead Clinton had enjoyed at the start of the Republican convention. On the other hand, a poll by the Gallup Organization for the same time period put Clinton a full fifteen points ahead of Bush, thus suggesting that the Republican convention had helped the President hardly at all.[21]

One point seemed really clear. Bill Clinton had maintained tight control over the Democratic convention and had come out with uniform praise in the media and a big "bounce" in all the public opinion polls. George Bush had maintained much less control over his convention, had been criticized for some of the more "right wing" things that he had allowed to go on there, and came out with no one knowing whether he had gotten a "bounce" in the polls or not. One lesson of 1992 was that presidential candidates should work to control their nominating conventions as tightly as possible.

25. Toward a Preprimary National Mini-Convention

It is true that the Republican and Democratic national conventions have evolved into "coronations" rather than true nominating conventions. It is also true, however, that the national conventions can be expected to continue in their present form well into the future. The two major political parties now regard their national conventions as an invaluable source of free advertising for the party presidential candidate, and the two parties have no intention whatsoever of giving up all that free advertising. Although the television networks are reducing the number of hours of broadcast time devoted to covering the national conventions, they still will want to televise in prime time the more colorful and exciting moments at the conventions, such as the keynote addresses, the balloting for the presidential and vice-presidential nominations, the acceptance speeches, and so forth.

It is best, therefore, to accept the party national conventions as meaningless institutions that do not do very much but will not go away. If reform is to take place, it will have to take the form of some sort of totally new party national convention that is added to the nominating system *without removing or changing the existing national conventions.*

As explained in Chapter 2, one of the least well-defined parts of the presidential nominating process is the lengthy period prior to the Iowa caucuses and the New Hampshire primaries. The various would-be nominees announce their candidacies during this period, travel around the nation giving speeches and holding rallies, and endeavor in every way possible to attract the attention, and the favor, of the news media. An important part of this process is the public opinion polls, which the news media use to track each candidate's popularity and chances of winning from the very moment the candidate enters the race.

As things stand at the present time, the news media have the most to say about which candidates advance and which candidates fall behind during this crucial precaucus, preprimary period. For that reason, I have labeled this particular portion of the presidential nominating process the "News Media Candidate Evaluation and Promotion Period."

A political party national convention that was truly relevant to the nominating process as it now exists would be held *prior to* the presidential caucuses and primaries, not after them. It would come immediately at the end of the News Media Candidate Evaluation and Promotion Period but before the caucuses and primaries have actually begun. The purpose of such a party national convention would be to rank the various candidates for the party's presidential nomination. These rankings, made by party professionals rather than the news media and the polls, as is done now, would serve as a guide to party members as they go about voting in the various presidential caucuses and primaries.

The suggestion here is that each political party hold a "Preprimary National Mini-Convention" in the middle of January of each presidential election year.[1] This new national mini-convention would not replace the present party national convention but would be held in addition to it.

The delegates to the Preprimary National Mini-Convention would be those members of the political party who currently hold major elected offices.[2] Party members who are United States senators and representatives all would be eligible to attend the convention and cast one vote. Also eligible would be the state governors who are members of the political party, the top two party leaders in each house of each of the fifty state legislatures, and the mayors of the 100 largest cities in the nation who are members of the political party.

If the president and vice president of the United States are currently members of the political party, they too could attend the mini-convention and cast their one vote.

If one assumes an equal balance between the two political parties throughout the major governing institutions of the nation, the delegates to a Preprimary National Mini-Convention would look like this:

Party members who are . . .

•	U.S. senators:	50
•	U.S. representatives	218
•	State legislators	200
•	Governors	25
•	Mayors	50
	Total:	543

Of course this is a theoretical model only. The numbers would vary as the particular political party won more or fewer Senate seats, more or fewer seats in the House of Representatives, and so forth. Also, because it has a unicameral, nonpartisan state legislature, the state of Nebraska would have to develop its own unique system for electing its state legislative delegates.

As the Preprimary National Mini-Convention is called to order, the emphasis would be on ranking the party candidates for president and nothing else. There would be no platform to argue over and adopt. There would be no discussion or revision of party rules. Because delegates to the convention would all be elected officials who are members of the party, there would be few if any arguments over who is or is not a bona fide delegate to the convention. In other words, there would be no credentials fights.

The Preprimary National Mini-Convention would be short and sweet. Each candidate for president would receive two nominating speeches, each a maximum of ten minutes long, after which there could be a short demonstration. As in the "good old days" of national conventions, the demonstration could include hired musicians playing marching music and the candidate's supporters carrying signs and marching up and down on the mini-convention floor. The two nominating speeches and the demonstration, however, could not exceed thirty minutes for each candidate.

Each candidate would then be allowed a maximum of thirty minutes to address the mini-convention, outlining his or her issue positions and stating why he or she would be the party's best candidate for president. Although it would not be an official part of the mini-convention proceedings, a candidate could hold a press conference and answer questions from the press and interested delegates.

Note that each candidate is limited to just one hour of mini-convention time, thirty minutes for being nominated and holding a demonstration and thirty minutes for speaking to the delegates. After the first candidate had been given his or her hour, the next candidate would be given his or her hour, and so on until the list of candidates was completed.

It would be necessary, of course, to limit the number of candidates who could be nominated to compete at the Preprimary National Mini-Convention. Otherwise, totally unqualified persons might announce their candidacy for the party nomination for president for no other purpose than to get to address the mini-convention. The best way to limit the list of candidates would be to require that, to be nominated and to get to speak to the convention, a candidate would have to submit a petition signed by 10 percent of the mini-convention delegates.

At the conclusion of the nominating speeches and the speeches by the candidates, the balloting would begin. Each delegate would have one vote. The states would be called in alphabetical order, and the votes for the various candidates would be reported by the leader of each state delegation.

At the end of the first ballot, a second ballot would be held with just the top four finishers in the running. This would give delegates who voted for the less popular candidates on the first ballot the opportunity to make a choice among the top four finishers on the second ballot. Once the results of the second ballot were announced, the mini-convention would then hear short campaign speeches (thirty minutes or shorter) from the four candidates whose names were on the second ballot.

The candidate with the lowest number of votes would give the first campaign speech; the candidate with the second lowest number of votes would give the second campaign speech, and so on. The candidate with the highest number of votes would, of course, give the fourth and final campaign speech.

Once that was over, the mini-convention delegates would speedily adjourn and go home.

The major purpose of the Preprimary National Mini-Convention would be to begin the process of winnowing the field of prospective party presidential candidates. The emphasis would be on determining the top four candidates for the party nomination rather than identifying a single promising candidate. Armed with the results of the second ballot at the Preprimary National Mini-Convention, party members could attend party caucuses and vote in party presidential primaries with a much clearer picture of what their choices are and which candidates the elected officials of their political party recommend.

One of the most important characteristics of the proposed Preprimary National Mini-Convention is the fact that the delegates are all elected officials. In other words, they are all men and women who have demonstrated skill and ability at getting a majority of their fellow citizens to vote them into public office. In addition, all but the newly elected will have occupied an elected office for a period of time and will have an improved sense of what the voting public is concerned about, at least in their particular state or local area. The delegates to the Preprimary National Mini-Convention thus will be the members of the political party who have faced the voters and won at the polling place. As such, they are the people whose opinions are most worthy of respect as to who should be the party's nominee for president.

Will holding a Preprimary National Mini-Convention put an end to the great power of news reporters and news editors during the News Media Evaluation and Promotion Period of presidential nominating campaigns? The answer is that it will not, but it will help to reduce the power of the news media during this critical stage of the nominating process. In addition to the evaluations being made in the news media, party members will have another important ingredient to help them make their choices in the caucuses and the primaries. That ingredient will be an official ranking of the candidates by their fellow party members who are elected officials.

26. The Clinton Buscapade

Following the successful conclusion of the Democratic National Convention in New York City in mid-July, the freshly nominated Democratic ticket of Bill Clinton and Al Gore boarded a bus and began a speech-giving, handshaking tour of America's industrial heartland. Additional buses carrying news reporters and campaign staffers trailed along behind. For six days and over one thousand miles, the Democratic bus caravan rolled across New Jersey, Pennsylvania, West Virginia, Ohio, Kentucky, Indiana, and Illinois, ending with a heavily attended rally in St. Louis, Missouri.

All along the route, groups of people waited at the edge of the highway to wave the candidates on as they passed by. Unexpectedly large crowds gathered at truck stops and roadside parks for scheduled stops at which the candidates gave speeches and did some handshaking. Politicians and reporters alike were surprised by the size of the crowds and the serious concern which people along the route expressed about the state of the nation. One night at Vandalia, Illinois, ten thousand people gathered at the old state capitol where Abraham Lincoln once served. When the buses arrived, the crowd lit candles and joined the candidates in singing "God Bless America."

Providing even more excitement to the bus tour was the fact that Clinton and Gore brought their attractive and personable wives with them. When the Democratic nominees were joined on the stage by Hillary Clinton and Tipper Gore, whoops and screams and whistles would erupt from the audience. The two couples appeared to be going on an enjoyable "double date" to visit and talk with the American people.

The Clinton-Gore "buscapade," as the news media labeled it, was so successful that the Democratic candidates revived it in August and in the fall campaign following the Republican convention. As late as one week before election day, Bill Clinton and Al Gore were back out on the road, busing through the lush green foothills of North Carolina, where the polls showed the race to be unusually tight.[1]

A high-powered movie producer from Hollywood, Mort Engelberg, was put to work searching out picturesque locations for stops. The result was a daily series of "carefully lit hay-bale sets and evocative small-town backdrops" where Bill Clinton and Al Gore presented their case to the American people.[2] News photographers had a field day as they shot nostalgic pictures of the buses and the candidates against a background that was "a rolling Norman Rockwell tableau, the placid, mythic beauty of small-town America."[3]

The buscapade was particularly effective in the evenings. People gathered at the edge of the road after work, often sitting in folding chairs while waiting for the buses to show up. Local radio stations would broadcast the location of the bus caravan at any given moment and suggest possible gathering places. If enough supporters were waiting at this major corner or in this particular downtown square, the candidates would spontaneously stop for a small amount of speech making and a large amount of handshaking and personal chatting.

One evening *Newsweek* interviewed John Bruce, a midwestern farmer, as he waited for the buses on the shoulder of U.S. Highway 61 in Wapello, Iowa. "I've only been here about an hour," Bruce said. "I was following them on the radio, heard when they left Burlington."

After farmer Bruce had shaken Bill Clinton's hand and the buses had rolled on into the darkness, Bruce described a change in voter sentiment that seemed to be taking place all over the nation: "Well, I wouldn't have supported him a few months ago. But then I saw this bus tour took out from the East, and I figured maybe they'll learn something. . . . I figure that anyone that would take the time to stop in the middle of the night and talk to us, instead of flying around to big cities in an airplane, can't be all bad."[4]

As the Democratic bus tour rolled from one local media market to another, television and radio stations preempted their regular programming to cover the buscapade live. Local stations that could not afford the thousands of dollars it costs to put a reporter on a campaign airplane were more than happy to pay $100 to $150 to put a reporter on the Clinton buscapade as it rolled through the local area. In most cases, "the Democrats were showered with largely uncritical, and often downright enthusiastic, reports from television, radio and newspapers." A television news anchor in La Crosse, Wisconsin, described "practically every move made by 'Bill' and 'Al.'"

Although the Democratic candidates would be in a particular area for only twenty-four hours or so, local media would build up the visit for almost a week beforehand, thereby maximizing the media impact. The final result "was the sort of abundant and friendly coverage that no paid commercial could match. The Bill Clinton-Al Gore bus tour [was], in essence, a free commercial on wheels."[5]

The Clinton-Gore buscapade was one of the unique developments of the 1992 presidential election campaign. Previously, as Iowa farmer Bruce so carefully pointed out, presidential candidates spent most of their time flying from major airport to major airport, striving mainly to get on television in large metropolitan media markets such as New York, Chicago, Atlanta, and Los Angeles. The Clinton campaign discovered a new postmodern political form: a bus tour back to small town America that would play big on television in the big metropolitan areas.

Perhaps most important, the buscapade enabled Clinton to strengthen his image as a representative of middle America rather than left-wing America. "The virtues expressed by the rural folks lining the highways—hope, desire for change, faith in the future—are, at once, old-fashioned and the very qualities Clinton and Gore are hoping to sell to a more cynical metropolitan electorate."[6] The images generated by the buscapade were so powerful and worked so well that Clinton and Gore made it one of the primary elements, if not *the* primary element, in their fall campaign.

In early September the major characteristic of the 1992 presidential election campaign was Bill Clinton's big lead over George Bush in the public opinion polls. The main message that was coming to the American people through the news media was the Clinton campaign's unbelievable momentum. As that momentum stayed steady, Bill Clinton had to fight the inclination to "sit on his lead."

The Clinton fall strategy thus had three main points. The first point was to make sure the economy was the major issue. To this end, a sign saying "The Economy, Stupid" was posted prominently in the Clinton campaign headquarters in Little Rock. The campaign was to focus on George Bush and his failed economic policies, not on Bill Clinton and his alleged character problems. The speeches and the advertising would all come back to one single idea: America could not afford four more years of George Bush as president.

The second point was to always be ready to respond to attacks from the Bush camp. Such attacks, the Clinton managers believed, were inevitable, given Clinton's large lead over Bush in the public opinion polls. A War Room was organized in the campaign headquarters in Little Rock with three television sets and a teletype bringing in wire-service reports. Throughout the day and on into the evening, the Clinton campaigners watched and listened to everything Bush had to say. Any attack on Clinton resulted in an instant response from the War Room. Reporters would be called and immediately given the Clinton answer to whatever Bush or one of his campaign lieutenants might have charged.

Richard L. Berke, a reporter for the *New York Times*, gave an example of how efficiently the Clinton War Room worked. Shortly after the Republican convention, Berke was in Ann Arbor, Michigan, covering the Bush campaign. Bush had just given a speech attacking Democratic vice-presidential candidate Al Gore. Berke was hard at work writing a newspaper article on the speech, mainly from the Bush point of view, when his telephone beeper went off. The call turned out to be from Gore, who had been alerted by the War Room as to what Bush had said and how the remarks could best be answered. As a result of this "instant response," Berke's story about the Bush speech contained Gore's responses side by side with Bush's charges, thus mitigating the overall impact of Bush's attack.[7]

The denizens of the Clinton-Gore War Room were particularly adept at intercepting Bush speeches and television commercials being sent across the country by satellite. As news accounts of Bush's speeches were sent to network headquarters in New York by satellite transmissions, the Clinton people would pick them up directly rather than waiting to see them on the television evening news. The Clinton managers thus gave themselves several hours of lead time in framing their responses to Bush's remarks. In the same way, when the Bush campaign would beam new television commercials to television stations across the country, the Clinton-Gore campaign would pick up the commercials off the satellite and start working on answering commercials long before the Bush commercials ever went on the air.[8]

The third point of the Clinton campaign strategy was to continue the policy, first adopted late in the spring presidential primaries, of using free television as much as possible. Throughout the fall campaign Clinton took advantage of every opportunity to appear on the *Today Show, Good Morning America,* the *Phil Donohue Show,* and others. The assumption was the same in the fall as it had been in the spring: The more people saw Bill Clinton on talk television, the more people would get to know him, come to like him, and judge him to be a more than acceptable alternative to George Bush.

By the middle of September the Clinton camp's three-pronged strategy was working so well that Clinton was still thirteen points ahead of Bush in the polling. Obviously there was no inclination at the Clinton headquarters in Little Rock to change the way things were going. All the pressure to change the campaign—to shake things up and move things around—was on the Bush-Quayle team.

27. THE BUSH CAMPAIGN: SEARCHING FOR A MESSAGE

Mid-September of 1992 found the Bush campaign for president in dire straits. Public opinion polls showed Bill Clinton with a giant lead. No matter what the President or his campaign managers did, George Bush seemed to be stalled at around 40 percent of the vote. "We're stuck," a top Bush campaign official told a friend. "Nothing's happening. It's stagnant out there."[1]

It was not as though the Bush organization was not trying. Immediately following the Republican convention, the President had moved to give his campaign new life by bringing his popular secretary of state, James A. Baker III, over to the White House as presidential chief of staff. Baker, who had managed Bush's highly successful 1988 campaign for the presidency, was expected to shape up not only the White House operation but also "to run a rake through the campaign," weeding out new and untried staffers and replacing them with proven veterans from the 1988 effort.[2]

Bush then tried to turn a negative into a positive. Pointing out what everyone already knew—that he was trailing badly in the public opinion polls—Bush began comparing himself to Harry Truman, the Democratic president who had scored a great come-from-behind victory over Republican Thomas E. Dewey in the 1948 presidential election. Bush began arguing that, as had Truman, he was going to confound the experts and prove the pollsters wrong by somehow winning this unwinnable election.

One way Truman won in 1948 was by blaming the nation's ills on the Congress, which was controlled by the Republicans at that time. Bush took his cue from Truman and began blaming the nation's ills in 1992 on the current Democratic-controlled Congress. "Harry Truman was frustrated by what he called the 'do-nothing Congress,'" Bush said. "The [current] gridlocked Congress hasn't listened to people either."[3]

At the same time he was criticizing the Democratic Congress for not solving the nation's problems, Bush tried to generate an activist image of a president working hard to end the economic recession. In early September he traveled to a General Dynamics Corporation plant in Fort Worth, Texas, to announce that he had approved the sale of 150 of the company's F-16 fighter planes to Taiwan. Bush trumpeted that the airplane contract would eventually be worth more than $6 billion and would create thousands of jobs in Texas, California, and Connecticut.

The Bush campaign strove hard to get the most publicity possible out of the announcement. Bush spoke from a platform with two of the steel gray fighter planes on either side of him. A giant banner above him read: "Jobs for America. Thanks Mr. President." That message was repeated on campaign buttons worn by the thousands of aircraft plant workers who gathered to hear Bush deliver the good news. The campaign buttons showed the American and Taiwanese flags, crossed at the staff, and sported the legend: "F-16's for Taiwan. Thanks Mr. President."[4]

As President Bush was making his announcement in Fort Worth, Defense Secretary Dick Cheney signaled from Washington that he was about ready to approve the sale of seventy-two F-15 jet fighter planes to Saudi Arabia, a $9 billion deal that would save thousands of jobs in the St. Louis, Missouri, and Tulsa, Oklahoma, aircraft plants where the planes were made.

George Bush also had some good news for the nation's wheat farmers. Speaking on the front lawn of a classic white clapboard farmhouse in Humboldt, South Dakota, with hay bales strategically scattered about to set the proper pastoral mood, the President said he would spend $1 billion to subsidize American wheat sales in foreign nations. In addition, he pledged $755 million in aid to farmers whose crops were destroyed by a recent hurricane in Florida and heavy rains in East Texas.

Because the economy appeared to be the major issue on the electorate's mind, Bush gave a major speech to the Economic Club of Detroit, Michigan, in which he proposed a number of government initiatives, one of them a tax cut, to speed an economic recovery. The proposals were bound up into a blue booklet and ballyhooed as "An Agenda for American Renewal." The plan had little long-term effect on the campaign, however, mainly because Bush's modified laissez-faire economics generated minimal excitement when compared to the more extensive government economic programs that Clinton was proposing.

Bush sought to counter the success of the Clinton buscapades by doing some campaigning from the back platform of a special railroad passenger train. During one September trip, the nineteen-car train slowly worked its way over a 233-mile, ten-town route through northern Ohio and southern Michigan. Standing on the observation platform of a restored 1924 sleeping car decorated with red, white, and blue bunting and the Seal of the President of the United States, Bush gripped an overhead handlebar for stability and waved and yelled to the large numbers of supporters who clustered at every railroad crossing.

Many of the people gathered along the tracks held their children aloft so they could get a better view of the train and the President. Many were holding handpainted signs expressing their support. Bush moved from one side of the observation platform to the other, seemingly determined to personally greet every person who had taken the trouble to come down to the tracks and watch him go by. "You gotta go the extra mile; take the extra step," Bush said about both his train ride and the campaign ahead. "Just get up there, it's easy to do. Your adrenalin flows on something like this."

Bush stayed out for hours on his observation car platform, holding one-way conversations as he rolled past his many admirers. When the train ran beside some of Michigan's many lakes, families waved from their pleasure boats and swimming rafts. "Children waved from the top of trees whose leaves [were] turning autumn red and gold. Flags flew from windows of farmhouses, and farm families, knee deep in mud or corn, held up banners saying, 'Hi' or 'Wave to me, Mr. President.'"[5]

As the train made its way through classic midwestern towns such as Marysville, Ohio, and Holly, Michigan, Bush unleashed what his strategists hoped would at last be a successful approach: an attack on Clinton as a tax-and-spend liberal who would take money from the middle class to pay for expensive government programs for poor people. Bush said: "We must not take a risk about this economy. Our economy could slide into a disaster if we go back to the misery days of Jimmy Carter, if we make the wrong choice. . . . They're going after the rich, but the middle class always gets up singing the blues. Big government gets the gold, and you get the shaft."

Harold Bryant, a Detroit mechanic, came to hear Bush speak as he passed through Plymouth, Michigan. Bryant said: "I think a lot of people are going to decide at the last minute that they just don't like the idea of a Democrat in there, thinking about that old Democratic tradition of raising our taxes."

Campaigning from the rear of a railroad train appeared to be lifting George Bush's spirits. "This is so exciting out here," the President said. "It's a little tiring, but it's just great. This is the heartland; I get a great wonderful feeling."

The news media kept pointing out, however, that time was beginning to run out for George Bush. Suddenly it was late in September. Election day was less than five weeks away, and the public opinion polls still showed Bill Clinton with a commanding lead. "But the calendar has become George Bush's enemy, almost as much as Bill Clinton," said *USA Today*. "And the President's search for spontaneous political combustion to close the gap with Clinton has become more urgent."[6]

George Bush's problem was not just the public opinion polls and the calendar, however. He was also bedeviled by the electoral college, that constitutionally required instrument through which the presidential votes of the American people must always be filtered. To properly understand the desperateness of George Bush's situation as the presidential campaign of 1992 entered its final month, it is essential to take an in-depth look at the electoral college and the way it greatly alters presidential campaign strategy.

28. The Distorting Effects
of the Electoral College

The American people think of a presidential election as a national election, and 90 percent of the time the news media in the United States cover the presidential election as if it were a national election. Candidates are portrayed as "campaigning across the country," and most media public opinion polls measure nationwide public opinion rather than isolating results from particular states.

In reality, there is no such thing as a "national" presidential election in the United States. Due to the existence of the electoral college, a presidential election is actually fifty-one separate elections, one in each of the fifty American states and the District of Columbia. The most important rule to remember is this: The presidential candidate who carries the popular vote in a particular state in almost all cases gets all of the electoral votes from that state.

The electoral college is provided for in the United States Constitution and dates from the earliest founding of the republic. The delegates from the thirteen original states who gathered in Philadelphia, Pennsylvania, in the summer of 1787 to write a national constitution did not trust the American people to make a wise choice for chief executive. After much debate it was decided to filter the selection of the president through a college of respected citizens who had been chosen by their fellow state citizens for that one task. According to the original conception, electors selected to the electoral college were to review the qualifications of the various candidates for president and then use their own judgment in determining which candidate would receive their one electoral vote.

In the more than two hundred years since the electoral college was first conceived by the nation's founders, many changes have occurred.[1] Most states have passed laws requiring the electors to vote for that candidate for president who won a plurality of the state's popular vote for president. In every state but two, the candidate who wins the popular vote gets all of that state's electoral votes. The only two exceptions are Nebraska and Maine, which give a portion of their electoral votes on the basis of which presidential candidates carry which congressional districts within the state.

In setting up the electoral college, the founders sought to balance the interests of the small states against the interests of the large states. To that end, each state was given two electoral votes to correspond to its two United States senators. This guaranteed that each state, no matter how small, would have two electoral votes, just as each state, no matter how small, is guaranteed two U.S. senators.

In addition, each state was given additional electoral votes equal to the number of representatives each state has in the United States House of Representatives. Since the number of members a state has in the House of Representatives is based on population, this meant that the more populous states would have more electoral votes than the less populous states.

This latter point is the most significant one when talking about the electoral college. The smallest states in terms of population, such as Wyoming and Alaska, have only three electoral votes each (two votes for each state's two United States senators and one vote for each state's one member of the United States House of Representatives). The largest states in terms of population, California and New York, have fifty-four and thirty-three electoral votes respectively. There thus is a tremendous disparity in the number of electoral votes cast by the various states. The obvious result of this great disparity is that presidential candidates spend most of their time, money, and organizing efforts in the states with the greatest number of electoral votes.

This point is one that bears emphasizing. One of the most unfair aspects of the electoral college is that it makes the votes of citizens who live in populous states with many electoral votes more important than the votes of citizens who live in less populous states with few electoral votes.[2]

There is another factor to keep in mind, however. That is the question of how close the race is in any particular state. A state can have a large electoral vote, but if public opinion polls show one candidate leading in that state by a large margin, neither the front-runner nor the trailing candidate will bother to campaign in that state very much. Instead, the candidates will concentrate their efforts in other populous or midsize-population states where polls show the race for that state's electoral votes to be a close one.[3]

To be elected president of the United States, a candidate does not need to win a majority of the popular vote nationwide. All a candidate needs to do is win a majority of the electoral college, which works out to 270 of the total 538 electoral votes. Candidates for president thus quickly develop what is called a "short list." This is a list of the states the candidate is most likely to carry, and has to carry, in order to end up with just over the 270 electoral-vote majority needed to win the electoral college and thereby win the election.

The men and women who are actually chosen as presidential electors do not even get a trip to Washington, D.C., for their efforts. On the second Monday of December, the electors in each state travel to the state capital and cast their votes there. The electoral-vote results from each state are then sent to Washington, where the official winner is certified and inaugurated into office on January 20 of the following year.

For years there has been some interest in Congress in initiating a constitutional amendment to abolish the electoral college and replace it with direct popular election of the president. As with any attempt to change the Constitution, however, there has been resistance, much of it coming from thoughtful scholars who believe it is wrong to abolish a hallowed institution created more than two hundred years ago by the nation's most respected early citizens, the founders.[4] Opposition also has come from senators and representatives from populous states, all of whom know full well that the electoral college gives increased influence over the outcome of presidential elections to voters in their states.

Complicating the effort to rid the nation of the electoral college is the fact that a constitutional amendment must first be passed by a two-thirds-vote of both houses of Congress. This means that two-thirds of the members of the House of Representatives, which is dominated by the populous states which benefit from the electoral college, would have to support such an amendment. It is not very likely that these states will let a constitutional amendment abolishing the electoral college be passed in the House of Representatives.

In addition, minority groups tend to be clustered in a small number of populous states, such as New York, Pennsylvania, and Illinois. Because they are key voting groups in states with many electoral votes, minority voters often get extra special attention from presidential candidates—attention that includes support for government programs that aid minority groups and pledges to appoint more minority-group members to the president's cabinet and other important government posts. Thus the American Jewish Congress has supported keeping the electoral college because Jews are concentrated in and have a major influence over the voting outcome in populous states such as New York and Florida.[5]

Most discussions about the electoral college center around what is known as the "disaster scenario." This scenario occurs when the winner of the popular vote loses the electoral college and thereby loses the election. One such disaster occurred in 1876, when Rutherford B. Hayes, a Republican, won the electoral college although his Democratic opponent, William Tilden, won 50.1 percent of the popular vote. The same thing occurred in 1888 when Republican challenger Benjamin Harrison took the electoral college but incumbent Democratic President Grover Cleveland won the popular vote.

There have not been any disasters in recent presidential elections, but there have been some exciting near misses. In the 1960 presidential election, Republican Richard Nixon almost defeated Democrat John F. Kennedy in the popular vote, despite the fact that Kennedy had an overwhelming lead in electoral votes. If incumbent Republican President Gerald Ford had won ten thousand more votes in Hawaii and Ohio in the 1976 presidential election, he would have won a majority of the electoral college even though Democratic challenger Jimmy Carter had a 2 million-vote lead in the popular vote.

The disaster scenario becomes more probable when there is a viable independent candidate running for president in addition to the Democratic and Republican candidates. This is because the United States Constitution requires that, if no candidate receives a majority of the electoral college vote, the election of the president will be decided in the House of Representatives with each state casting one vote. If a strong third-party candidate wins a number of states and the other states divide their votes evenly between the Republican and Democratic candidates, there is no electoral college majority and the election is thrown into the House of Representatives.

In recent years the closest the nation came to a strong independent candidate pushing the election into the House of Representatives was in 1968 when Alabama governor George Wallace, running on a platform of opposition to racial integration, came within fifty-four thousand votes of denying Republican candidate Richard Nixon an electoral college majority. If that election had gone into the House of Representatives, independent candidate Wallace had made it clear that he would throw his support to the Republican or Democratic candidate who would make the most concessions to his anti-integration ideology.

Early in the 1992 presidential election independent candidate Ross Perot was riding high in the polls and looked as though he might carry many of the states with a large number of electoral votes. At that time, genuine fear was expressed by a number of political commentators that, if President Bush and Bill Clinton closely split the electoral votes in the non-Perot states, the 1992 presidential election might end up in the House of Representatives.

Most states require their presidential electors to vote for the presidential candidate who won the state's popular vote. Some states, however, have no such formal legal requirement, and occasionally an elector will do what the founders had in mind and cast his or her vote for a personal choice rather than the state's popular winner. Thus in 1976, an elector for losing Republican candidate Gerald Ford cast his vote for Ronald Reagan, whom Ford had defeated in the 1976 Republican presidential primaries and caucuses. In 1988, an elector for Michael Dukakis, that year's losing Democratic candidate, cast his vote for that year's Democratic vice-presidential candidate, United States Senator Lloyd Bentsen of Texas.

Average citizens grow weary of hearing about every last detail and nuance of the electoral college. Presidential candidates and their campaign staffs must never lose interest in this arcane and complex political institution, however. It is only through mastering the electoral college, and carefully studying its effects on the presidential election process, that one can master the art of winning a presidential election.

29. The Clinton and Bush Electoral College "Short Lists"

"People tend to think of a presidential campaign as one national effort," said George Stephanopoulos, the Clinton campaign's communications director, "but internally, at this point, all we think about every day is about separate states, putting the 270 electoral votes we need together state by state."[1]

Stephanopoulos gave that quote to the press in late September of 1992, just at the moment the presidential election was really heating up and starting down the home stretch toward election day, now just six weeks away. The realities of the electoral college coupled with the latest public opinion polls had given the Clinton-Gore camp the following electoral college strategy.

Start with California, traditionally a Republican state in recent presidential elections. A deep and lingering economic recession made the state of the economy the top issue with California voters. In addition, a bitter debate over a bankrupt state treasury was swirling around Republican Governor Pete Wilson. The result was that Democrat Bill Clinton had a double-digit lead over Republican George Bush in the California public opinion polls. California's fifty-four electoral votes, the largest number of any state, appeared to be safely in the Democratic candidate's pocket.

Next on the Clinton electoral vote list were the ten states (and the District of Columbia) which Michael Dukakis carried in 1988 in his losing effort against George Bush. If any states were going to vote Democratic in 1992, it was going to be these. They were Hawaii (4 electoral votes), Washington (11), Oregon (7), Minnesota (10), Iowa (7), Wisconsin (11), West Virginia (5), District of Columbia (3), New York (33), Rhode Island (4), and Massachusetts (12). Taken together, these ten states plus D.C. gave Bill Clinton another 107 surefire electoral votes.

Next, look at the South. Prior to the Reagan-Bush years, the South had been the most Democratic part of the country, and it still was Democratic when it came to electing members of Congress, state governors, and state legislators. In the 1980s, however, the Reagan brand of economic and social conservatism had turned the South into the most Republican part of the country where presidential elections were concerned.[2] The only two southern states the Democrats could really count on carrying in 1992 were Clinton's home state of Arkansas and Al Gore's home state of Tennessee. Arkansas's six electoral votes added to Tennessee's eleven put seventeen more electoral votes in the Democratic column.

The Clinton wish list was looking very good at this point. California, plus the ten states (and D.C.) that Dukakis carried in 1988, plus Arkansas and Tennessee totaled 178 electoral votes. Fewer than 100 more were needed to hit the magic number of 270. Because the High Plains states (Kansas, Nebraska, and so on) and the Rocky Mountain West (Idaho, Utah, Wyoming, and the others) tended to vote Republican in presidential elections, the obvious place for Clinton to look for those last necessary electoral votes was in the Middle Atlantic states and the Midwest.

Pennsylvania (23), Maryland (10), Illinois (22), and Missouri (11) were all quickly added to the Clinton short list. George Bush had won these four states in 1988, but by less than five percentage points. Then Ohio (21) and Michigan (18) were added in, two states that had been particularly hard hit by the economic recession, the one issue most damaging to Bush's chances for reelection. These six Middle Atlantic and Midwestern states totaled 105 electoral votes. Added to the 178 electoral votes of the states already on the Clinton short list, they produced a final total of 283 electoral votes, 13 more than the 270 needed for victory.

One cannot say for certain that the states listed in table 29.1 comprised the actual short list adopted by the Clinton campaign. Quite understandably, campaign organizations keep such information and strategizing as secret as possible. In addition, presidential campaigns make alterations to their short lists as the campaign develops and public opinion polls show changed situations in various states. Numerous

TABLE 29.1
The Probable Clinton Electoral College Short List

State	Electoral Votes
1. California	54
2. Hawaii	4
3. Washington	11
4. Oregon	7
5. Minnesota	10
6. Iowa	7
7. Wisconsin	11
8. West Virginia	5
9. District of Columbia	3
10. New York	33
11. Rhode Island	4
12. Massachusetts	12
13. Arkansas	6
14. Tennessee	11
15. Pennsylvania	23
16. Maryland	10
17. Illinois	22
18. Missouri	11
19. Ohio	21
20. Michigan	+ 18

Total: 283 (270 needed to win)

newspaper and magazine articles, however, presented a variety of lists similar to this one, showing the states which Clinton had to carry to win the 1992 presidential election.[3]

The Bush campaign, of course, began developing its short list the same way the Democrats did—starting with the safest states first and building from there. Thanks to the electoral legacy handed to him by Ronald Reagan, George Bush looked to the conservative South as the best place to find Republican votes in a presidential election. The Bush short list thus began with Texas (32 electoral votes), Florida (25), North Carolina (14), and Virginia (13). These states, the four largest in the South, put 84 electoral votes in the Bush column.

But much more from the South than those four states was needed. With polls showing California's fifty-four electoral votes safely in Bill Clinton's hands, Bush needed to pick up a number of midsize states all over the nation to compensate. That meant that every southern state except for Clinton's Arkansas and Gore's Tennessee ended up on Bush's short list. Thus Oklahoma (8), Louisiana (9), Mississippi (7),

Alabama (9), Georgia (13), and South Carolina (8) were added, bringing the Bush electoral vote total from the South to 138.

After the South, the most solidly Republican parts of the country in presidential elections are the High Plains and the Rocky Mountain West. Unfortunately for the Republicans, these states comprise vast land areas but, due to their relatively small populations, have very few electoral votes. Bush needed to win almost every one of them, again mainly because he was not going to win California. The result was a staggeringly long list of states added to Bush's short list, which now was not so short.

The High Plains states on Bush's must-win list were North Dakota (3), South Dakota (3), Nebraska (5), and Kansas (6). The Rocky Mountain states were Idaho (4), Wyoming (3), Utah (5), and Arizona (8). These 37 electoral votes, added to the 138 Bush was counting on in the South, brought the Bush wish list to 175 electoral votes, 95 votes short of the 270 needed to win the election.

A quick twelve votes could be picked up in Indiana, Vice President Dan Quayle's home state, even though some public opinion polls showed Indiana a toss-up. The Bush-Quayle campaign managers probably figured that if they could not win in Indiana, they had no chance of winning the election at all. With Indiana's 12 figured in, only 83 more electoral votes were needed to hit that magic 270.

It was not much, but three more electoral votes could be counted on in Alaska, which had been voting strongly Republican in recent years.

Although public opinion polls showed Bush behind Clinton in most of the midwestern states, it was in the Midwest that he had the best chance of catching Clinton. As a result, Missouri (11), Wisconsin (11), Michigan (18), and Ohio (21) were added to the Bush critical list. The 61 votes of those four states brought the Bush theoretical total to 251. To put the campaign safely over the top, the Bush campaign managers added New Jersey (15), Connecticut (8), and Colorado (8), giving the Bush-Quayle short list a total of 282 electoral votes, 12 more than the 270 needed to win.

As with the Clinton probable short list, one cannot say for certain that the states listed in Table 29.2 comprised the exact Bush short list. This much can be said for certain. Ten days before election day, the Bush campaign told the Associated Press that it was particularly targeting Texas, Florida, Georgia, North Carolina, Colorado, Missouri, Wisconsin, Michigan, Ohio, New Jersey, and Connecticut.[4]

It is significant to note that there are only twenty states on the probable Clinton short list, but there are twenty-seven states on the

TABLE 29.2
The Probable Bush Electoral College Short List

State	Electoral Votes
1. Texas	32
2. Florida	25
3. North Carolina	14
4. Virginia	13
5. Oklahoma	8
6. Louisiana	9
7. Mississippi	7
8. Alabama	9
9. Georgia	13
10. South Carolina	8
11. North Dakota	3
12. South Dakota	3
13. Nebraska	5
14. Kansas	6
15. Idaho	4
16. Wyoming	3
17. Utah	5
18. Arizona	8
19. Indiana	12
20. Alaska	3
21. Missouri*	11
22. Wisconsin*	11
23. Michigan*	18
24. Ohio*	21
25. New Jersey	15
26. Connecticut	8
27. Colorado	8

Total: 283 (270 needed to win)

* States on both the Clinton short list and the Bush short list.

probable Bush short list. The reason the Bush list was so much longer than the Clinton list was because of Clinton's big lead in California. Bush had to strive to win a large number of midsize states in order to compensate for not having California's fifty-four electoral votes. The task of putting together an electoral college majority without California is so difficult that campaign insiders refer to it as "threading the needle."

By now, the major effect of the electoral college on presidential election campaigns should be obvious. Both candidates tend to concentrate their efforts in states which wind up on both candidates' short lists. In the case of the 1992 presidential election, the four states that ended up on both the Clinton and the Bush short lists were Missouri, Wisconsin, Michigan, and Ohio.

The other side of the coin is that presidential candidates tend to waste no effort whatsoever in states where, according to public opinion polls, one candidate or the other has a big lead. This particularly happened to California in 1992. Bill Clinton's lead over George Bush was large at the beginning of the campaign and never narrowed significantly. As a result, neither candidate invested much time or money in the Golden State.

Veteran campaign watchers know that the simplest way to divine the candidates' electoral college strategies is to monitor their respective travel schedules. Labor Day weekend is the traditional jumping-off point for presidential general elections. Labor Day 1992 found Bill Clinton campaigning in Missouri and Ohio. Not surprisingly, George Bush also started off in the Midwest, stumping through Ohio, Michigan, and Wisconsin.[5]

The electoral college also influences the way the various candidates purchase and run their television advertising. In the 1992 presidential election campaign, the Clinton campaign limited its television advertising to just twenty states—the twenty states where polls showed the race was close. States that saw a particularly large number of Clinton television advertisements were Michigan, Ohio, Missouri, and Connecticut. The Clinton campaign aired no commercials in New York and California, even though both those states were on the Clinton short list, because Clinton was leading in the polls in those two states by such wide margins.

The Bush-Quayle campaign was forced to take a somewhat different approach. Because Bush was lagging behind Clinton in the polls in so many of the states on the Bush short list, national television advertising had to be purchased in an effort to catch up in a large number of states simultaneously. The Bush campaign purchased time on national television on such shows as ABC's *Monday Night Football*. It was nearly impossible to pursue a targeted strategy when running behind in so many states. "They're trying to get their numbers up generally while they determine which states they're going to seriously compete in," explained Don Sipple, a Republican media consultant.[6]

By the time there was only one month to go before election day, the Clinton strategists stopped looking at their short list and began looking at Bush's. The large lead which Clinton gained over Bush at the close of the Democratic convention had not faded. Clinton was leading Bush in the polls not only in the states on the Clinton short list but also in states in the South, the West, and New England that, in recent presidential elections, had been regarded as safely Republican.

The Clinton forces thus did some campaigning and ran some television ads in states not on their short list, mainly to knock the Bush campaign off balance. Locally tailored Clinton ads began airing in Texas, Bush's home state and considered safe for the Republicans. The ads attacked Bush's poor economic record nationally and his failure to create more jobs in the Lone Star State. When public opinion polls showed that Clinton might have a chance of winning Florida, a state previously thought safe for Bush, the Clinton campaign ran television ads specifically directed at Florida's large number of elderly voters.

"Every time we go to a Bush state," said Clinton communications director George Stephanopoulos, "we pin Bush down another day in his own bunker. Look at the places where Bush is spending his time now: Mississippi, Alabama, North Carolina, Texas. . . . We are forcing him to spend great amounts of time defending his own turf."[7] It went without saying that, if the Clinton forces could tie George Bush up in what were once thought to be safe Republican states, Bush would have less time to campaign in the crucial swing states of the Midwest—Missouri, Wisconsin, Michigan, and Ohio.

USA Today summed up the overall effect of the electoral college on the 1992 presidential election advertising campaigns this way: "The result is a patchwork. Voters in battleground states see far more ads than anyone else. [Because of Clinton's wide lead in the polls,] voters in traditionally Republican strongholds see more ads—from both Clinton and Bush—than they're used to. Voters in states where Clinton has apparently insurmountable leads see little more than what filters through on network programs or cable."[8]

By late September of 1992, it was obvious that President George Bush was not just running against Bill Clinton, his popular Democratic opponent. He also was running against the distorting effects of the electoral college, and the Clinton campaign was exploiting those distortions as effectively as possible.

30. A Tale of Two Rallies

Colorado had the good fortune in 1992 of being on George Bush's short list of states which he had to win in order to get a 270-vote majority in the electoral college. The result was that a steady stream of presidential candidates, vice-presidential candidates, and candidates' wives visited the state throughout the fall campaign. In one spectacular week in mid-September, George Bush and Bill Clinton each held a major political rally in the Denver area. The Bush rally was held in the Denver suburbs on Tuesday, September 15, 1992. The Clinton rally was held in downtown Denver just two days later, on Thursday, September 17.

The Bush rally was staged in a modern industrial park in one of Denver's more upscale suburbs. The parking lot of Jeppesen Sanderson, Inc., a high-tech manufacturer of airline charts and pilot training videos, had been cleared of automobiles and closed off with temporary fencing. Those who wanted to see President Bush and hear his talk had to show an admission ticket and pass through a metal detector in order to get into the rally area. The tickets were mainly distributed by Republican Party officials in Colorado and were somewhat hard to come by.

Clearly, the emphasis at the Bush rally was on security. By choosing a location deep in a suburban industrial park, the rally organizers greatly reduced the probability of uninvited guests walking by and deciding to come to the rally. Virtually everyone in attendance was an invited guest or an official member of the press. To make it even more difficult for "crashers," people who came by private automobile had to park in distant parking lots and ride a shuttle bus to the rally area. No ticket? No bus ride. As is typical when the president of the United States travels, police and security officials were everywhere.

Despite the high security, the setting for the rally was quite charming. The parking lot was well-paved and heavily landscaped. Colorful sunburst locust trees, their yellow leaves shimmering in the bright western sunshine, were scattered throughout the parking lot along with an occasional grove of evergreen trees. The modern office and factory buildings of the industrial park provided a pleasant backdrop for the festivities. The customary wooden booths were present at which the Republican faithful could buy hot dogs, hamburgers, soft drinks, and Bush-Quayle campaign paraphernalia while waiting for the President to arrive.

As always seems to happen at George Bush political rallies, early comers were entertained by a series of musical groups playing and singing songs from the 1950s and 1960s. Most notable was Forever Plaid, a four-man singing group reminiscent of such male quartets of yesteryear as The Four Lads and The Four Freshmen. Dressed in red, blue, and green plaid tuxedos, Forever Plaid not only sang in harmony but also did little dancesteps in unison across the stage. The older people at the rally were delighted. The younger people either paid no attention or were turned off by it all.

After vocalizing such golden oldies as "Moments to Remember," "No, Not Much," "Shangri-La," and "Three Coins in the Fountain," the four young men took a break and explained to all who would listen that they were currently starring in a musical comedy titled *Forever Plaid* playing in downtown Denver. When pressed on the subject, they confessed they were not backing George Bush for president but had volunteered their services in order to promote their show. "And we're strictly bipartisan," said one member of the group. "Thursday night we'll be singing at a reception in Denver where Bill Clinton will be the guest of honor."

Forever Plaid was followed by a number of country-and-western musical groups. One of them, The Tom Stipe Band, made a point of singing songs with titles like "Should Have Stood By Her" and "Family Ties." Lead singer Tom Stipe said he was an avid Bush supporter who consciously chose music that would reflect "strong Republican family values."

It was good there was plenty of entertainment at the Bush rally, because the President was a long time coming. It was a warm September day without a single cloud in the sky, and the waiting crowd, which eventually grew to about five thousand persons, started to get a little sun-baked. Two marching bands from local high schools had been recruited to play patriotic music in the moments just before the President arrived. At last the presidential limousine appeared and the bands began to play. George Bush stepped out of the limousine, waved to the crowd, mounted the speaker's platform, took off his suitcoat, and began his talk.

Bush's speech was barely fifteen minutes long. He began by noting that the Communist threat had come to an end during his tour of duty in the White House. He said: "I'm proud to be the first president to visit Colorado and say the Cold War is over and freedom finished first."

Bush then launched into a vigorous attack on Bill Clinton's economic policies, describing Clinton's ideas as "that tired old tax-and-spend philosophy" that would "feed the overfed bureaucrats in Washington, D.C."[1] Bush said Clinton "wants to give the government more power." As for himself, Bush said he was interested in "giving you, the American people, more power."

Bush labored to work some humor into his attacks on Clinton. After charging that Clinton's grandiose spending plans would surely raise everyone's income taxes, Bush looked seriously at his audience and said: "I think every day is the Fourth of July and America's best days are ahead of her. Bill Clinton thinks every day is April 15th [the day income tax returns are due]."

Then the President attacked the Arkansas governor for his lack of knowledge of foreign policy. Bush particularly emphasized the point that Clinton had never taken a clear stand on whether or not he supported United States military involvement in the Persian Gulf War. "The only reason Clinton wants to get into the Oval Office," Bush said, "is so he'll have a place to run around in circles in."[2]

The overall theme of Bush's speech was that Clinton never makes a definite statement and thus should not be trusted with the presidency of the United States. The President emphasized that there were big differences between him and his Democratic opponent. "A Grand Canyon divides me and my opponent on the issues," Bush said. "You see it in every issue that we care about: education, health care, economic growth, creating jobs." Bush also took a jab at the public opinion polls that showed him running far behind Clinton. "The polls may show us behind today," he said, "but I know we are going to be ahead in November, because we have the right ideas."[3]

Almost as soon as it had begun, George Bush's quarter-hour address to his Colorado supporters was over. A group of elementary school children had been lined up at the foot of the stairs leading down from the speaker's platform. The President came down the steps and spent no more than five minutes posing for photographs with the children and shaking hands with their teachers. There was no opportunity at all for members of the general audience to try to shake Bush's hand or shout personal encouragement to him. The minute the photographers' flashbulbs stopped popping and the television cameras switched off, the President was back in his limousine and off to a $5,000-a-plate fund-raising luncheon at a nearby hotel.

The five thousand people who had waited for as long as three hours on a sun-soaked parking lot to see George Bush had not seen very much of him. He was at the rally for little more than twenty minutes. Saddest of all was the fate of the four-man singing group, Forever Plaid, that had entertained the crowd so enthusiastically before the President's arrival. They very much wanted to be photographed with George Bush, but the best they could do was gather around the limousine as the President was leaving and have a picture snapped as Bush was getting into the car. Only three of the Plaids were able to get into the photograph, and the President was paying no attention to them as he went by.[4]

This failure of George Bush to really "connect" with his audience, even an audience of five thousand carefully selected supporters, was not unique to the Denver rally. According to Stephen Hirsh, the White House news producer for ABC News, the Bush effort was not "taking off" anywhere it went. Hirsh explained: "There's no focus to the Bush campaign. It's not well organized. It's not reaching the critical mass [needed to generate real enthusiasm and excitement]. The really big crowds aren't turning out to see George Bush. The campaign lacks color. It lacks splash. There's no flash of brilliance on the Bush side of things. Most of all, there's too much emphasis only on what's in front of the camera. Bush is not shaking hands or having much human contact with his audience."[5] Hirsh gave the impression that Bush's failure to spend more time with his rally audiences was hurting him—badly.

Two days later Bill Clinton held his Colorado rally in downtown Denver. The setting was the Greek amphitheater in Denver's Civic Center Park, the same place where Ross Perot had held his petition-turning-in ceremony for Colorado some two months earlier. The site of the Bush rally had been remote and protected. The Clinton rally site, in contrast, was much more open and accessible. Anyone, whether a homeless person or a high-powered businessman, could easily walk the few short blocks from the heart of downtown Denver to the Clinton rally site. The rally was scheduled from noon to 1 P.M. in order to catch a big lunch hour "walk-in" audience.

And big the audience was. By just before the noon hour more than thirty thousand persons were milling about the bronze statuary and still-in-bloom flower beds in Civic Center Park. At thirty thousand this crowd was six times the size of the crowd that had gone to hear President Bush. Many people brought blankets and a basket of food and prepared to enjoy the festivities picnic-style, sitting or lying on the grass. Outside the Greek amphitheater, a large system of loudspeakers had been set up so that those who could not get into the amphitheater could easily hear Clinton's speech if not see him give it.

Tickets were required to get into the amphitheater itself. As with all presidential campaign rallies, the areas closest to the podium were limited to staunchly committed supporters and the press. The Democratic Party had been in charge of distributing the tickets, and the amphitheater had quickly filled with a large group of well-dressed and enthusiastic Clinton supporters. There was some disappointment expressed when people without influence in the Colorado Democratic Party learned they were not going to get into the amphitheater without a ticket, and that tickets were hard to come by.

There was no live vocal entertainment before the Clinton rally as there had been at the Bush rally. A small jazz band, with a saxophone lead, provided the prespeech entertainment. This was background music only, setting a mood and allowing personal conversations to proceed unaffected.

Because of the large number of people present and Bill Clinton's comfortable lead in the public opinion polls, the Clinton rally very quickly achieved what ABC's Stephen Hirsh had called "critical mass." There was a definite feeling of excitement in the air—a sense that something really important was about to take place. With each passing minute, more and more people walked from downtown Denver into the park, adding to the excitement. People were everywhere, sitting on park benches, standing on grassy knolls, and climbing up statues and lampposts to get a better view.

Because of its openess, the Clinton rally had the feeling of the public marketplace and the country fair. A group from ACT UP was present, outside the amphitheater, waving signs and yelling slogans for gay and lesbian rights. A pro-life activist was handing out the customary photographs of an aborted fetus, but not too far away young women from NARAL (the National Abortion Rights Action League) were handing out green and white posters saying "I Vote Pro-Choice." One man carried a handmade sign that read, "Not every sperm needs a name." This "Y'all come!" atmosphere contrasted strongly with the tight security so prevalent at the Bush rally.

Right on schedule, Bill Clinton appeared on the stage in the Greek amphitheater with Denver mayor Wellington Webb, a Democrat, and

Colorado governor Roy Romer, also a Democrat. Mayor Webb opened the official proceedings by declaring it "Bill Clinton Day" in Denver. Governor Romer added to the already prevalent mood of success by announcing that, at thirty thousand persons, this was the largest rally in Colorado political history, even larger than the crowd of twenty-five thousand people who had turned out to see Democratic President Harry Truman in Denver in 1948.

Promptly at 12:30 P.M. Bill Clinton began his speech. He went right to the economic issue, charging that the failed economic policies of the Reagan and Bush administrations had left the nation with unacceptably high unemployment. He then attacked the Republican National Convention held the previous August in Houston. Clinton picked up on the news media's theme that the Republican confab was pitched so strongly to the religious right that it promoted "religious warfare." The Democratic nominee then moved on to the family values issue, promising that his presidency would be "pro-family and pro-choice" all at the same time.[6]

As he had done throughout his entire campaign for the presidency, Clinton rattled off a stream of statistics and mentioned a wide variety of United States government programs that he supported and would expand. Unlike President Bush, who did not relate his Colorado speech to Colorado issues, Clinton focused on a number of items of local concern. One was the National Renewable Energy Laboratory in Golden, Colorado, which conducts research on developing viable alternative fuels. "It has been allowed to die on the vine under Reagan and Bush," Clinton charged. "It will flourish like a flower in the desert under Clinton and Gore."[7]

The Democratic nominee even referred to Bush's comment two days earlier that a "Grand Canyon" divided the two candidates on the issues. "Boy, is he right about that," Clinton said. He then noted that, whereas the Republican approach is to remove government from as much of everyday life as possible, his approach was to make government a positive force in people's lives. He explained: "I have done my best for nearly a year now to offer the American people a new approach, one that goes beyond trickle-down economics without going back to tax-and-spend economics, one that says we have to invest in our people and their jobs and their education and their health care."[8]

After speaking nonstop for twenty minutes, Clinton waded into the crowd in the Greek amphitheater for a round of handshaking. It was literally a "round" of handshaking, because the Clinton managers had constructed a circular boardwalk at the foot of the speaker's platform about 100 feet in diameter. The audience had been allowed to fill the large area in the center of the circular boardwalk as well as the area outside, but only Bill Clinton was allowed on the boardwalk itself.

As Clinton walked slowly around the boardwalk, he reached into the crowd on both sides to shake hands. So great was the crowd's enthusiasm, and so large the number of hands extended in his direction, that he mainly grabbed mobs of hands simultaneously. There was a constant chorus of cheers and greetings from the audience. With so many people present, it took Clinton a full half hour to make just one circumnavigation of the boardwalk. He then made a second trip around as additional persons plunged into the crowd and struggled to get close enough to the boardwalk to touch his hand and hear his voice. In all, Clinton spent fifty-five minutes doing two round-trips around the boardwalk. By the time he was finished, his shirt was soaked through with perspiration.

The raised circular boardwalk was an extremely successful media device. The effect of putting Bill Clinton, and no one else, on the board-walk was to have his head and shoulders stand out above everyone else's in the still photographs and the television coverage. The ubiquitous press platform was located so that every photographer and camera operator had a perfect shot of Clinton and his adoring supporters.

Throughout this exciting and emotionally charged handshaking session, a medley of recorded songs played on the loudspeaker system. Popular hits of the past ten years, such as "Man in the Middle" and "Lean on Me," had been specifically chosen to appeal to voters between the ages of twenty and forty. Sung by recording artists like Michael Jackson and Fleetwood Mac, the songs were filled with lyrics that related well to the election campaign: "I'll be your friend," "You just might have a problem that I understand," "It's up to you," "We all shine on," "Everyday people," "Our numbers are many, but our hearts beat as one," and "Gonna make a difference, gonna make it right."[9]

Anyone who attended both the Bush rally and the Clinton rally in Colorado in September of 1992 could not help but be struck by the contrast in the way the two men related to their respective audiences. Bill Clinton gave almost an hour to handshaking and greeting, and the crowd responded with boundless enthusiasm. George Bush gave only enough time to get a few fast photographs and television takes, and most of his crowd left the rally vaguely disappointed.

The Clinton rally ended with the feeling that here was a candidate enjoying surging success. The Bush rally ended with the feeling that a desperate struggle lay ahead, and things needed to change—and change a lot—if the struggle were going to end successfully.

The night of his big Denver rally, Bill Clinton attended a $5,000-a-plate fund-raising dinner. As they had said they would, the Forever Plaid singing group provided a portion of the entertainment. Bill Clinton took the two to three minutes required to pose for a photograph with the quartet. All four of the young men were in the photograph with Clinton, who was smiling broadly and had his arm around the shoulder of one of the Plaids.[10]

31. THE RETURN OF ROSS PEROT

On Thursday, October 1, 1992, with slightly more than a month to go before election day, Ross Perot jumped back into the presidential race. He made his announcement from his campaign headquarters in Dallas, Texas, flanked by his wife, Margot, three of his five children, and his vice-presidential candidate, retired Rear Admiral James Stockdale.

Perot was able to reenter the election because, even though he had withdrawn his candidacy the previous July 16, his volunteer organization continued working and put his name on the ballot in all fifty states and the District of Columbia. Between the time Perot dropped out of the race and the time he got back in, the Texas computer billionaire spent $7 million of his own money to keep his political movement rolling along.[1]

"I know I hurt many of you who worked so hard through the spring and summer when I stepped aside on July 16," Perot said in his reentry speech. He claimed he was once again running for the White House because neither President George Bush nor Democratic nominee Bill Clinton was willing to prescribe the bitter medicine needed for the United States economy. To Perot, the required cure was a 50-cent-a-gallon tax increase on gasoline and massive cuts in government spending. Perot explained: "I thought that both political parties would address the problems that faced the nation. We gave them a chance. They didn't do it. . . . The American people are ready to address [the budget deficit] and fix it and both of the other parties say it's political suicide to talk about it. I'm not interested in political suicide, but I do understand the American people are ready to deal with this."

Unconventional as ever, Perot read a prepared speech and then walked out without answering questions from the news media. He returned after news reporters accused him of purposely avoiding them.

Asked if he had come back into the contest just to harm President Bush's reelection prospects, Perot denied that he disliked George Bush. He pointed out that, throughout the earlier portion of his candidacy, he had only criticized Bush for his performance as president and had never attacked him personally.

At the end of the impromptu questioning, Perot said he would likely join President Bush and Democratic nominee Clinton in any upcoming presidential debates. "Sure, I'll be glad to participate," Perot said as he strode out the door.[2]

The second phase of Ross Perot's campaign for the presidency got off to a roaring start with $24 million of paid television advertising in the first two weeks. A few days before getting back in the race, Perot brought together a group of Dallas advertising executives which he called the 270 Group. The "270" referred to the number of electoral votes required to win the election.

In addition to a well-done series of sixty-second television commercials, Perot and his advertising team produced a number of "infomercials," thirty-minute paid television commercials designed to look like regular news programming. Sitting at an office desk with bookshelves and a window in the background, Perot spent the entire half hour just talking plain Texas talk to his audience. He devoted the earlier shows in his infomercial miniseries to discussing the national economy, the later shows to describing his life and his values.

The first "Perot Show" aired on October 6, 1992, and amazed everyone by attracting 16 million viewers. It was the second most popular network show in its time slot. The entire program consisted of Ross Perot using some two dozen flip charts and a metal pointer to dissect the causes of the economic recession.

Unlike most political advertising, this program appeared to respect the intelligence of the American people and their ability to comprehend the seriousness of the fiscal crisis facing the nation. Holding up one economic chart after the other, Perot talked about such weighty subjects as the never-ending increases in the national debt and recent patterns in government spending (more and more spending each fiscal year). As Perot presented one gloomy economic fact after another, he made clear his concern about and disgust with the way the nation was being run. He said: "We used to have the world's greatest economic engine. We let it slip away and with it went millions of jobs and taxpayers. Let's take a little time to figure out what's happened to the engine. Let's raise the hood and go to work. Let's diagnose the problem. I can tell you before we look at the engine, an engine tune-up ain't going to fix it. We're going to have to do a major overhaul."

Perot's call to America to "raise the hood and go to work" on the United States economy became one of the hallmarks of his revived presidential effort. Perot frequently referred to the comment himself, and it was repeated over and over again by newspaper reporters and television commentators covering the Perot campaign. The idea that the American economy needed a "major overhaul" and not just a "tune-up" was one that Perot succeeded in planting in the national consciousness for the remainder of his presidential effort.

In his matter-of-fact, homespun attack on the state of the economy, Perot did not mention either President Bush or Democratic challenger Bill Clinton. He did, however, criticize both major political parties for allowing a stalemate to develop between a Republican White House and a Democratic Congress. He explained: "The American people are good, and yet over time we have created a country that's a mess. We have a situation in which our President blames Congress, Congress blames the President, the Democrats and Republicans blame each other. Nobody steps up to the plate and accepts responsibility for anything, including the $4 trillion debt which you and I must pay for."[3]

This first Perot infomercial and the ones that followed became one of the big surprises of the 1992 presidential election campaign. In recent decades no candidate for president had ever devoted a half hour of paid national network television time to an uninterrupted speech. The ruling political wisdom was that a single "talking head" was the most boring thing in television and would drive viewers away rather than attract them. Ross Perot launched the second coming of his presidential campaign with an innovative and unique form of "sole-proprietor" political television that drew large audiences and convinced many listeners that the United States economy was, indeed, in dire straits.

Political commentators were quick to note, however, that Perot was skillfully using his paid infomercials to avoid the kind of press and public questioning faced by candidates who campaign the old-fashioned way with live speeches and direct interviews with the media. By sticking almost exclusively to thirty-minute paid programs, Perot was attempting to sell himself to the American people without being accessible to penetrating and possibly embarrassing questions from news reporters. As one newspaper columnist put it: "There's an undemocratic queasiness about the way Perot will apparently run— buying hunks of TV time . . . and avoiding the public rowdiness Clinton and even Bush endured for 10 months."[4]

The minute Ross Perot put himself back in the presidential race, political analysts began speculating as to whether his renewed candidacy would help Republican George Bush or Democrat Bill Clinton. A *Washington Post*-ABC News poll, conducted just before Perot made his surprise reentry, showed Perot stealing nine votes from Clinton for every six votes stolen from Bush, thus suggesting Perot would mainly help Bush's faltering candidacy.[5] Other analysts argued that Perot would harm Clinton in the Midwest, which Clinton needed to win the election, but would simultaneously hurt Bush in Texas and Florida, the two southern states that represented the "base" of Bush's support in the electoral college.

At least on the surface, the Clinton campaign appeared to be much more worried about the renewed Perot candidacy than the Bush campaign was worried about it. Beginning in August there had been negotiations between the Clinton camp and the Perot camp to find a way to let Perot stay out of the race, throw his support to Clinton, and still be able to claim a moral victory. By mid-September Clinton and Perot were talking directly to each other on the telephone, but they failed to reach agreement on the tough issues separating them. Perot came back into the race despite the strong efforts of the Clinton camp to get him to stay out.[6]

Later in the campaign, during an appearance on the *CBS Morning News*, Bill Clinton said there was no question that Ross Perot was pulling more votes from him than from George Bush. Clinton explained: "[The President] hopes that the anti-Bush vote will be divided [between Clinton and Perot] and he can sneak right up the middle."[7]

The Bush campaign, for its part, did seem to think that Perot's reentry might shake up the race and force voters to think anew about whom they were voting for. This would be good for President Bush, because Clinton was continuing to run far ahead in the public opinion polls, particularly in California and the big northeastern and midwestern states with large numbers of electoral votes. Perot's renewed candidacy would tend to "break things up, shake things up," a senior Bush campaign adviser said.[8]

Ross Perot reentered the 1992 presidential election just at the time the two major candidates were completing their negotiations for a series of nationally televised debates. The same day Perot aired his first infomercial, his campaign managers formally accepted an invitation from Republican President George Bush and Democratic challenger Bill Clinton to join the upcoming debates.

32. BUSH'S LAST CHANCE: THE 1992 PRESIDENTIAL DEBATES

There is one element in presidential election campaigning that somewhat reduces the limiting effects of the electoral college. The presidential debates, broadcast live on national television into every one of the fifty states, force the candidates to make nationwide appeals and behave as though they are running for a national office. For that brief period in mid-October that the presidential debates are taking place, electoral college "short lists" take a backseat as the presidential contenders work at looking good to a vast audience of the nation's voters.

Not that the electoral college "short lists" are completely forgotten. Obviously, debating presidential candidates work very hard at saying things they think will increase their popularity in the big states with many electoral votes. The big difference is that every voter in the United States, no matter what state he or she lives in, can watch the debates on television and thereby relate to the campaign—and the candidates—in a very direct way.

Televised presidential debates are a relatively new addition to presidential election campaigns.[1] The first one was held in 1960, when Republican candidate Richard Nixon, the incumbent vice president, agreed to a series of television debates with his Democratic opponent, Senator John F. Kennedy of Massachusetts.

Kennedy was relatively unknown at the time, and the television debates enabled him to present his case to the American people in a direct, personal, and appealing fashion. Nixon suffered in those first debates from having a poor makeup job which, in the era of black-and-white television, made him look unshaven and sinister. When Kennedy narrowly won the 1960 presidential election, many observers gave much of the credit to Kennedy's winning performance in the television debates.[2]

In fact, Kennedy's use of the first televised presidential debates to steal the White House from Richard Nixon put a sixteen-year hex on presidential candidate debating on national network television. It was not until 1976 that Gerald Ford, the incumbent Republican president, agreed to debate Jimmy Carter, a former Democratic governor of Georgia. Ford had succeeded to the presidency when Richard Nixon had resigned following the Watergate scandal, and Ford believed he could improve his "presidential stature" with the American people by agreeing to debate his less well-known opponent.

Once again a presidential debate proved to be a key factor in who eventually won the election. In answer to a direct question from a newspaper reporter, Gerald Ford made a very definite statement that Eastern Europe was no longer under Soviet domination. This was a remark which, at a time when the former Soviet Union had troops stationed throughout the region, appeared stupid at worst and uninformed at best. A week of "clarifications" by the Ford campaign failed to change the impression that the incumbent president might not know as much about foreign affairs as he ought to know. Democrat Carter narrowly won the election, and Ford's "gaffe" in the presidential debates was given a large share of the credit.[3]

Since incumbent President Gerald Ford had been willing to debate Jimmy Carter in 1976, Carter was more or less obligated to agree to debate when he came up for reelection in 1980. Lightning struck a third time, however, when Carter's Republican opponent, former California governor Ronald Reagan, turned to the television cameras and asked a question of the audience which proved to be devastating to Carter's hopes of being returned to the White House. Reagan intoned: "Are you better off than you were four years ago?" The question, in effect, was asking voters to compare their present situation with what things were like when Carter was first elected four years earlier. Reagan asked his question at a time when the nation was experiencing "stagflation"—a slumping economy coupled with double-digit inflation. Millions of television-watching voters answered Reagan's question with a resounding "No!" and went out and voted for Reagan on election day. Reagan ended up winning the election over Carter handily.[4]

The 1976 and 1980 presidential debates set a powerful precedent that has not been violated since. All presidential candidates, even well-known incumbents or those with wide leads in the public opinion polls, are regarded as obligated to participate in television debates. Two clear rules of strategy have emerged over the years, however. Number one: Don't say anything that sounds stupid (the way Ford did in 1976). Number two: Watch out for "zingers" (like the one Reagan launched at Carter in 1980).

As the 1992 presidential debates were about to get underway, the prevailing opinion was that they represented George Bush's last hope of somehow whittling down Bill Clinton's comfortable lead in the public opinion polls. The debates were an opportunity for Bush to go before a national television audience and, with a superlative performance on his part or a major failure on Clinton's part, catch up quickly in a large number of states all at once. If this did not happen in the television debates, it was said, Bush's last chance to catch Clinton would be gone.

All three candidates had major goals they wanted to achieve in the debates. Bill Clinton wanted to continue to hammer on the economic issue and confirm the national mental image of Bush as an economic incompetent. The Bush campaign wanted to make more of an issue of Clinton's character, striving to "change this from a referendum on the times to a referendum on two people."[5] Ross Perot wanted to attack both of the other candidates, but particularly the calamitous budget deficits that had built up during Bush's presidential years.

The first of three presidential debates was held on Sunday evening, October 11, 1992, in the field house at Washington University in suburban St. Louis, Missouri. Before a large audience, more or less equally divided among supporters of the three candidates, George Bush, Bill Clinton, and Ross Perot responded to questions from representatives of the news media and then rebutted each other. All three candidates were aware that one of the most important events in the fall campaign was about to begin.

The first dramatic exchange in the debate was not long in coming. During the week leading up to the first debate, President Bush had been making a point of the fact that Bill Clinton had participated in anti-Vietnam War demonstrations in 1969 while studying as a Rhodes Scholar at Oxford University. Furthermore, Clinton had paid a visit to Moscow while at Oxford. Bush was quick to inject this issue into the debate. He said: "I think it's wrong to demonstrate against your own country or organize demonstrations against your own country in foreign soil. I just think it's wrong. . . . I couldn't do that. And I don't think most Americans could do that."[6]

Clinton responded by accusing Bush of impugning his patriotism. He then said that Bush's attack was reminiscent of Senator Joseph McCarthy's witch-hunting attacks on Communists forty years earlier. In a slick turnabout, Clinton noted that George Bush's own father, the late Senator Prescott Bush, had roundly criticized McCarthy for carelessly accusing people of not being loyal Americans. Clinton said: "When Joe McCarthy went around this country attacking people's patriotism, he was wrong. He was wrong. And a senator from Connecticut stood up to him named Prescott Bush. Your father was right to stand up to Joe McCarthy. You were wrong to attack my patriotism. I was opposed to the war, but I love my country."

Presidential debaters are always hoping to get "the big sound bite," that one part of the debate that is played over and over again on television news programs in the hours and days following the debate. Clinton's accusation that President Bush was behaving like Joe McCarthy became "the big sound bite" of the 1992 presidential debates. In addition to being played repeatedly on television, the McCarthy charge played prominently in all the newspaper stories and political columns concerning the debates.

As the first debate continued, independent candidate Ross Perot slowly began to play more of a leading role. He made a number of pithy remarks that made good television news quotes and were repeated in the next day's newspaper stories. Throughout the debate Bush had been emphasizing the idea that a president needed to be experienced. When it was his turn to speak, Perot picked up strongly on the experience issue: "I don't have any experience in running up a $4 trillion debt. I don't have any experience in gridlock government, where nobody takes responsibility for anything and everybody blames everybody else. I don't have any experience in creating the worst public school system in the industrialized world, the most violent crime-ridden society in the industrialized world. But I do have a lot of experience in getting things done."

When not fending off attacks from both Clinton and Perot, President Bush sought to convince the voters that he was preparing to take real action to end the nation's economic problems. He promised to keep James A. Baker III, who had done such a good job as Bush's secretary of state, at the White House as a sort of domestic policy czar. At the very end of the debate, Bush introduced the theme that he hoped would eventually discredit Clinton and thereby revive the flagging Bush campaign. The President said: "I hope as president that I've earned your trust. . . . I hope I've earned your trust because a lot of being president is about trust and character. And I ask for your support for four more years to finish the job."

The minute the first debate was over, the collected news analysts and political commentators of America set about the task of deciding which of the three candidates had won. There was unusual unanimity. George Bush had not performed poorly in the first debate, but he had needed a big victory in order to start catching Bill Clinton in the public opinion polls and had not gotten such a victory. Clinton had been slightly more impressive than Bush, but all he really needed to do was not commit a major gaffe, and he never even came close to saying the wrong thing or otherwise messing up. Final conclusion: Clinton won because nothing happened to disturb his big lead in the polls.

The candidate who appeared to have benefited most from the first debate was Ross Perot. Many viewers told pollsters they thought Perot was the clear winner, as did a Kansas State University professor of speech who graded the debate for Gannett News Service.[7] Perot's peppery speaking style and opposition to both political parties had given him most of the best lines. The judgment that Ross Perot had won was so universal that, two nights later, the Bush camp was spinning the idea that, by winning the debate, Perot was beginning to steal lots of votes from Clinton and thereby help the Bush candidacy.

Perhaps the biggest winner was the concept of holding presidential debates. According to overnight television rating services, the first debate drew a larger audience than an American League baseball playoff game being televised on a competing channel. In fact, it was no contest. The debate, carried by ABC, NBC, and Fox, gained a 38.4 rating. The baseball game, playing on CBS, had a much smaller 8.3 rating. Each rating point represented 436,000 homes.[8]

Two nights after the first presidential debate, on Tuesday evening, October 13, 1992, the three vice-presidential candidates had their turn to debate. Dan Quayle, the incumbent Republican vice president, immediately went on the attack. In his opening statement, he charged that "Bill Clinton does not have the strength or the character to be president." Quayle then began developing the theme that Clinton was just another tax-and-spend liberal. Clinton will "raise taxes, increase spending, and enlarge government," Quayle said. "Can you really trust Bill Clinton?"[9]

Democratic vice-presidential candidate Al Gore, who appeared to be overprepared, did not respond to Quayle's lively attack on Clinton's character, a failure which later was said to have greatly upset Clinton. Gore did a creditable job, however, of lambasting the Republicans on the economic issue. "When it came to the recession," Gore noted, "they were like a deer caught in the headlights, paralyzed into inaction." Later on Gore turned to Quayle and pointedly asked: "When are you guys going to start worrying about our people—here—in America—and get our country moving again."

The most interesting debater was Ross Perot's vice-presidential running mate, retired Navy Admiral James Stockdale, who made a number of humorous comments about his obvious lack of political experience. His opening comment was: "Who am I? Why am I here?" Later on, when he had run out of things to say, Stockdale told the television audience he was "out of ammunition." His most telling point, which drew a loud round of applause, came when Republican Quayle and Democrat Gore got into a shouting match over Bill Clinton's conflicting statements about the recent Persian Gulf War. In the midst of all the yelling, Stockdale chirped: "I think America is seeing right now why this nation is in gridlock."

Commentators noted a grim irony in the vice-presidential debate. The Republicans finally got their attack on Bill Clinton's character going, but it was Dan Quayle rather than George Bush who started scoring points. Sadly for the Bush campaign, its best attack on Clinton came in a vice-presidential debate with a much reduced television audience.

The second presidential debate was held two days after the vice-presidential debate, on Thursday, October 15, 1992, in Richmond, Virginia. The Clinton forces were getting nervous as the second debate began. Ross Perot was starting to move up in the polls, and as he did so he was stealing votes from Clinton in the West and among younger voters all across the country. In addition, after his strong performance in the vice-presidential face-off, Dan Quayle was proving a popular guest on the morning television talk shows.

Clinton thus needed a victory in the second presidential debate, and he got it. One reason was that "it followed a format that he had suggested and had already mastered: questions from an invited studio audience of selected uncommitted voters."[10] Bush got in trouble when a young Black woman asked him how the national debt was affecting him personally. The question was confusing—she probably meant to ask how the economic recession, rather than the national debt, was affecting him personally. "I'm not sure I get it," Bush replied, and asked the woman to repeat the question. His eventual answer was rambling and unspecific.

When it was his turn to respond, Clinton walked toward the young woman and answered the question as if it had been about the economic recession. He "established eye contact and talked warmly about how much pain the national debt caused in a small state like Arkansas, where the governor personally knew people who lost their jobs when companies went bankrupt." In other words, "Clinton connected."[11]

A very telling event occurred toward the end of the second debate. Shortly after Clinton had scored so effectively in his answer to the young Black woman, the television cameras caught Bush looking at his watch. That one simple "moment" on national television spoke volumes. Time was running out for the president. Bush had been "late getting organized, late appointing James Baker to pull his floundering campaign together, late settling on a theme—a good three months behind on almost everything."[12] It was now late in the second of three presidential debates, and everyone could see that the President's campaign had yet to catch fire and really start moving forward.

The third presidential debate was held the following Monday, October 19, 1992, in East Lansing, Michigan. On this night, George Bush went on the attack, much as Dan Quayle had done in the vice-presidential debate. The President charged that Clinton's economic plan would "raise taxes on all incomes over $36,600 per year, bring back high interest rates, and bring back the high inflation of the Carter years." Bush argued that his economic plan would "lead America and the world out of the recession." The President concluded that his plan would "grow the economy." Bill Clinton's plan would "grow the government."[13]

"Mr. and Mrs. America," Bush said, "when you hear him say we're going to tax only the rich, watch your wallet. Because his figures don't add up and he's going to sock it right to the middle-class taxpayer and lower, if he's going to pay for all the spending programs he proposes."[14]

Seeking to denigrate Bush's promise to make James Baker III his domestic policy czar, Clinton stated: "The person responsible for domestic economic policy in my administation will be Bill Clinton." Bush got his best sound bite of all three debates when he replied: "That's what worries me."[15]

Clinton's bland performance in the final presidential debate was attributed to his deciding to "coast on his lead, doing and saying nothing to stir things up."[16] The result of the coasting was that Bush began catching up in the polls for the first time since the summer. His campaign had become focused at last—on the twin issues of taxes and trust. The only question was whether there was enough time left, just two weeks, for Bush to catch up to Clinton and win the election.

In reality, the situation for George Bush following the debates was nowhere near as favorable as it first appeared. Because the presidential debates were a national phenomenon, Bush was beginning to catch up with Clinton only in the national public opinion polls. In California and the states of the Northeast with the most electoral votes, Clinton remained far ahead of Bush. When the last presidential debate ended, Bush lost his national platform. "From this point on," wrote David S. Broder of the *Washington Post*, "Bush will have no forums of the kind the three debates and their gigantic audiences provided. The only saturation coverage his remarks will receive will come in the communities he visits. And there are too many places where his standing needs bolstering for him to visit in the remaining time."

Broder hammered away on this idea that, now that the debates were over, the electoral college was badly skewing the presidential election in favor of Bill Clinton. "The minute [they] wound up the third and final presidential debate last Monday night," Broder wrote, "the national campaign was over. From now on, it is 51 separate races—in the 50 states and the District of Columbia—and that is a big problem for George Bush."[17]

33. The End of the Path

The national momentum which George Bush had generated in the final presidential debate continued to grow. As election day neared, he surged to within five points of Bill Clinton in one of the national polls. The President was campaigning hard and "on his message," attacking Clinton on the "trust and taxes" issue at every opportunity.

The message that Bush was delivering personally on television talk shows and at campaign rallies was further supported with television advertising in the key states Bush felt he must win to gain a majority in the electoral college.[1] One widely distributed advertisement hammered extra hard on the trust issue. It consisted of a series of average Americans talking about Bill Clinton. The script read:

> Man #1: "If you're going to be president you have to be honest."
> Man #2: "Bill Clinton hasn't been telling anything honestly to the American people."
> Woman #1: "The man just tells people what they want to hear."
> Man #2: "About dodging the draft."
> Woman #2: "I think he's full of hot air."
> Man #3: "I wouldn't trust him to be commander in chief."
> Woman #3: "I think that there's a pattern, and I just don't trust Bill Clinton."

> Woman #4: "I don't think he's honorable. I don't think he's trustworthy."
> Man #4: "You can't have a president who says one thing and does another."
> Woman #4: "Scares me. He worries me. You know, and he'll just go one way or another."

This particular ad used ordinary-looking people to slap the "you can't trust him" label on Bill Clinton. One woman even mentioned "a pattern," suggesting that not telling the truth was a recurring facet of Clinton's behavior. President Bush was saying the word "pattern" over and over again in his campaign statements about Clinton's lack of trust-worthiness. By using ordinary people in the ad, the Bush campaign was able to make harsh attacks on the Democratic candidate's character appear somewhat less abrasive.[2]

The Clinton campaign's polling and focus groups revealed that Bush's attacks and the TV ads on the trust issue really were beginning to harm the Democratic candidate.[3] Furthermore, voters seemed to have such a low opinion of Clinton's character that ads attempting to portray him as trustworthy simply did not work. The Clinton camp thus went back to their strongest issue—the economy—and renewed the attack on Bush on that point. One Clinton television spot showed a young man reading classified ads in the newspaper in the kitchen while his mother looked on. The young man turned to the camera and said:

> Since I graduated I've done telemarketing. I was a bicycle messenger.
> I hope in the future to get a job in my field and from there start my own life, but there are no jobs. I feel trapped, having to live at home. The Republicans really do not know what the average American is going through.
> The Democratic plan is the plan that makes the most sense. I really believe that the Democrats would bring a lot of hope and enthusiasm to this country.

The ad ended with these words on the television screen: "The Democratic Party. A plan that works for a change."

This ad illustrated an idea that became a principal Clinton theme as the 1992 presidential campaign came to a close. This was the idea that Bill Clinton had a definite plan to end the economic recession and that the plan would work. The ad was designed to divert the viewer's attention from Bill Clinton personally—neither his picture nor his name appeared anywhere in the ad—and focus the viewer's thoughts on George Bush's failed economic policies.

Bush's skillful handling of the "trust and taxes" issue not only was gaining votes for Bush but also was rapidly shifting votes from Clinton to Ross Perot. Ten days to go before election day, Perot hit 20 percent support in the public opinion polls and looked likely to go even higher. At the Clinton campaign headquarters in Little Rock, the view was "that 20 [percent] for Perot spelled danger for Clinton and 25 [percent] could be death."[4] Clearly, Bush's best hope for winning the election was that Perot would continue stealing votes from Clinton and thereby allow Bush to eke out a narrow victory in a tight three-way race.

At this point in the campaign, Ross Perot made an important campaign decision. His first two half-hour television shows had been on the flagging national economy and the burgeoning national debt. The popularity of these two television programs was a major factor in the Texas billionaire's late surge in the polls. Instead of continuing to attack on economic issues, however, Perot devoted his subsequent half-hour programs to "warm and fuzzy" descriptions of his life and his family. Perot the economic doomsayer suddenly turned into Perot the loving husband, father, and employer.

In the ads, Perot presented himself to the television audience as a self-effacing civic and corporate hero who had devoted his life almost as much to philanthropy as to making money. "Money is the most overrated thing in the world," Perot told his viewers. "You need enough money to take care of your family, but beyond that, the only worthwhile use of having money . . . is to do constructive things for others."

Perot also emphasized his business philosophy in his final series of thirty-minute television shows. He said he always followed a "three musketeers" policy, "one for all and all for one," and he claimed he boosted employee morale by treating his workers as if they were members of his family. He said his management style was to live the motto: "I care about what you can do and what you've done lately."[5]

Just at the moment when his half-hour ads were playing to large audiences and he was gaining in the polls, Perot took another one of those inexplicable turns that completely wrecked a surging campaign. Appearing on CBS's 60 Minutes just nine days before election day, Perot said he had withdrawn from the presidential race the previous July, not because it would be best for America, but because he had heard "rumors" that Republican "dirty tricksters" planned to ruin his daughter's upcoming wedding. Perot had little or no solid evidence for the charge—he would only attribute the rumors to "friends"—but he felt at the time that the safest course of action was to abort his candidacy. Supposedly, Perot told an incredulous viewing audience, the Republicans were going to release a faked lewd photograph of his daughter to the tabloids just a few days before her wedding day.

Overnight, the terms "crazy" and "paranoid" once again seemed to apply to Ross Perot. People could not believe that a major contender for the United States presidency would take such totally unsubstantiated rumors so seriously—and act so wildly. Perot then compounded the problem the day after the *60 Minutes* fiasco by telling reporters that the sources for these rumors were none of their concern. Perot sagged badly in the polls, so badly that he no longer had a chance of carrying even one state and its electoral votes. As Perot's candidacy quickly faded, so did the Bush campaign's hopes of winning a close three-way race.

Six days before election day, the message of the public opinion polls was mixed. Republican hopes surged as a Gallup poll for CNN and *USA Today* showed Bush just two points behind Clinton nationwide. Other major newspaper and television network polls gave Clinton a comfortable, but rapidly diminishing, six- to seven-point lead.[6]

Informed observers of American presidential politics were not fooled by any of these national samples, however. Individual state polls indicated Bush was trailing Clinton in fourteen of the twenty-nine or so states he needed to win in order to gain a majority in the electoral college. The hoopla in the press over the tightening national polls was just that—hoopla and hype. When one looked at the prospective electoral college results, there was absolutely no hope for George Bush to win with only six days to go before the voting. *Newsweek* reported that, "according to the Bush campaign's own polling data, the gap between Bush and Clinton had not closed in many key states."[7]

Not that the Bush campaign was about to give up. Bush campaigned vigorously across Ohio, a state which he had to win and where the polls showed the race was close. By now the Republican assault on Clinton had come down to one word: trust. In a flurry of quick rallies in Lima, Toledo, and Columbus, Bush hammered on the theme that Clinton was trying to "be all things to all people." In Strongsville, a town near Cleveland, Bush stood across from the Town Hall and said to a cheering crowd: "I'll tell you what's going to decide this election: it's going to be character and trust."

Also, in the final week of the campaign, Bush began to criticize Clinton for his "sorry record" during the twelve years he was governor of Arkansas. "Governor Clinton better clean up his mess in Arkansas before fooling around with the United States of America," the President said.[8] The Bush organization backed up this theme with what many observers thought was one of Bush's best television attack ads. It showed Arkansas as a barren wasteland, with a hungry vulture perched in a dried-up tree. As dust storms swirled across this forlorn and empty montage, an announcer recited the sorry statistical status of employment, income, education, and civil rights in Clinton's Arkansas.

At first the Clinton campaign responded directly to Bush's all-out and free-swinging attack on the trust issue. The Clinton line was that Bush was untrustworthy himself. "Every time Bush talks about trust, it makes chills run up and down my spine," Clinton told a large crowd at an evening rally in Louisville, Kentucky. "The very idea that the word 'trust' could come out of Mr. Bush's mouth after what he's done to this country and the way he's trampled on the truth is a travesty of the American political system."[9]

As had the Bush camp, the Clinton forces came up with an attack television ad on the trust issue. The ad showed clips of President Bush making optimistic pronouncements about the national economy, but after each Bush prediction an announcer pointed out how the promised result was never achieved. The ad concluded with a question that had an obvious answer: "Can we afford four more years?"[10]

The final weekend before election day, however, the Clinton campaign went back to its most solid issue: the economy. Over and over again it played a television ad in which the names of famous economists who supported Clinton's economic plans scrolled continuously down the screen. The ad left the impression that almost every leading economic thinker in America was behind Bill Clinton and his fiscal remedies. The ad concluded by noting that an independent panel of economic experts convened by *Time* magazine saw Clinton as having the best economic proposals.[11]

The Friday before election day produced the biggest surprise event of the 1992 presidential election campaign. A federal grand jury in Washington, working with special investigator Lawrence Walsh, handed down a new criminal indictment of former Secretary of Defense Caspar Weinberger, who had served under Ronald Reagan at the time George Bush was vice president. The indictment charged Weinberger with making false statements to Congress during its investigation of the Iran-Contra affair.

Iran-Contra was a government scandal in which the Reagan Administration was accused of secretly selling antitank missiles to Iran and using the money to finance anti-Communist rebels in Nicaragua, a program which the Congress had voted to eliminate. If the Reagan people really were helping anti-Communists in Nicaragua, they were violating a law of Congress, and that would have been a scandal of major proportions.

George Bush had contended throughout his presidency that he had no knowledge of the Iran-Contra dealings that took place while he was vice president. Bush consistently claimed he was "out of the loop." The new Weinberger indictment, coming four days before election day, contained a note of Weinberger's stating that Bush had been present at a meeting where important Iran-Contra decisions had been made. It suggested that Bush was more familiar with the details of the Iran-Contra affair than he had previously acknowledged.

This surprise disclosure completely deflated George Bush's efforts to raise questions about Bill Clinton's truthfulness and win votes on the "trust" issue. The news media gave the story prominent play, particularly CBS, which devoted the first fifteen minutes of its Friday evening television newscast to the new Weinberger indictment and its implications concerning Bush's honesty.[12] Clinton immediately seized on the new disclosure by calling a news conference during a campaign stop in Pittsburgh, Pennsylvania. Clinton said: "Secretary Weinberger's note clearly shows that President Bush has not been telling the truth when he says he was out of the loop."[13] Later, Clinton charged that the new indictment "not only directly contradicts the President's claims [but] diminishes the credibility of the presidency."[14]

The effect of this last-minute disclosure on Bush's standing in the public opinion polls was immediate. Overnight the Republican President's late surge in the polls sputtered and died.[15] The Saturday before election day, a campaign aide brought Bush the grim new figures. The President made no effort to hide his vexation, even though there were news personnel present. He took off his baseball cap and threw it down on the table.[16] By Monday morning the situation was totally lost. The Gallup Poll for CNN and USA Today, which the previous week had shown Bush within two points of Clinton nationwide, now had Clinton with a comfortable seven-point lead.[17] The situation with the electoral college, which had never looked good for Bush, now was completely hopeless. Whenever newspaper reporters pointed out to the Clinton campaign that Bush was still fairly close to Clinton in one or two of the national polls, the Clinton people would emphasize that the Democratic nominee "held steady leads in more than enough states to fashion an Electoral College majority."[18]

Adding to George Bush's problems was the fact that, even before the new Weinberger indictment, the news editors of America had looked at Bush's woeful position in the electoral college and decided that Bill Clinton was going to be elected the next president of the United

States. The result was a series of major stories strongly hinting that Clinton had already won the election, even though the election had not been held yet.

Newsweek began this process two weeks before election day when it devoted its cover story to the idea that the Bush campaign was "Running Out of Time."[19] That same week Time ran a banner headline saying the campaign was ending up with "Clinton in Control."[20] One week later Newsweek put a large picture of Bill Clinton on its cover with the headline: "President Clinton? How He Would Govern." Only the question mark after Clinton's name suggested that perhaps the election was still in the future.[21]

Not to be outdone, Time put Clinton on its cover the weekend before election day along with the headline, "Bill Clinton's Long March." The accompanying story had the sort of length and detail that suggested Time considered Clinton all but elected.[22] In its day-before-election-day issue, U.S. News & World Report had the honesty to point out that all the other newspapers and magazines were running "the current spate of it's-all-over stories." After making this charge, U.S. News ruminated at great length on what the results might be "if Clinton wins big."[23]

Amazingly, the news editors who decided to run all these Clinton's-got-it-won stories did so at a time when the public opinion polls showed the race tightening and one prominent national poll, the Gallup Poll, had Bush within two points of Clinton. How could they be so confident that Clinton was going to win? The answer, of course, was their knowledge of the electoral college and the fact that Clinton had comfortable leads in the vast majority of the states with large numbers of electoral votes.

If anyone had any doubts that the electoral college was still controlling Clinton's and Bush's activities the last days before the election, they only needed to look at the two candidates' travel schedules. Bush started out in the crucial Midwest, giving a major address in Auburn Hills, Michigan. He moved on to Stratford, Connecticut, and Madison, New Jersey, hoping to win more votes in those two crucial East Coast states. Then it was back to the Midwest with stops in Akron and Cincinnati, Ohio, and Louisville, Kentucky. Bush made a final stop in Baton Rouge, Louisiana, and then headed home to Houston, Texas, where he would wait while the nation voted.

Although Bill Clinton now was painfully hoarse from giving so many speeches and talking with so many voters, his last two days' travel schedule was even more ambitious than Bush's. As Bush had done, Clinton started in the Midwest, at Cincinnati, Ohio, and then moved to the East, stopping in Philadelphia and Wilkes-Barre, Pennsylvania, and East Rutherford, New Jersey. Next it was back to the Midwest, with rallies in Cleveland, Ohio; and Romulus, Michigan; and St. Louis, Missouri; and Paducah, Kentucky.

Clinton was so determined to win the election that he did not stop campaigning as the sun set the evening before election day. On his campaign roared to McAllen and Fort Worth, Texas, followed by a late-night stop in Albuquerque, New Mexico. At 5 A.M. on election day, Bill Clinton spoke to a large and enthusiastically wide-awake crowd at the airport in Denver, Colorado. He concluded his travels in his hometown of Little Rock, Arkansas, where he would spend the long hours of election day waiting for the nation's verdict.[24]

Bush's and Clinton's final travel schedules left no doubt as to what the electoral college race had come down to. The final areas of battle were the Midwest—principally Ohio, Michigan, and Kentucky—and the East—particularly New Jersey. Because these four states were all fairly large in terms of population and the polls showed the race in each of them to be close, they received the lion's share of the last-minute attention from both campaigns.

Suddenly, after more than a year of frenetic political activity, it was election day. The news media reported an unusually heavy turnout of voters and an unexpectedly high level of interest in the presidential election and its outcome. As darkness began to fall on the East Coast and then westward across the nation, Americans gathered in front of their television sets and by their radios to learn who had won and by how much.

The fun began shortly after 7 P.M. eastern standard time, when the polls closed in a large number of East Coast states. As the votes began to come flooding in, the television networks began making predictions and "calling" states as having voted for one candidate or the other. Thus by 7:15 P.M. CBS called both Vermont and New Hampshire for Clinton. To the well-informed, however, neither of these two results meant very much, because neither Vermont nor New Hampshire were on Bush's electoral college "short list." There was still an outside chance for lightning to strike and Bush to win the election.[25]

Just before 8 P.M. eastern time, however, the election was over for anyone who knew anything about the electoral college. CBS called Georgia, a key state on Bush's short list, for Clinton. Hope immediately faded for every politically astute Republican across the country.

Scant minutes later, shortly after 8 P.M. EST, Bush's doom was totally sealed when CBS gave both Michigan and New Jersey to Clinton. The next thirty minutes saw two more of Bush's short list states,

Missouri and Connecticut, fall into the Clinton fold.

At 8:45 P.M. eastern time Clinton was leading Bush in the electoral college by 238 to 33. That meant that California, which would report in late but would certainly give its 54 electoral votes to Clinton, would put Clinton over the top of the 270 electoral votes needed to win. As it turned out, however, enough of the states on Bush's short list went to Clinton that the Arkansas governor did not need California.

Colorado went Democratic just before 9 P.M. EST, closely followed by Louisiana and Wisconsin. The race was tight in Ohio, but when the Buckeye State finally went to Clinton, the Democratic candidate had all the electoral votes he needed even without California. CBS declared Clinton the certain winner at 10:48 P.M. eastern time, a full twelve minutes before the polls even began to close in California.

As soon as the major television networks had all called the race for Clinton, George Bush went to his election night hotel in Houston, Texas, and graciously conceded the election. Speaking to a ballroom filled with subdued supporters, the now lame-duck President said: "The people have spoken, and we respect the majesty of the democratic system. I ask that we stand behind the new president." When asked about his future plans, Bush said he planned "to get very active in the grandchild business—and find ways to help others."

About ninety minutes later, when there was absolutely no doubt that he had won the election, Bill Clinton appeared before some forty thousand supporters at the old Arkansas statehouse in Little Rock. It was the same spot where he had announced his candidacy for president a year earlier. Standing outdoors on a cold, clear night before a backdrop of red, white, and blue bunting, Clinton seemed genuinely moved by George Bush's concession speech and his call for solidarity behind the new president-elect. "I ask all of you to join with me to express our gratitude for a lifetime of service," Clinton said, noting that Bush had served both as a young torpedo plane pilot in World War II and as commander-in-chief of the armed services during the Persian Gulf War.

Clinton then looked into the audience and returned to the major theme—change—which had brought him to this sweet moment of victory. "My fellow Americans," he said, "on this day with high hopes and brave hearts, in massive numbers, the American people have voted to make a new beginning."[26]

As soon as all the votes were counted, the political commentators went to work dissecting and analyzing the election results. The final tally in the popular vote showed Bill Clinton with 43 percent, George Bush with 38 percent, and Ross Perot with 19 percent. Conservative newspaper columnists were quick to point out that 57 percent of the

TABLE 33.1
The 1992 Presidential Election Electoral College Results

Clinton		Bush	
1. Arkansas	6	1. Alabama	9
2. California	54	2. Alaska	3
3. Colorado	8	3. Arizona	8
4. Connecticut	8	4. Florida	25
5. Delaware	3	5. Idaho	4
6. District of Columbia	3	6. Indiana	12
7. Georgia	13	7. Kansas	6
8. Hawaii	4	8. Mississippi	7
9. Illinois	22	9. Nebraska	5
10. Iowa	7	10. North Carolina	14
11. Kentucky	8	11. North Dakota	3
12. Louisiana	9	12. Oklahoma	8
13. Maine	4	13. South Carolina	8
14. Maryland	10	14. South Dakota	3
15. Massachusetts	12	15. Texas	32
16. Michigan	18	16. Utah	5
17. Minnesota	10	17. Virginia	13
18. Missouri	11	18. Wyoming	3
19. Montana	3		
20. Nevada	4	*Total*	*168*
21. New Hampshire	4		
22. New Jersey	15		
23. New Mexico	5		
24. New York	33		
25. Ohio	21		
26. Oregon	7		
27. Pennsylvania	23		
28. Rhode Island	4		
29. Tennessee	11		
30. Vermont	3		
31. Washington	11		
32. West Virginia	5		
33. Wisconsin	11		
Total	*370*		

American people voted against Bill Clinton, going either for Bush or Perot. Liberal commentators were equally quick to respond that, although Clinton only won 43 percent of the popular vote, he won 100 percent of the White House.

The electoral college was another matter. Clinton got 370 electoral votes compared to only 168 for George Bush and 0 for Ross Perot. Just as the electoral college overfavored the leader in the public opinion polls during the campaign, it overfavored the winner of the popular vote on election night. Clinton may have received only 43 percent of the popular vote, but he garnered a whopping 69 percent of the electoral college.[27]

Why had Bill Clinton won and George Bush lost? Most analysts contended that the major factor was the sour economy and President Bush's failure to appear to be doing very much about it. The Clinton campaign managers had it exactly right when they put up that sign in the Little Rock headquarters saying "The Economy, Stupid."[28]

Bush also was hampered by the fact that he had prepared to be a "foreign policy" president rather than a "domestic policy" president. For most of his career in government he had served in diplomatic posts or as director of the Central Intelligence Agency, which is totally focused on foreign affairs. As vice president, he had mainly traveled overseas to visit world leaders rather than touring the United States and talking to local politicians. As president, he had drawn on his knowledge of things international to organize the broad coalition of nations that helped the United States win the Persian Gulf War. But, as *New York Times* reporter Richard L. Berke pointed out, "Bush never communicated to the American people what he was doing in foreign policy and how important it was."[29]

In the end, Bush's foreign policy emphasis worked against his domestic efforts. While serving as president "he was comfortable with the status quo to the point of complacency." As long as the economy was healthy, "Bush's hands-off attitude brought little public protest. But when the economy soured—and the recovery stalled—Bush's inaction was viewed as indifference to people's needs."[30]

The economy and Bush's failure to do something conspicuous about it were not the only explanations for Clinton's big victory. The Arkansas governor was greatly admired for the quality and tone of his victorious campaign. He had set out to win the South back to the Democratic Party in presidential elections. He achieved a significant part of that goal by carrying, not just his home state of Arkansas and Al Gore's home state of Tennessee, but also Georgia and Louisiana.

Most important, outside the South, Bill Clinton reunited Black Democrats with working-class White Democrats and thereby restored the biracial voting alliance that is crucial to a Democratic Party presidential victory. Particularly in the Northeast, the Midwest, and California, Clinton ran almost even with Bush among White voters but polled so strongly among Blacks and other minority groups that he easily won the key states in those regions with the most electoral votes.[31] Bush was left with a small chunk of the electoral college pie that consisted of only the South (mainly Florida and Texas) and the low electoral vote states of the High Plains (Kansas, Nebraska, the Dakotas, and so on) and the Rocky Mountain West (Arizona, Idaho, Utah, and so on).

A number of political analysts praised Bill Clinton for projecting an image to the voters that was neither "too liberal" nor "too left wing." Throughout the campaign Clinton described himself as "a different kind of Democrat" and a "new Democrat," thus separating himself in many voters' minds from the more demanding liberal groups in the Democratic Party. According to Thomas Byrne Edsall, Clinton succeeded in keeping the support of these left-wing groups—"among them homosexuals, women, the disabled, and those who advocate more help for the homeless"—but did not favor them so strongly that he lost the votes of "the white working class and lower middle class that had traditionally provided the core of the [Democratic] Party's support."[32]

Political scientist Gerald M. Pomper attributed Clinton's success in 1992 to his ability to unite the "new" Democratic Party of the 1960s and 1970s with the "old" Democratic Party of the 1930s, 1940s, and 1950s. Clinton got the votes of the "new" advocates of social liberalism, mainly women's rights supporters, as well as the votes of the "old" advocates of economic liberalism, the New Deal Democrats. In Pomper's view, Clinton "modernized" the traditional economic appeals of the Democratic Party, making them appropriate "for a nation with higher average incomes and higher expectations."[33]

Another political scientist, John Kenneth White, saw Clinton winning because of the "mood" he created in his campaign for the White House. "But already this much is clear: Americans responded to Clinton's call to have the 'courage to change,' and supported him—not for his detailed issue positions, but because he believed in the values of opportunity, community, and responsibility, and for his confidence that we can do better as a people and a country. . . . [Voters] seem willing to support a leader who strikes the correct moral or reaffirming tone."[34]

Bill Clinton turned out to be a much better television campaigner than George Bush, particularly on morning shows, talk shows, and phone-in-style town halls.[35] If that was not trouble enough for Bush, Ross Perot developed the half-hour political infomercial and used it to hammer home Bush's alleged economic failings. "It is sad that George

Bush . . . would go out befuddled by twin plagues of a new age, Information and Intimacy Overload. And flummoxed as well by two post-modern media archetypes: Ross Perot, who may well be the ultimate talk-show guest, and Bill Clinton, who seems destined to become the ultimate American talk-show host."[36]

The long and tortuous 1992 path to the United States presidency had at last come to an end. Bill Clinton had won the election, but he had not yet won the support and the confidence of the American electorate. Even after the election was over, polls continued to show that the voters still were not overly enthusiastic about any of the three candidates. As president, however, Clinton would be judged by his record in office, not the skillful election campaign that had put him there.

34. Toward an Amendment for the Popular Election of the President

Once again in 1992 the presidential election process used in the United States avoided the "disaster scenario" implicit in that venerable old institution known as the electoral college. Despite the fact that Ross Perot mounted an inconsistent but well-financed independent candidacy, all of the electoral votes went to one or the other of the two major party candidates. One of them, Democratic nominee Bill Clinton, won a clear majority of the electoral votes and thereby won the election. The remote but ever present possibility that a presidential election might have to be settled in the United States House of Representatives was avoided one more time.

But just because the electoral college did not produce calamitous results in 1992 does not mean the institution should be retained. In fact, many things occurred in the 1992 fall general election campaign that strongly suggested that the electoral college should be abolished. Its greatest drawback is that it makes voters in large- and midsize-population swing states much too important and voters in small-population states and states strongly committed to one candidate or the other of no importance whatsoever. As are so many other aspects of the presidential selection system in the United States, the electoral college is unfair and does not treat the voters in the various states in an equal manner.

The citizens of each state of the United States should have the power to directly vote for their president. Candidates running for president should know that every citizen has an equal vote, for then the candidates would focus their campaigns nationally rather than concentrating on a limited number of closely contested states with large numbers of electoral votes.

How unfair was the 1992 presidential election campaign because of the existence of the electoral college? Which states' voters participated the most, and which states' voters were neglected the most? Table 34.1 identifies those states that received maximum campaign attention in 1992, those that received a moderate amount, those that received virtually no attention because they strongly supported George Bush, and those that received virtually no attention because they strongly supported Bill Clinton.

Table 34.1 indicates that maximum campaigning took place in only twelve states and moderate campaigning in ten. That means that voters in only twenty-two states, with approximately 45 percent of the national population, were exposed to the 1992 presidential campaign in an intense way.

The table also shows that twelve states were so committed to George Bush and seventeen states so committed to Bill Clinton that there was virtually no presidential campaigning in those states and very little television advertising. That suggests voters in twenty-nine states, with approximately 55 percent of the national population, were, to all intents and purposes, nonparticipants in the 1992 presidential election campaign. They got to vote, and they got to watch on television what was happening in other states, but that was about all they got.

The effects of the electoral college are more far-reaching than most Americans realize. It is an institution that no longer serves the historical purpose for which it was created and that has had many unintended and unfair consequences. It should be eliminated and replaced by direct popular election of the United States president.

The job of eliminating the electoral college belongs to the United States Congress. A constitutional amendment is required, and, as previously noted, such an amendment first would have to be passed by a two-thirds vote in both the Senate and the House of Representatives. Following this challenging achievement, the constitutional amendment would then have to be approved by three-fourths of the state legislatures (thirty-eight out of fifty) before becoming part of the United States Constitution.

An Amendment for the Popular Election of the President would provide for presidents to be elected exactly the way governors and United States senators are elected in most of the states. Votes for president would be tabulated on a national rather than a state basis, and

TABLE 34.1
Campaign Attention to the Fifty States
in the 1992 Presidential Election

Maximum Campaign Attention		Moderate Campaign Attention	
State	Electoral Votes	State	Electoral Votes
Colorado	8	Alabama	9
Connecticut	8	Indiana	12
Georgia	13	Louisiana	9
Florida	25	Maine	4
Kentucky	8	Montana	3
Michigan	18	Nevada	4
Missouri	11	New Hampshire	4
New Jersey	15	New Mexico	5
North Carolina	14	South Carolina	8
Ohio	21	Vermont	+ 3
Texas	32		
Wisconsin	+11	Total	61
Total	184		

Minimal Campaign Attention (safe for Bush)		Minimal Campaign Attention (safe for Clinton)	
State	Electoral Votes	State	Electoral Votes
Alaska	3	Arkansas	6
Arizona	8	California	54
Idaho	4	Delaware	3
Kansas	6	District of Columbia	3
Mississippi	7	Hawaii	4
Nebraska	5	Illinois	22
North Dakota	3	Iowa	7
Oklahoma	8	Maryland	10
South Dakota	3	Massachusetts	12
Utah	5	Minnesota	10
Virginia	13	New York	33
Wyoming	+ 3	Oregon	7
		Pennsylvania	23
Total	68	Rhode Island	4
		Tennessee	11
		Washington	11
		West Virginia	+ 5
		Total	225

whoever gets the most votes wins. In a three- or four-way race, a plurality of votes rather than a majority of the total votes cast would be sufficient to determine the winner.[1] In the highly unlikely event of a tie for first place in the national popular vote, the winner would be chosen in the House of Representatives from among the two candidates who tied.

The president and vice president are the only officials of the United States government who are elected on a national basis. For that reason alone they should be elected by a national constituency expressing its will through a national popular vote. Individual state interests already are quite well represented in the United States Senate and the United States House of Representatives, where every member comes from and serves the interests of a particular state. It is time to abolish the electoral college and place the president and vice president under a nationally-oriented, rather than a state-oriented, electoral system.

35. REFORMING THE FLAWED PATH

In one sense, the 1992 presidential selection process was a complete success. Although the 1992 road to the White House was as long and complex as ever, in the end one candidate stood out above all the others and was elected president of the United States. As it was designed to do, the presidential selection process produced one—and only one—winner.

There also was no question that, by the time Tuesday, November 3, 1992, rolled around, Governor Bill Clinton of Arkansas was the popular choice of a plurality of American voters to take over the White House. Although it was true that Clinton did not receive a majority of the popular votes, he received substantially more than any of the other candidates who ran for president in 1992. The person who was *elected* president was the person whom the largest number of Americans wanted to *be* president.

This book has recommended three major reforms designed to eliminate major flaws in the presidential election process. The first reform is the adoption of a Model Calendar of State Presidential Primaries and Caucuses (see Chapter 19). This reform makes a sincere effort at scheduling presidential primaries and caucuses in such a way that every voter in every state would have the opportunity to participate in a presidential primary or caucus in a meaningful way.

The second reform is the creation of a Preprimary National Mini-Convention in both the Democratic and Republican parties (see Chapter

25). Although the present national party conventions serve no nominating purpose (the nominees are selected in the early primaries and caucuses), they retain considerable importance as week-long national television advertisements for the two political parties. In addition to the summer national conventions, both parties should hold mini-conventions of their elected officials just before the spring primaries and caucuses begin. The function of these winter mini-conventions would be to rank the major contenders for the party nomination for president, thereby giving the average voter something of a guide as to who the more qualified candidates might be.

The third reform, the adoption of an Amendment for the Popular Election of the President, would eliminate the electoral college and replace it with a popular election of the president of the United States (see Chapter 34). This would be the most difficult of the three reforms to achieve because it would require a two-thirds vote in both houses of Congress and majority support in three-fourths of the state legislatures.

How would the presidential selection system in the United States function if these three reforms were adopted and implemented? How would the "new" system differ from the present system? And, most important, what kinds of presidential candidates would be more likely to be nominated and win the general election with these three reforms in place?

Begin with the Preprimary National Mini-Convention, since it would be the first formal event in this new presidential selection process. This reform will cause candidates for president to focus their preprimary campaigns on elected officials who are members of their political party as well as on the news media. Under the present system, the candidates focus their preprimary campaigns almost exclusively on the news media.

Under this reform, there will be many more presidential candidate visits to and meetings with prominent elected officials in the party, particularly United States senators and representatives, governors, key state legislators, and big-city mayors. In many cases, elected officials who are going to the mini-convention will call press conferences and officially announce the candidate they are supporting for the party nomination for president. An important side effect will be increased media attention to and therefore more national publicity for the elected officials in the political party that the presidential candidates will be so avidly visiting and courting.

This increased importance and influence of elected officials in the party is one of the most significant benefits of the Preprimary National Mini-Convention. In his classic study of how the presidential selection process is evolving in the United States, *Consequences of Party Reform,* Nelson W. Polsby stated that the "proliferation of primaries weakens the influence of state and local politicians on the choice of delegates and increases the influence of the news media." Polsby further noted that substituting a "media elite" for a "state party leader elite" replaces an elite that is mainly responsible to the voters (state party leaders) with an elite that is mainly responsible to editors and stockholders (the media).[1]

The Preprimary National Mini-Convention thus would bring party leaders who are elected officials back into the nominating process, restoring some of the power and influence they possessed before national conventions were replaced by presidential primaries as the principal means of nominating candidates for president. In doing so, the mini-convention would increase the importance of the political parties in the contemporary nominating process and, concommitantly, in American politics generally.

One of the major effects of the Preprimary National Mini-Convention would be to advance the presidential candidacies of established party leaders at the expense of "outsider" candidates with little or no national reputation. Because elected officials from all fifty states would be voting at the mini-convention, candidates with well-established national reputations and a broad base of support would have the best chance of being one of the "final four" candidates ranked by the mini-convention. Lesser-known candidates with only statewide or regional support (such as Georgia governor Jimmy Carter in 1976) would not be expected to do very well at the mini-convention.

There also should be a greater emphasis at the mini-conventions on selecting candidates who can win the general election in November. Many of the elected officials casting ballots at the mini-convention will be running for reelection on the same ballot with the party's presidential candidate. To a much greater extent than regular party members voting in a presidential primary or caucus, elected officials will have a vested interest in putting the most popular presidential candidate possible at the top of the party ticket in the November general election. Elected officials will be much less likely than the average voter in a party presidential primary to cast their votes on an ideological or philosophical basis. Elected officials will vote for a presidential candidate who looks like a winner—because they will want to win too.

It should always be kept in mind, however, that the mini-convention will be making a recommendation to party voters rather than actually nominating a party candidate for president. The final decision as to who will be the party nominee for president will still be made in the presidential primaries and caucuses. The mini-conventions will increase the chances of the eventual presidential nominee having a national reputation and a broad base of support, but they will not guarantee that result. "Outsider" candidates with only state or regional support will still be able to run in the primaries and caucuses and hope that a surprise victory in an early primary or caucus will give a substantial boost to their candidacy.

The Preprimary National Mini-Convention will strengthen the position of popular incumbent presidents but weaken the position of unpopular incumbents unfortunate enough to look as if they are going to lose the November general election. Elected officials in a political party will enthusiastically rally around a popular incumbent who appears likely to pull in lots of votes at the top of the party ticket. These same elected officials will be quick to dump an unpopular incumbent who threatens to drag some of them down to defeat. Both parties will benefit from having a well-publicized mechanism by which elected officials can express displeasure with an unpopular incumbent president and begin the process of denying him or her the party nomination for president. The mini-convention also will serve to begin the process of finding a more popular candidate to run in place of an unpopular incumbent.

A president will, of course, recognize throughout the four years of his or her first term the controlling influence which elected officials in the party will have at the Preprimary National Mini-Convention when the president runs for renomination and reelection. This will cause presidents to pay extra attention to the ideas and concerns of their fellow elected officials in the party, thereby keeping presidents in closer touch with what is going on in the nation. The assumption here is that party members who are elected officials will be in close touch with the electorate and will be quick to inform the president of the electorate's wishes and opinions. They will be double-quick to inform the president when his or her policies are not going over well with the electorate.

Following the Preprimary National Mini-Convention, the second step in a reformed presidential selection system would be an officially established Model Calendar of State Presidential Primaries and Caucuses. The most important aspect of this reform is that it would substitute a rationally structured plan for the present system of primaries and caucuses that evolved randomly and haphazardly.

The basic institutions of government in the United States did not come into being in an unintentional or disorganized way. A group of rational and well-educated human beings, now known as the founders, gathered at Philadelphia, Pennsylvania, in the summer of 1787 at the Constitutional Convention. They worked hard at creating a logical and workable structure of government. They debated at great length what a government should be and how various proposed governmental institutions might actually function once adopted.

It is important to note that the presidential nominating system currently in use in the United States was not developed in the same rational and logical way that most of the other institutions of American government and politics were created. The present system of presidential primaries and caucuses evolved over time in a highly accidental and decentralized way.[2] State legislatures for the most part acted completely independently of each other when deciding such questions as whether to hold a primary or a caucus and how early or late to hold it. When rational human beings tinkered with this ever-evolving nominating system, they worked mainly to increase the influence of a particular state (or a particular region) or increase the chances of victory of a particular candidate. At no time has a single organization or group of people met and worked to structure a unified, reasonable, coordinated presidential nominating system for the United States.

The Model Calendar of State Presidential Primaries and Caucuses would, of course, create such a rational and unified nominating system. Presidential primaries and caucuses would be spread over five Tuesdays, each of the Tuesdays two weeks apart, with small-population states voting early in the calendar and the largest-population states voting on the final day.

One of the most important results of adopting a model calendar would be that it would put an end to state governors and/or legislatures tinkering with the present system in an effort to advance a particular candidate or achieve a particular political purpose. Since the date of a particular state's primary or caucus would be determined by an agreement among all the states, individual states would lose the ability to play around with the primary and caucus calendar.

Under the model calendar, there would be no more Super Tuesdays, that eventually successful effort by southern state legislatures to increase southern influence over the presidential primary process by scheduling a large number of southern primaries on the same day. The model calendar also would eliminate the kind of thing that happened in Georgia in 1992, when the Peach State moved its presidential primary forward one week to give Bill Clinton an early victory and "a bridge to Super Tuesday."

Because the model calendar proposed here schedules the states with the largest numbers of delegates on the fifth and final Tuesday, it will encourage the two or three leading candidates in the earlier primaries to stay in the race until the final day. It also will encourage candidates with support in populous states to get in the race and stay in the race in a way they are not encouraged to do by the present system, which puts a premium on winning early in relatively small-population states. The model calendar thus should encourage more governors of populous states and United States senators from populous states to run for their party's nomination for president.

Many reasons have been given as to why New York governor Mario Cuomo stayed out of the 1992 race for the Democratic nomination for the presidency. One reason often cited was the lengthy calendar of primaries and caucuses stretching out over sixteen weeks. Another was the fact that New York State, where Cuomo would have been expected to enjoy strong support, voted in the middle of the primary calendar rather than at the beginning.

If the Model Calendar of State Presidential Primaries and Caucuses had been in effect in 1992, Governor Cuomo might very well have entered the Democratic contest. The primary and caucus season would have been only some ten weeks rather than sixteen weeks long, a real attraction to a candidate with the responsibility of being a sitting governor of a populous state. Furthermore, Cuomo could have expected to do well on the fifth and final primary day when New York and all the other populous states would have been voting. With his national reputation as a leading Democratic liberal and his legendary public speaking skills, Cuomo might have calculated that he could "clean up" on that final Tuesday. These factors might have been enough to get Cuomo into the 1992 race.

The model calendar will somewhat weaken the chances of relatively unknown candidates who concentrate on Iowa or New Hampshire and seek to launch a candidacy on early momentum. It is true that, under the model calendar, Iowa and New Hampshire would still have their isolated and favored positions at the beginning of the primary and caucus process. It is also true that "outsider" candidates will continue to pursue "Iowa bounce" and "New Hampshire surge" strategies. The problem for them will be the fourteen smaller-population states voting or caucusing on the first Tuesday of the model calendar's five-Tuesday cycle. With so many states from many different regions voting and caucusing at once, candidates with well-established national reputations should do better than lesser-known candidates who might have won in Iowa or New Hampshire.

Perhaps most important, the model calendar will reduce the undue influence of the limited number of populous states, mainly

Florida and Texas, that vote relatively early in the nominating process now in use. In both 1988 and 1992, the eventual winners in both the Republican and Democratic nomination races "broke out of the pack" on Super Tuesday in Florida and Texas. After a brief "mop up" period, the nomination races were essentially over and a large number of state primaries and caucuses became "irrelevant."

By placing Florida and Texas and eight other populous states on the fifth Tuesday in the cycle, the model calendar reduces the likelihood that any candidate will win a large number of delegate votes early in the process and "wrap up" the nomination before the fifth Tuesday's voting and caucusing takes place. In other words, by putting all the states with the largest numbers of delegates on the final Tuesday, the model calendar attempts to keep the Democratic and Republican races for the presidential nomination alive and exciting until the very last primaries and caucuses are held.

It is a bit early to make predictions on who will receive the Republican and Democratic nominations for president in 1996, but it is interesting to speculate on whom the model calendar might favor if it were put into operation for 1996. On the Republican side, the model calendar would favor candidates with already established national reputations, such as Senate Republican Leader Robert Dole of Kansas or House Republican Whip Newt Gingrich of Georgia. Leading figures from the Reagan and Bush administrations, such as former Secretary of State James Baker, former Secretary of Defense Dick Cheney, former Secretary of Housing and Urban Development Jack Kemp, and former Secretary of Education Lamar Alexander also would be expected to do well. "Outsider" candidates, such as small state governors whose names are barely known to the general public when the race begins, would not be expected to do as well as they do under the present nominating system.

The model calendar would have much less effect on the Democratic Party in 1996, given the fact that Bill Clinton is in his first term as president and will most likely run for renomination and reelection in 1996. If Clinton does well and is a popular president, he would be easily renominated no matter what nominating system were in effect. If his presidency is unpopular, however, and his prospects for reelection become doubtful, the model calendar would particularly encourage governors and United States senators from populous states—those states that hold primaries on that blowout fifth Tuesday—to challenge President Clinton for the 1996 Democratic nomination.

The state governors and state legislatures will have to act quickly if they want to have a Model Calendar of State Presidential Primaries and Caucuses in place for the 1996 presidential nominations. In October of 1993, the key state of California moved its presidential primary from the first Tuesday in June to the fourth Tuesday in March (March 26, 1996).[3] Barring other changes in the 1996 primary and caucus calendar, California will vote one week after Illinois and Michigan on Midwest Tuesday (March 19, 1996) and one week before New York (April 2, 1996).

The implications of this unilateral move by California are very great. With California having almost 20 percent of the delegate votes needed for a majority in both the Democratic and Republican national conventions, it is hard to see how the race for the nomination in both parties would not be over once California had voted. This would reduce to total irrelevance in the presidential nominating process every primary or caucus after California's. The state with the most to lose would be New York, which holds its primary on the first Tuesday in April. California would replace New York as the last "relevant" primary, again assuming that no other changes were made between the 1992 and the 1996 primary calendar.

The third recommended reform is the adoption of an Amendment for the Popular Election of the President. Such an amendment to the United States Constitution would abolish the electoral college and replace it with direct popular election of the president. This change would mainly affect the way presidential candidates campaign, and in doing that could affect the outcome of the election.

If the electoral college were abolished, the votes of the citizens of small-population states would be just as valuable as the votes of citizens of populous states. Instead of concentrating on a limited number of middlesize- and large-population states where the vote was close, presidential candidates would seek votes in every state across the country. Individual state polls would decrease in importance and candidates for president would pay much closer attention to national polling predictions. Candidates would focus their appeals more at the national level than at the state level, seeking additional votes anywhere they could find them.

Most importantly, the party candidates would run their television and radio spot ads nationally rather than mainly in close states with large numbers of electoral votes. This last point is crucial because it is through television and radio advertisements that most Americans are exposed to and influenced by presidential campaigns.

If there had been no electoral college in the 1992 presidential election, George Bush might have been able to make a more credible challenge to Bill Clinton in the last week before election day. With six days to go, Bush pulled within two percentage points of Clinton in some of the national public opinion polls. This fact was meaningless, however, because Clinton held a commanding lead over Bush in the polls in key states with many electoral votes. The result was that the news media continued to play the election as going to Clinton rather than being a close race.

Without the electoral college and its "help the leader" effects, the last week of the 1992 presidential election would have had a completely different atmosphere. When Bush pulled to within two points of Clinton in the national polls, the news media would have portrayed the race as "going down to the wire." Both candidates would have turned their attention to national television and national television advertising, seeking additional votes in any state where they could find them. The news media would have paid much more attention to Bush's last-minute effort to raise the "trust" issue against Clinton, and the Clinton forces would have had to work harder to blunt that issue. Furthermore, there would have been no "it's-all-over stories" in the national newsmagazines implying that Clinton had already won the election.

Thinking that the race between Bush and Clinton was a close one, a large number of Perot voters might have been tempted to cast a "deciding" vote between Bush and Clinton rather than "waste" their vote on Perot. If, because of the growing importance of the "trust" issue, more of those switched Perot votes had gone to Bush rather than Clinton, it could have changed the final outcome of the election.

This is all speculation, of course, but it does make the point that presidential election campaigns in the United States would be very different if the electoral college were abolished and the president were elected by a direct popular vote.

So here are three reforms for the flawed path to the presidency. They are the Preprimary National Mini-Convention, the Model Calendar of State Presidential Primaries and Caucuses, and an Amendment for the Popular Election of the President. All three are mainly oriented to the simple idea that every American should have the opportunity to *participate* in presidential elections as fully as possible. Over and over again in 1992, the American people indicated that they wanted to be a larger part of the presidential election process. They attended rallies and watched television debates in unexpectedly large numbers. By adopting these three reforms and making the presidential selection system more participatory and more equitable, American political leaders will be making it more democratic—and the United States, now more than ever, is a democracy.

APPENDIX
ELECTION AND CAUCUS RESULTS

TABLE 1
1992 Democratic Primary Results

	Turnout	Brown	Clinton	Harkin	Kerrey	Tsongas	Other
New Hampshire (February 18)	167,819	8.1	24.7	10.2	11.1	33.2	12.7
South Dakota (February 25)	59,503	3.9	19.1	25.2	40.2	9.6	2.0
Colorado (March 3)	239,643	28.8	26.9	2.4	12.3	25.6	3.8
Georgia (March 3)	454,631	8.1	57.2	2.1	4.8	24.0	3.8
Maryland (March 3)	567,224	8.2	33.5	5.8	4.8	40.6	7.2
South Carolina (March 7)	116,414	6.0	62.9	6.6	0.5	18.3	5.7
Florida (March 10)	1,123,857	12.4	50.8	1.2	1.1	34.5	-
Louisiana (March 10)	384,417	6.6	69.5	1.0	0.8	11.1	11.0
Massachusetts (March 10)	794,093	14.6	10.9	0.5	0.7	66.3	7
Mississippi (March 10)	191,357	9.6	73.1	1.3	0.9	8.1	7
Oklahoma (March 10)	416,129	16.7	70.5	3.4	3.2	-	11.9
Rhode Island (March 10)	50,709	18.8	21.2	0.6	0.9	52.9	5.5
Tennessee (March 10)	318,482	8.0	67.3	0.7	0.5	19.4	4.0
Texas (March 10)	1,482,975	8.0	65.6	1.3	1.4	19.2	4.5
Illinois (March 17)	1,504,130	14.6	51.6	2.0	0.7	25.8	5.2
Michigan (March 17)	585,972	25.8	50.7	1.1	0.5	16.6	2.4
Connecticut (March 24)	173,119	37.2	35.6	1.1	0.7	19.5	5.8
Puerto Rico (April 5)	63,398	1.6	95.6	0.0	1.3	0.1	1.3
Kansas (April 7)	160,251	13.0	51.3	0.6	1.4	15.2	18.5
Minnesota (April 7)*	204,170	30.6	31.1	2.0	0.6	21.3	14.4[1]
New York (April 7)	1,007,726	26.2	40.9	1.1	1.1	28.6	2.0
Wisconsin (April 7)	772,596	34.5	37.2	0.7	0.4	21.8	5.4
Pennsylvania (April 28)	1,265,495	25.7	56.5	1.7	1.6	12.8	1.7

District of Columbia (May 5)	61,904	7.2	73.8	-	-	10.4	8.5
Indiana (May 5)	476,850	21.5	63.3	-	3.0	12.2	-
North Carolina (May 5)	691,875	10.4	64.1	0.9	0.9	8.3	15.4
Nebraska (May 12)	150,587	21.0	45.5	2.8	-	7.1	23.5
West Virginia (May 12)	306,866	11.9	74.2	0.9	1.0	6.9	5.0
Oregon (May 19)	347,698	31.4	45.3	-	-	10.5	12.7
Washington (May 19)*	147,981	23.1	42.0	1.3	1.0	12.8	19.8[1]
Arkansas (May 26)	502,617	11.0	68.0	-	-	-	20.9
Idaho (May 26)*	55,124	16.7	49.0	-	-	-	34.3
Kentucky (May 26)	369,438	8.3	56.0	1.9	0.9	4.9	28.0
Alabama (June 2)	450,899	6.8	68.2	-	-	-	25
California (June 2)	2,752,029	40.2	47.5	-	1.2	7.4	3.8
Montana (June 2)	116,899	18.5	46.9	-	-	10.8	23.9
New Jersey (June 2)	399,913	19.5	59.2	-	-	11.1	10.2
New Mexico (June 2)	180,770	16.9	52.8	1.9	-	6.3	22.2
Ohio (June 2)	1,032,851	19.0	61.2	2.4	2.2	10.6	4.6
North Dakota (June 9)*	31,562	-	12.6[2]	-	-	-	87.4[1]

[1] Perot write-in votes totaled 2.1 percent of the Democratic primary vote in Minnesota, 19.1 percent in Washington and 28.4 percent in North Dakota (which was the winning total).

[2] Clinton's vote in North Dakota came on write-ins.

* Indicates a nonbinding "beauty contest" primary.

- Indicates that the candidate or an "other" option was not listed on the ballot.

Note: Results are based on official returns except for California, Montana, New Jersey, New Mexico, North Dakota, Ohio, Oregon, and Puerto Rico, where results are nearly complete but unofficial. Percentages may not add up to 100 due to rounding.

Source: Congressional Quarterly Weekly Report, July 4, 1992 (Democratic Convention Special Issue), p. 69.

TABLE 2

1992 Democratic First-Round Caucus Winners

Caucus States	Turnout	Brown	Clinton	Harkin	Kerrey	Tsongas	Other
Iowa (February 10)	*30,000	1.6	2.8	76.4	2.5	4.1	12.6
Maine (February 23)	13,500	30.3	14.8	5.2	3.0	29.0	17.8
Idaho (March 3)	3,090	4.5	11.4	29.7	8.0	28.4	18.0
Minnesota (March 3)	*50-60,000	8.2	10.3	26.7	7.6	19.2	28.2
Utah (March 3)	31,638	28.4	18.3	4.0	10.9	33.4	5.0
Washington (March 3)	*60,000	18.6	12.6	8.2	3.4	32.3	24.7
American Samoa (March 3)	N.A.	-	4.3	-	8.7	-	87.0
North Dakota (March 5-19)	*5,000	7.5	46.0	6.8	1.2	10.3	28.3
Arizona (March 7)	36,326	27.5	29.2	7.6	-	34.4	1.3
Wyoming (March 7)	*1,500	23.0	28.5	14.2	-	11.7	22.7
Democrats Abroad (March 7-9)	*4,000	12.2	26.6	6.9	-	36.8	17.5
Nevada (March 8)	*6-7,000	34.4	26.6	-	-	19.6	19.4
Delaware (March 10)	*2,500	19.5	20.8	-	-	30.2	29.6

Hawaii (March 10)	3,014	13.6	51.5	12.7	0.4	14.3	7.5
Missouri (March 10)	*20-25,000	5.7	45.1	-	-	10.2	39.0
Texas (March 10)	N.A.						
Virgin Islands (March 28)	343	4.1	39.7	-	-	-	56.3
Vermont (March 31)	*6,000	46.7	16.8	-	-	9.3	27.2
Alaska (April 2)	*1,100	33.1	30.9	-	-	1.3	34.7
Virginia (April 11, 13)	N.A.	11.6	52.1	-	-	-	36.3
Guam (May 3)	*1,000	20.0	49.0	-	-	-	31.0

* Turnout estimate.
- Indicates that the candidate was not listed on the caucus ballot or that his votes were not tabulated separately.
N.A. - not available.

Note: By and large, caucus results were compiled by the state parties and reflect either the share won of delegates to the next stage of the caucus process or a tally of the presidential preferences of caucus participants. No results were available from the March 10 precinct caucuses in Texas. In most cases, the turnout figures are estimates.

Source: Congressional Quarterly Weekly Report, July 4, 1992 (Democratic Convention Special Issue), p. 70.

TABLE 3
1992 Republican Primary Results

	Turnout	Buchanan	Bush	Duke	Other
New Hampshire (February 18)	174,165	37.4	53.0	-	9.7
South Dakota (February 25)	44,671	-	69.3	-	30.7
Colorado (March 3)	195,690	30.0	67.5	-	2.5
Georgia (March 3)	453,987	35.7	64.3	-	-
Maryland (March 3)	240,021	29.9	70.1	-	-
South Carolina (March 7)	148,840	25.7	66.9	7.1	0.3
Florida (March 10)	893,463	31.9	68.1	-	-
Louisiana (March 10)	135,109	27.0	62.0	8.8	2.1
Massachusetts (March 10)	269,701	27.7	65.6	2.1	4.7
Mississippi (March 10)	154,708	16.7	72.3	10.6	0.4
Oklahoma (March 10)	217,721	26.6	69.6	2.6	1.2
Rhode Island (March 10)	15,636	31.8	63.0	2.1	3.1
Tennessee (March 10)	245,653	22.2	72.5	3.1	2.0
Texas (March 10)	797,146	23.9	69.8	2.5	3.8
Illinois (March 17)	831,140	22.5	76.4	-	1.2
Michigan (March 17)	449,133	25.0	67.2	2.4	5.4
Connecticut (March 24)	99,473	21.9	66.7	2.3	9.1
Puerto Rico (April 5)	262,426	0.4	99.2	0.3	0.1
Kansas (April 7)	213,196	14.8	62.0	1.8	21.4
Minnesota (April 7)	132,756	24.2	63.9	-	11.9[2]
Wisconsin (April 7)	482,248	16.3	75.6	2.7[1]	5.5
Pennsylvania (April 28)	1,008,777	23.2	76.8	-	-

District of Columbia (May 5)	5,235	18.5	-	81.5	-
Indiana (May 5)	467,615	19.9	-	80.1	-
North Carolina (May 5)	283,571	19.5	-	70.7	9.8
Nebraska (May 12)	192,098	13.5	1.5	81.4	3.7
West Virginia (May 12)	124,157	14.6	-	80.5	4.9
Oregon (May 19)	304,159	19.0	2.2	67.1	11.8
Washington (May 19)	129,655	10.2	1.2	67.0	21.6[2]
Arkansas (May 26)	54,876	11.9	-	83.1	5.0
Idaho (May 26)	115,502	13.1	-	63.5	23.4
Kentucky (May 26)	101,119	-	-	74.5	25.5
Alabama (June 2)	165,121	7.6	-	74.3	18.1
California (June 2)	2,156,464	26.4	-	73.6	-
Montana (June 2)	90,975	11.8	-	71.6	16.6
New Jersey (June 2)	310,270	15.0	-	77.5	7.5[2]
New Mexico (June 2)	86,967	9.1	-	63.8	27.1
Ohio (June 2)	924,572	16.8	-	83.2	27.1
North Dakota (June 9)	47,808	-	-	83.4	16.6[2]

[1] Duke withdrew from the race April 22.

[2] Write-in votes for Ross Perot totaled 2.7 percent of the Republican primary vote in Minnesota, 19.6 percent in Washington, 7.5 percent in New Jersey and 8.1 percent in North Dakota.

- Indicates that the candidate or an "other" option was not listed on the ballot.

Note: Results are based on official returns except for Ohio, where results are nearly complete but unofficial.

Source: Congressional Quarterly Weekly Report, August 8, 1992 (Republican Convention Special Issue), p. 63.

TABLE 4
Official 1992 Presidential Election Results

State	Clinton		Bush		Perot	
	Votes	Percent	Votes	Percent	Votes	Percent
Alabama	690,080	40.9	804,283	47.6	183,109	10.8
Alaska	78,294	30.3	102,000	39.5	73,481	28.4
Arizona	543,050	36.5	572,086	38.5	353,741	23.8
Arkansas	505,823	53.2	337,324	35.5	99,132	10.4
California	5,121,325	46.0	3,630,575	32.0	2,296,006	20.6
Colorado	629,681	40.1	562,850	35.9	366,010	23.3
Connecticut	682,318	42.2	578,313	35.8	348,771	21.6
District of Columbia	192,619	84.6	20,698	9.1	9,681	4.3
Delaware	126,054	43.5	102,313	35.3	59,213	20.4
Florida	2,071,651	39.0	2,171,781	40.9	1,052,481	19.8
Georgia	1,008,966	43.5	995,252	42.9	309,657	13.3
Hawaii	179,310	48.1	136,822	36.7	53,003	14.2
Idaho	137,013	28.4	202,645	42.0	130,395	27.0
Illinois	2,453,350	48.6	1,734,096	34.3	840,515	16.6
Indiana	848,420	36.8	989,375	42.9	455,934	19.8
Iowa	586,353	43.3	504,891	37.3	253,468	18.7
Kansas	390,434	33.7	449,951	38.9	312,358	27.0
Kentucky	665,104	44.6	617,178	41.3	203,944	13.7
Louisiana	815,971	45.6	733,386	41.0	211,478	11.8
Maine	263,420	38.8	206,504	30.4	206,820	30.4
Massachusetts	1,318,639	47.5	805,039	29.0	630,731	22.7
Maryland	988,571	49.8	707,094	35.6	281,414	14.2
Michigan	1,871,182	43.8	1,554,940	36.4	824,813	19.3
Minnesota	1,020,997	43.5	747,841	31.9	562,506	24.0
Mississippi	400,258	40.8	487,793	49.7	85,626	8.7

Missouri	1,053,873	44.1	811,159	33.9	518,741	21.7
Montana	154,507	37.6	144,207	35.1	107,225	26.1
Nebraska	216,864	29.4	343,678	46.6	174,104	23.6
Nevada	189,148	37.4	175,828	34.7	132,580	26.2
New Hampshire	209,040	38.9	202,484	37.6	121,337	22.6
New Jersey	1,436,206	43.0	1,356,865	40.6	521,829	15.6
New Mexico	261,617	45.9	212,824	37.3	91,895	10.1
New York	3,444,450	49.7	2,346,649	33.9	1,090,721	15.7
North Carolina	1,114,042	42.7	1,134,661	43.4	357,864	13.7
North Dakota	99,168	32.2	136,244	44.2	71,084	23.1
Ohio	1,984,919	40.2	1,894,248	38.3	1,036,403	21.0
Oklahoma	473,066	34.0	592,929	42.6	319,878	23.0
Oregon	621,314	42.5	475,757	32.5	354,091	24.2
Pennsylvania	2,239,164	45.1	1,791,841	36.1	902,667	18.2
Rhode Island	213,299	47.0	131,601	29.0	105,045	23.2
South Carolina	479,514	39.9	577,507	48.0	138,872	11.5
South Dakota	124,888	37.1	136,718	40.2	73,295	21.8
Tennessee	933,521	47.1	841,300	42.4	199,968	10.1
Texas	2,281,815	37.1	2,496,071	40.6	1,354,781	22.0
Utah	183,429	24.7	322,632	43.4	203,400	27.3
Vermont	133,592	46.1	88,122	30.4	65,991	22.8
Virginia	1,038,650	40.6	1,150,517	45.0	348,639	13.6
Washington	993,037	43.4	731,234	32.0	541,780	23.7
West Virginia	331,001	46.7	241,974	35.4	108,829	15.9
Wisconsin	1,041,066	41.1	930,855	36.8	544,479	21.5
Wyoming	68,160	34.0	79,347	39.6	51,263	25.6
Total	44,908,233	43.0	39,102,282	37.4	19,741,048	18.9

Source: *Congressional Quarterly Weekly Report*, January 23, 1993, p. 190.

NOTES

CHAPTER 1

1. ABC News/Washington Post Poll, *Colorado Springs Gazette Telegraph*, December 18, 1991, p. A1.

2. ABC News/Washington Post Poll, *Colorado Springs Gazette Telegraph*, December 18, 1991, p. A1.

3. The idea that the Great Depression and President Franklin D. Roosevelt's New Deal created a Democratic majority in the United States oriented to economic concerns is ably described in Samuel Lubell, *The Future of American Politics*, 2nd edition revised (Garden City, NY: Doubleday, 1956). See particularly Chapter 3, "Revolt of the City," pp. 29-60.

4. For an interesting 1989 prediction of how George Bush would do in foreign policy as president, see Erwin C. Hargrove, "George Bush and the Cycle of Politics and Policy," in Michael Nelson, ed., *The Elections of 1988* (Washington, D.C.: Congressional Quarterly Press, 1989), pp. 172-173. Hargrove described Bush as "a man who wishes to take maximum advantage of new opportunities without establishing any vision of his own." Hargrove's view was prescient in light of the fact that Bush succeeded greatly in practical terms in foreign policy, but, when the Soviet Union disintegrated, Bush was unable to communicate to the American people what a post-Cold War American foreign policy should be like. See also Kevin Phillips, *The Politics of Rich and Poor: Wealth and the American Electorate in the Reagan Aftermath* (New York: Random House, 1990), p. 221. Phillips was one of the first analysts to note that the breakup of the Soviet Union "reduced the political importance of the longtime Republican reputation for a strong defense against Soviet aggression."

5. The isolationist themes sounded by Patrick Buchanan in New Hampshire in 1992 previously had enjoyed considerable popularity among certain

groups in the Republican Party. See Chapter 7, "The Myth of Isolationism," in Samuel Lubell, *The Future of American Politics*, 2nd edition revised, pp. 137-167. Also see Chapter 8, "The 'New Isolationism,'" in Samuel Lubell, *The Hidden Crisis in American Politics* (New York: W. W. Norton, 1970), pp. 249-265.

6. Robin Toner, "Buchanan Off and Running against Bush," *Denver Post*, December 11, 1991, p. 2A. Associated Press, "Buchanan Throws his Hat in Ring," *Colorado Springs Gazette Telegraph*, December 11, 1991, p. A9. Associated Press, "Buchanan Blames Bush for U.S. Economic Woes," *Denver Post*, December 9, 1991, p. 13A.

7. Jack W. Germond and Jules Witcover, *Mad As Hell: Revolt at the Ballot Box, 1992* (New York: Warner Books, 1993), p. 35.

CHAPTER 2

1. For extensive coverage of Bill Clinton's childhood, college years, and career as governor of Arkansas, see David Maraniss, "Bill Clinton, Running on the Fast Track," *Washington Post National Weekly Edition*, February 3-9, 1992, pp. 12-13; Donald Baer and Steven V. Roberts, "The Making of Bill Clinton," *U.S. News & World Report*, March 30, 1992, pp. 28-34; David Maraniss, "Bill Clinton, Born to Run," *Washington Post National Weekly Edition*, July 20-26, 1992, pp. 6-10; and Elizabeth Kolbert, "Early Loss Casts Clinton as a Leader by Consensus," *New York Times*, September 28, 1992, p. A1. For a campaign biography on Clinton see Charles F. Allen and Jonathan Portis, *The Comeback Kid: The Life and Career of Bill Clinton* (New York: Birch Lane, 1992).

2. For a description of the political consultant who helped Bill Clinton and other southern Democrats to found the Democratic Leadership Council, see Michael Duffy, "A Public Policy Entrepreneur: Domestic-Issues Coordinator Al From Yanked the Democrats Back to the Center," *Time*, December 14, 1992, p. 51.

3. There is considerable literature supporting the idea that the South is a most important component in Democratic Party hopes for winning the presidency. Earl Black and Merle Black argued that "the most reasonable strategy for the Democrats would be to concentrate on Northern states but to allocate some campaign resources to a small number of Southern states—Arkansas and Tennessee, for example, plus any others that might be experiencing severe economic difficulties in the election year—where majority biracial coalitions might be constructed. Denying the Republicans a complete sweep of the South is probably the most realistic outcome that the Democrats can hope for in the near future." Earl Black and Merle Black, *The Vital South: How Presidents Are Elected* (Cambridge, MA: Harvard University Press, 1992), p. 362. Also see Kevin P. Phillips, *The Emerging Republican Majority* (New Rochelle, NY: Arlington House, 1969); Harry S. Dent, *The Prodigal South Returns to Power* (New York:

John Wiley and Sons, 1978); Robert P. Steed, Laurence W. Moreland, and Tod A. Baker, eds., *The 1984 Presidential Election in the South* (New York: Praeger, 1986); Robert H. Swansbrough and David M. Brodsky, eds., *The South's New Politics: Realignment and Dealignment* (Columbia, SC: University of South Carolina Press, 1988); and Laurence W. Moreland, Robert P. Steed, and Tod A. Baker, eds., *The 1988 Presidential Election in the South* (New York: Praeger, 1991).

4. Rhodes Cook, "The Nominating Process," in Michael Nelson, ed., *The Elections of 1988* (Washington, D.C.: Congressional Quarterly Press, 1989), pp. 32-34. Cook's term "The Exhibition Season" was continued by Ryan J. Barilleaux and Randall E. Adkins in "The Nominations: Process and Patterns," in Michael Nelson, ed., *The Elections of 1992* (Washington, D.C.: Congressional Quarterly Press, 1993), pp. 31-32, 37-40.

5. Ross K. Baker, "Sorting Out and Suiting Up: The Presidential Nominations," in Gerald M. Pomper et. al., *The Election of 1992: Reports and Interpretations* (Chatham, NJ: Chatham House, 1993), pp. 40-43.

6. Following her husband's election as president of the United States in November 1992, Hillary Clinton requested that the news media identify her as Hillary Rodham Clinton, Rodham being her maiden name. During the campaign, however, she was identified in the news media as Hillary Clinton and is so identified in this book.

7. Dan Balz and E. J. Dionne Jr., "Gathering Momentum, Money and Media Scrutiny," *Washington Post National Weekly Edition*, January 20-26, 1992, p. 12.

8. The Clinton emphasis on support for the "middle class" may have stemmed from the research and writing of Kevin Phillips, who argued strenuously in the early 1990s that the Reagan and Bush presidencies favored wealthy Americans at the expense of the middle class. "Widespread resentment over extreme wealth was inevitable," Phillips wrote in 1990, "though still unfocused." Kevin Phillips, *The Politics of Rich and Poor: Wealth and the American Electorate in the Reagan Aftermath* (New York: Random House, 1990), p. 210.

9. Associated Press, "Clinton Joins the Ranks Running for President," *Colorado Springs Gazette Telegraph*, October 4, 1991, p. A5.

10. Associated Press, "Clinton Notches a Knockout at Party Meeting," *Colorado Springs Gazette Telegraph*, November 24, 1991, p. A3.

11. Wire Services, "Cuomo's a No Go for 1992," *Denver Post*, December 21, 1992, p. 1A.

12. Author's notes, panel discussion on "View from the Media," The Colorado Symposium on the Presidential Election, University of Colorado at Colorado Springs, December 12, 1992.

13. The preprimary leader in the public opinion polls possesses enhanced status in the eyes of political scientists and other astute political observers, mainly because the "preprimary poll leader [becomes] the nominee 85 percent of the time." See Nelson W. Polsby and Aaron Wildavsky, *Presidential Elections: Strategies of American Electoral Politics*, 5th edition (New York: Charles Scribner's Sons, 1980), p. 87.

CHAPTER 3

1. According to Clif Larson, the Iowa Democratic state chairman at the time the Iowa caucuses were created, the January date was selected to allow adequate time to prepare for subsequent caucuses and the state convention in mid-May. There was an awareness that such an early caucus date would bring Iowa more attention from the news media, but no one foresaw it becoming such an important event so quickly. See William G. Mayer, "The New Hampshire Primary: A Historical Overview," in Gary R. Owen and Nelson W. Polsby, eds., *Media and Momentum: The New Hampshire Primary and Nomination Politics* (Chatham, NJ: Chatham House Publishers, 1987), pp. 20-25. Also see Hugh Winebrenner, *The Iowa Precinct Caucuses: The Making of a Media Event* (Ames, IA: Iowa State University Press, 1987), pp. 38-40, and Peverill Squire, ed., *The Iowa Precinct Caucuses and the Presidential Nominating Process* (Boulder, CO: Westview Press, 1989), pp. 1-3.

2. Rhodes Cook, *Race for the Presidency: Winning the 1992 Nomination* (Washington, D.C.: Congressional Quarterly Press, 1991), pp. 7-9. Cook described the Iowa caucuses as "one of the most successful political inventions of recent times."

3. For a complete description of Carter's efforts in Iowa in 1976, see Jules Witcover, *Marathon: The Pursuit of the Presidency 1972-1976* (New York: Viking Penguin, 1977), pp. 206-229.

4. For a detailed description of the Iowa Republican caucuses in 1980, see Chapter 5, "The Functional Equivalent of a Primary," in Jack W. Germond and Jules Witcover, *Blue Smoke and Mirrors: How Reagan Won and Why Carter Lost the Election of 1980* (New York: Viking Press, 1981), pp. 93-115.

5. News Services, "Iowa Takes Political Back Seat," *Colorado Springs Gazette Telegraph*, February 10, 1992, p. A3.

6. Robert S. Boyd, Knight-Ridder News Service, "'Have-not' Harkin Runs for President," *Denver Post*, September 16, 1991.

7. Ruth Marcus, "Tom Harkin: Fighter for the Underdog or Rank Opportunist?" *Washington Post National Weekly Edition*, March 2-8, 1992, p. 13. This article gives a long and detailed account of Harkin's youth and political career. Also see Dan Balz, "Tom Harkin: A Democrat and Proud of It," *Washington Post National Weekly Edition*, July 1-7, 1991, p. 14.

8. Carl P. Leubsdorf, "Shrewd Harkin Seizes Political Opportunities," *Denver Post*, February 9, 1992, p. 19A.

9. Robert S. Boyd, Knight-Ridder News Service, "'Have-not' Harkin Runs for President," *Denver Post*, September 16, 1991, p. 1A.

10. *Florida Times Union*, Jacksonville, reprinted in the *Washington Post National Weekly Edition*, March 2-8, 1992, p. 14.

CHAPTER 4

1. This colorful account of the distant origins of the New Hampshire presidential primary is from William G. Mayer, "The New Hampshire Primary: A Historical Overview," in Gary R. Orren and Nelson W. Polsby, *Media and Momentum: The New Hampshire Primary and Nomination Politics* (Chatham, NJ: Chatham House Publishers, 1987), p. 10. Also see Charles Brereton, *First Step to the White House: The New Hampshire Primary 1952-1980* (Hampton, NH: Wheelabrator Foundation, 1979), p. 2, and Neal R. Peirce, *The New England States* (New York: Norton, 1976), pp. 315-323.

2. According to Brereton, "the New Hampshire primary law enacted in 1949 was tailor-made to advance the political fortunes of General Dwight D. Eisenhower in 1952." Charles Brereton, *First Step to the White House: The New Hampshire Primary 1952-1980* (Hampton, NH: Wheelabrator Foundation, 1979), p. 4.

3. For a statistical study of the extent to which New Hampshire overwhelmingly dominates media coverage of the nominating process, see William C. Adams, "As New Hampshire Goes . . . ," in Gary R. Orren and Nelson W. Polsby, *Media and Momentum: The New Hampshire Primary and Nomination Politics* (Chatham, NJ: Chatham House Publishers, 1987), pp. 42-59. Adams concludes that New Hampshire's "exaggeration" in the nominating process is "startling."

4. The term "Big Mo" was coined by George Bush to describe the advantage he had gained by winning the 1980 Iowa Republican caucuses. See Larry M. Bartels, *Presidential Primaries and the Dynamics of Public Choice* (Princeton, NJ: Princeton University Press, 1988), p. 27, and Jeff Greenfield, *The Real Campaign: How the Media Missed the Story of the 1980 Campaign* (New York: Summit Books, 1982), pp. 39-40.

5. The law was passed in 1975 when Massachusetts and Vermont, seeking to create a New England regional presidential primary, had the audacity to schedule their primaries the same day as New Hampshire's.

6. For a long and detailed account of the youth and early political career of Paul Tsongas, see Bill McAllister, "Paul Tsongas, Against All Odds," *Washington Post National Weekly Edition*, February 17-23, 1992, p. 12.

7. Hadley and Stanley argue that the uproar over Gennifer Flowers actually helped Bill Clinton gain recognition among the voters. "Finally, the widely reported Gennifer Flowers incident made Bill Clinton a household word; his name recognition soared to 86 percent of all voters (89 percent among Democratic voters and those leaning Democratic), and his support among Democrats for the nomination rose over three weeks from 17 to 42 percent." Charles D. Hadley and Harold W. Stanley, "Surviving the 1992 Presidential Nomination Process," in William Crotty, ed., *America's Choice: The Election of 1992* (Guilford, CT: Dushkin Publishing Group, 1993), p. 34.

8. News Services, "Clinton Denies Report of Affair," *Colorado Springs Gazette Telegraph*, January 27, 1992, p. A3.

9. David Maraniss and Bill McAllister, "Just When He Thought the Worst Was Behind Him," *Washington Post National Weekly Edition*, February 24–March 1, 1992, p. 13.

10. Knight-Ridder News Service, "N.H. Finale: 47% in GOP Reject Bush," *Denver Post*, February 20, 1992, 1A.

11. *Boston Herald*, February 19, 1992, p. 1.

12. Carl M. Cannon, Knight-Ridder News Service, "Clinton's Strong Finish May Be More Telling than Buchanan's," *Denver Post*, February 19, 1992, p. 6A.

13. Noel Eisenberg, Tsongas campaign worker in New Hampshire, interview by the author, Colorado Springs, September 10, 1993.

14. William G. Mayer argues that one of the major purposes of the New Hampshire primary, from the viewpoint of the news media, is to get a nominating race down to a two-person contest. The New Hampshire winner becomes the front-runner and the second-place finisher becomes a rallying point for those opposed to the front-runner. Having a two-person race also gives the media an exciting and continuing story to report. William G. Mayer, "New Hampshire: A Historical Overview," in Gary R. Orren and Nelson W. Polsby, *Media and Momentum: The New Hampshire Primary and Nomination Politics* (Chatham, NJ: Chatham House Publishers, 1987), p. 25.

15. Personal observation of the author.

16. Orren and Polsby argue that the small size and concentrated nature of the population in New Hampshire are one of the most important things that make it attractive to "outsider" candidates for president. "The New Hampshire primary has been fertile ground for 'outsider' candidates—mavericks, insurgents, relatively weak partisans. . . . It . . . helps that New Hampshire is small and manageable logistically." Gary R. Orren and Nelson W. Polsby, "New Hampshire: Springboard of Nomination Politics," in Gary R. Orren and Nelson W. Polsby, *Media and Momentum: The New Hampshire Primary and Nomination Politics* (Chatham, NJ: Chatham House Publishers, 1987), p. 4.

17. Scott Shepherd and Julia Malone, Cox News Service, "Results Filtered Through Expectations," *Colorado Springs Gazette Telegraph*, February 18, 1992, p. A3.

CHAPTER 5

1. Associated Press, "Brown, Tsongas in Cliffhanger," *Colorado Springs Gazette Telegraph*, February 24, 1992, p. A1.

2. Associated Press, "Brown, Tsongas in Cliffhanger," *Colorado Springs Gazette Telegraph*, February 24, 1992, p. A1.

CHAPTER 6

1. Ted Muenster, South Dakota state chairman, Bob Kerrey for President, quoted by Fred Brown, "Democrats Turn Their Attention to South Dakota," *Denver Post*, February 24, 1992, p. 1A.

2. For a long and detailed account of Bob Kerrey's youth and political career, see Guy Gugliotta, "Everything Going for Him, If Only Things Would Get Going," *Washington Post National Weekly Edition*, February 10-16, 1992, pp. 13-14. For a discussion of Kerrey's campaign for president, see Thomas B. Edsall, "Kerrey May Be Too Honest for His Own Good," *Washington Post National Weekly Edition*, February 10-16, 1992, p. 15.

3. Carl M. Cannon, Knight-Ridder News Service, "In Kerrey, Democrats see the Right Ingredients," *Denver Post*, October 6, 1991, p. 4A.

4. Scott Shepherd, Cox News Service, "Kerrey Hopes to Inject Some Magic into '92 Race," *Colorado Springs Gazette Telegraph*, September 29, 1991, p. A12.

5. Carl M. Cannon, Knight-Ridder News Service, "In Kerrey, Democrats See the Right Ingredients," *Denver Post*, October 6, 1991, p. 4A.

6. News Services, "Candidates Focus on Farm Issues," *Colorado Springs Gazette Telegraph*, February 24, 1992, p. A3.

CHAPTER 7

1. Thomas C. Cronin and Robert D. Loevy, *Colorado Politics and Government: Governing the Centennial State* (Lincoln: University of Nebraska Press, 1993).

2. Fred Brown, "Senator Seeks Early Presidential Primary," *Denver Post*, January 30, 1990, p. 3B.

3. In retrospect, senator Bird's decision to put the Colorado presidential primary to a vote of the people may have avoided a gubernatorial veto. Democratic Governor Roy Romer turned out to be a strong supporter of Bill Clinton for the Democratic nomination for president. If Romer had calculated that Clinton, a southerner, would not do very well in an early primary in a western state such as Colorado, Romer might very well have vetoed the Colorado presidential primary bill.

4. *Democratic Party of the United States v. Wisconsin ex rel. Lafollette*, 450 US 107 (1981).

5. "Poll/Colorado Issues," *Denver Post*, October 7, 1990, p. 12A. John Sanko, "Voters Hot on Tax Curb, Cool on Gambling," *Rocky Mountain News*, October 7, 1990.

6. The fifteen states were Iowa, Maine, Minnesota, Idaho, Washington, North Dakota, Arizona, Wyoming, Nevada, Delaware, Hawaii, Missouri, Vermont, Alaska, and Virginia.

7. Eric Anderson, "Tsongas Campaigns in Denver," *Denver Post*, May 2, 1991, p. 13A.

8. Renate Robey, "Presidential Ad War Heats Up," *Denver Post*, February 22, 1992, p. 4B.

9. Fred Brown, "Surge Put Brown Third in Colorado," *Denver Post*, February 28, 1992, p. 4A.

10. Renate Robey and Eric Anderson, "Colo. Campaigns' Range: Well-Heeled to Shoestring," *Denver Post*, February 16, 1992, p. 1C.

11. The Sangre de Cristo center was named for a spectacular, snowcapped mountain range located southwest of Pueblo. When Spanish explorers first saw the red color of a morning sunrise reflecting off the snowcapped mountains, they named the mountains Sangre de Cristo, or "Blood of Christ."

12. The term "share-out" was introduced into political analysis by Theodore H. White in *The Making of the President 1968* (New York: Atheneum, 1969), p. 84.

13. Jim Buynak, "Wife Stumps for Clinton in Springs," *Colorado Springs Gazette Telegraph*, March 2, 1992, p. A3.

14. Mona Charen, "Activist Wife Undermines Clinton's Credibility," *Colorado Springs Gazette Telegraph*, June 5, 1992, p. B9.

15. Barry Noreen, "Brown Brings His Message to Town," *Colorado Springs Gazette Telegraph*, February 27, 1992, p. A1.

16. Barry Noreen, "Brown Brings His Message to Town," *Colorado Springs Gazette Telegraph*, February 27, 1992, p. A1.

17. Eugene Burdick, *The Ninth Wave* (New York: Dell, 1956), p. 346-359.

18. All quotes from the Saturday television debate are from Fred Brown, Eric Anderson, and Renate Robey, "Sharp Comments Traded during Democrats' Forum," *Denver Post*, March 1, 1992, p. 1A.

19. Chart entitled "Democratic Front-Runners," *Denver Post*, March 4, 1992, p. 11A.

20. Chart entitled "Democratic Candidates," *Denver Post*, March 4, 1992, p. 11A.

21. Genevieve Anton, "Brown Crashes the Party," *Colorado Springs Gazette Telegraph*, March 4, 1992, p. A1.

22. Genevieve Anton, "Brown Crashes the Party," *Colorado Springs Gazette Telegraph*, March 4, 1992, p. A1.

23. Jeff Thomas, "Surprising Colorado Muddles Race," *Colorado Springs Gazette Telegraph*, March 4, 1992, p. A5.

24. Jeff Thomas, "Surprising Colorado Muddles Race," *Colorado Springs Gazette Telegraph*, March 4, 1992, p. A5.

25. "Late Price Cut Can't Save Buchanan Lunch," *Colorado Springs Gazette Telegraph*, February 26, 1992, p. A1.

26. Genevieve Anton, "Quayle Makes Whistle-Stop in Denver," *Colorado Springs Gazette Telegraph*, February 20, 1992, p. A3.

27. Dan Njegomir, "Kemp Carries Bush's Flag to Springs," *Colorado Springs Gazette Telegraph*, February 27, 1992, p. A3.

28. These ideas were contained in a campaign memorandum written by a Nixon speech writer, Raymond K. Price. See Joe McGinniss, *The Selling of the President 1968* (New York: Trident Press, 1969), pp. 30-33.

29. *Variable*, June, 1992, a western politics newsletter published by Ciruli Associates, 1380 Lawrence Street, Suite 650, Denver, Colorado 80204.

30. George Stephanopoulos, the communications director for the Clinton campaign, subsequently argued that Jerry Brown's victory in Colorado ended Paul Tsongas's chance to remain in the race and thus guaranteed the 1992 Democratic nomination to Bill Clinton. When asked later if he agreed with Stephanopoulos, Paul Tsongas said he did and added: "That was the moment the brass ring was lost." See Jack W. Germond and Jules Witcover, *Mad As Hell: Revolt at the Ballot Box, 1992* (New York: Warner Books, 1993), pp. 258-259. Robert Sherrill thought this revelation about the critical nature of the Colorado Democratic presidential primary was so important he included it in his review of Germond and Witcover's book. See Robert Sherrill, "The Nitty Ditty Nitty

Gritty Election," a review of *Mad as Hell: Revolt at the Ballot Box, 1992,* by Jack W. Germond and Jules Witcover, *Washington Post National Weekly Edition,* August 30-September 5, 1993, p. 35.

CHAPTER 8

1. Robert D. Loevy, *To End All Segregation: The Politics of the Passage of the Civil Rights Act of 1964* (Lanham, Maryland: University Press of America, 1990), pp. 261-266. Also see Lyndon Baines Johnson, *The Vantage Point: Perspectives on the Presidency 1963-1969* (New York: Popular Library, 1971), p. 159.

2. Theodore H. White saw the shooting and wounding of George Wallace while campaigning in the 1972 Maryland Democratic presidential primary as the turning point in the 1972 presidential election. When Wallace's severe wounds forced him to drop out of the race, White argued, the Nixon forces saw themselves capable of defeating any candidate the Democrats might nominate. Theodore H. White, *The Making of the President 1972* (New York: Atheneum, 1973), pp. 316-318.

3. For a good description of Brown's victory over Carter in Maryland in 1976, see Jules Witcover, *Marathon: The Pursuit of the Presidency 1972-1976* (New York: Viking Penguin, 1977), pp. 353-358.

4. This and subsequent quotes by Michael Gordon, Democratic member of the Maryland house of delegates from Rockville-Gaithersburg, from an interview by the author, June 24, 1992.

5. This and subsequent quotes by Nathan Landow, chairman of the Maryland Democratic Party, from an interview by the author, June 24, 1992.

6. For an extensive article on Tsongas's campaign, and problems, in the 1992 Maryland Democratic presidential primary, see David Shribman, "Tsongas Struggles to Prove His National Appeal In Maryland Race as New Hampshire Cheers Fade," *Wall Street Journal,* February 27, 1992, p. A12.

CHAPTER 9

1. This and subsequent quotes by Bob Holmes, Member of the Georgia house of representatives from Atlanta, from an interview by the author, June 24, 1992.

2. Cynthia Wright, executive counsel to Georgia governor Zell Miller, interview by the author, June 24, 1992.

3. Associated Press, "Southern Voters Judge Candidates on Patriotism, Morality," *Colorado Springs Gazette Telegraph,* March 3, 1992, p. A3.

4. Associated Press, "Southern Voters Judge Candidates on Patriotism, Morality," *Colorado Springs Gazette Telegraph*, March 3, 1992, p. A3.

5. Associated Press, "Southern Voters Judge Candidates on Patriotism, Morality," *Colorado Springs Gazette Telegraph*, March 3, 1992, p. A3.

6. News services, "Colorado Vote May Help Define Democratic Race," *Colorado Springs Gazette Telegraph*, March 3, 1992, p. A1.

7. At a later date, the *New York Times* published a very positive statement that Governor Zell Miller's support in Georgia was a critical part of Bill Clinton's campaign for the 1992 Democratic nomination. "Governor Miller, a veteran in Georgia politics, helped save Mr. Clinton's candidacy when he came limping South after a second-place finish in New Hampshire. Mr. Clinton's big victory in Georgia's March 3 primary helped set the stage for a big victory in the March 10th 'Super Tuesday' contests across the South, which largely sealed the nomination for Mr. Clinton." "Democrats to Name 3 Keynote Speakers," *New York Times*, June 26, 1992, p. A13.

8. Associated Press, "Blacks Help Clinton in Georgia," *Colorado Springs Gazette Telegraph*, March 4, 1992, p. A5.

9. Germond and Witcover agree that the change in the date of the Georgia primary was a critical part of Clinton's winning the 1992 Democratic presidential nomination. "[Zell] Miller conveniently had persuaded his legislature to move the Georgia primary date forward, out of the clutter of Super Tuesday, a move that . . . set [Clinton] up to emerge as the clear front-runner after Super Tuesday." Jack W. Germond and Jules Witcover, *Mad As Hell: Revolt at the Ballot Box, 1992* (New York: Warner Books, 1993), p. 248.

10. Associated Press, "Buchanan Goes on the Attack," *Colorado Springs Gazette Telegraph*, February 28, 1992, p. A3.

11. Associated Press, "Buchanan Goes on the Attack," *Colorado Springs Gazette Telegraph*, February 28, 1992, p. A3.

12. Associated Press, "Bush Blasts Protectionism Vowed by Rival," *Colorado Springs Gazette Telegraph*, March 1, 1992, p. A6.

13. Associated Press, "Supporter of Bush Accuses Rival of Flirting with Fascism," *Colorado Springs Gazette Telegraph*, March 2, 1992, p. A3.

14. Associated Press, "Bush Blasts Protectionism Vowed by Rival," *Colorado Springs Gazette Telegraph*, March 1, 1992, p. A6.

CHAPTER 10

1. For an analytical epitaph to the Kerrey campaign, see Mary McGrory, "Bob Kerrey, the Candidate Who Had It All Untogether," *Washington Post National Weekly Edition*, March 16-22, 1992, p. 25.

CHAPTER 11

1. For a detailed account of the southern Democratic creation of Super Tuesday, see Harold W. Stanley and Charles D. Hadley, "The Southern Presidential Primary: Regional Intentions With National Implications," *Publius*, Summer 1987, pp. 83-100.

2. A good discussion of Super Tuesday in the South in 1988 can be found in Gerald M. Pomper, "The Presidential Nominations," in Gerald M. Pomper et al., *The Election of 1988: Reports and Interpretations* (Chatham, NJ: Chatham House Publishers, 1989), pp. 38-44.

3. All quotes about Texas from *USA Today* in Bill Nichols, "Texas: Clinton Likely to Win 'Bubba vote,'" *USA Today*, March 6, 1992, p. 5A.

4. George Oster, Florida Democratic Party political director, quoted in Adam Nagourney, "Florida: Tsongas Showing Strength," *USA Today*, March 6, 1992, p. 5A.

5. Tom Fielder and Martin Merzer, "Spotlight Swings to Florida," *Miami Herald*, March 7, 1992, p. 1A.

6. Adam Nagourney, "Florida: Tsongas Showing Strength," *USA Today*, March 6, 1992, p. 5A.

7. Adam Nagourney, "Florida: Tsongas Showing Strength," *USA Today*, March 6, 1992, p. 5A.

8. Tom Fiedler and Dan Holly, "Democrats Intensify Vote Hunt," *Miami Herald*, March 9, 1992, p. 1A.

9. Margaret Carlson, Priscilla Painton, and Walter Shapiro, "The Long Road," *Time*, November 2, 1992, pp. 28-43.

10. All quotes from Martin Merzer, "Trail Mix," *Miami Herald*, March 9, 1992, p. 12A.

11. Tom Fiedler and Anne Bartlett, "Florida's Turn to Be Counted," *Miami Herald*, March 10, 1992, p. 1A.

12. "Ad Watch," *Miami Herald*, March 7, 1992, p. 21A.

13. Tom Fiedler and Martin Merzer, "Spotlight Swings to Florida," *Miami Herald*, March 7, 1992, p. 1A.

14. Tom Fiedler and Anne Bartlett, "Florida's Turn to Be Counted," *Miami Herald*, March 10, 1992, p. 1A.

15. New York Times News Service, "Questions Raised about Clinton Land Deal," *Orlando Sentinel*, March 9, 1992, p. A-5.

16. Tom Fiedler and Anne Bartlett, "Florida's Turn to Be Counted," *Miami Herald*, March 10, 1992, p. 1A.

17. Rick Pierce, "Clinton's Backers Celebrate," *Fort Lauderdale Sun-Sentinel*, March 11, 1992, p. 4A.

18. Tom Davidson, "Florida Declares Clinton Front-Runner," *Fort Lauderdale Sun-Sentinel*, March 11, 1992, p. 4A.

19. All exit poll data from Wire Services, "Racial, Ethnic Vote Goes to Clinton," *Fort Lauderdale Sun-Sentinel*, March 11, 1992, p. 5A.

20. Associated Press, "Democrat Harkin Expected to Fold His Campaign Today," *Miami Herald*, March 9, 1992, p. 13A.

21. Johanna Neuman, "Israel Issues May Weigh in at Polls," *USA Today*, March 6, 1992, p. 4A.

22. Agence France-Presse, "Remember The Alamo (photograph)," *Miami Herald*, March 7, 1992, p. 1A.

23. Martin Merzer, "Trail Mix," *Miami Herald*, March 7, 1992, p. 21A.

CHAPTER 12

1. Adam Nagourney, "Democratic Hopefuls Stump in Key Midwest: For Clinton, Early Efforts in Illinois Pay Off," *USA Today*, March 13, 1992, p. 8A.

2. Bill Nichols, "Democratic Hopefuls Stump in Key Midwest: Tsongas Not Well-Received in Michigan," *USA Today*, March 13, 1992, p. 8A.

3. Bill Nichols, "Democratic Hopefuls Stump in Key Midwest: Tsongas Not Well-Received in Michigan," *USA Today*, March 13, 1992, p. 8A.

4. Steve Daley, "Primary Takes a Nasty Turn," *Chicago Tribune*, March 16, 1992, Section 1, p. 1.

5. John King, Associated Press, "Rivals Blast Clinton's Conduct before Midwestern Primaries," *Tampa Tribune*, March 16, 1992, p. 1.

6. Steve Daley, "Primary Takes a Nasty Turn," *Chicago Tribune*, March 16, 1992, Section 1, page 1.

7. Steve Daley, "Primary Takes a Nasty Turn," *Chicago Tribune*, March 16, 1992, Section 1, p. 1.

8. Steve Daley, "Primary Takes a Nasty Turn," *Chicago Tribune*, March 16, 1992, Section 1, p. 1.

9. All Paul Tsongas quotes from Glenn F. Bunting, "Tsongas Pulls Out of Race: It's Down to Clinton and Brown," *San Francisco Chronicle*, March 20, 1992, p. 1.

10. Glenn F. Bunting, "Tsongas Pulls Out of Race: It's Down to Clinton and Brown," *San Francisco Chronicle*, March 20, 1992, p. 1.

CHAPTER 13

1. Susan Yoachum and Jerry Roberts, "Demos Debating Clinton's Next Move," *San Francisco Chronicle*, March 20, 1992, p. 1.

2. Wire Services, "Brown Rides Crest of Conn. Win, Steps up His Attacks on Clinton," *Denver Post*, March 26, 1992, p. 4A.

3. Sandy Grady, "Upset Proves Democrats Still Looking," *Denver Post*, March 26, 1992, p. 7B.

4. Robin Toner, "Democrats Rebuff Clinton in the Connecticut Primary as Brown Wins a Close Vote," *New York Times*, March 25, 1992, p. 1A.

5. Christopher Graff, Associated Press, "Brown Captures Vermont Caucuses," *Denver Post*, April 1, 1992, p. 1A.

6. Associated Press, "Brown Beats Clinton in Vermont," *Colorado Springs Gazette Telegraph*, April 1, 1992, p. A3.

CHAPTER 14

1. Wire Services, "Clinton Tried Pot in '60s," *Denver Post*, March 30, 1992, p. 1A.

2. Sandy Grady, "Forget About a 'Brokered' Convention," *Denver Post*, April 7, 1992, p. 7B.

3. "Campaign Notebook," *Colorado Springs Gazette Telegraph*, March 29, 1992, p. A3.

4. Observed on television by the author.

5. Knight-Ridder News Service, "Campaign Trail Lined with Stress," *Colorado Springs Gazette Telegraph*, March 30, 1992, p. A3.

6. Knight-Ridder News Service, "Campaign Trail Lined with Stress," *Colorado Springs Gazette Telegraph*, March 30, 1992, p. A3.

7. Sam Roberts, "Brown and Clinton Trade Blows in New York Contest," *New York Times*, March 26, 1992, p. A13.

8. Wire Services, "Clinton Tries to Shoot Down Brown's Flat Tax Plan," *Denver Post*, March 29, 1992, p. 6A. Also see "Campaign Notebook," *Colorado Springs Gazette Telegraph*, March 29, 1992, p. A3.

9. Gwen Ifill, "Campaign Attacks by Brown Assailed by his Party Chief," *New York Times*, March 27, 1992, p. A1.

10. Wire Services, "Clinton Tries to Shoot Down Brown's Flat Tax Plan," *Denver Post*, March 29, 1992, p. 6A.

11. Douglas Jehl, "Clinton: I Can Take a Punch and Give One," *Denver Post*, April 3, 1992, p. 6A.

12. Wire Services, "Clinton Tries to Shoot Down Brown's Flat Tax Plan," *Denver Post*, March 29, 1992, p. 6A.

13. "Campaign Notebook," *Colorado Springs Gazette Telegraph*, March 29, 1992, p. A3.

14. Philip J. Trounstine, Knight-Ridder News Service, "Jackson for V.P. Draws Jewish Backlash," *Denver Post*, April 3, 1992, p. 6A.

15. Associated Press, "Brown Blasts Report on Contributions," *Colorado Springs Gazette Telegraph*, April 4, 1992, p. A3.

16. Cox News Service, "Brown, Clinton Put on the Defensive," *Colorado Springs Gazette Telegraph*, April 6, 1992, p. A3.

17. Douglas Jehl, "Clinton: I Can Take a Punch and Give One," *Denver Post*, April 3, 1992, p. 6A.

18. Sandy Grady, "Forget About a 'Brokered' Convention," *Denver Post*, April 7, 1992, p. 7B.

19. Cox News Service, "Brown, Clinton Put on the Defensive," *Colorado Springs Gazette Telegraph*, April 6, 1992, p. A3.

20. Jack W. Germond, "N.Y. Debate Surprisingly Low Key as Weary Clinton Backs Down," *Denver Post*, April 1, 1992, p. 5A.

21. Jack W. Germond, "N.Y. Debate Surprisingly Low Key as Weary Clinton Backs Down," *Denver Post*, April 1, 1992, p. 5A.

22. Jill Dutt and Alan Eysen, "Tsongas Considers Getting Back in Race," *Denver Post*, April 4, 1992, p. 1A.

23. Sandy Grady, "Clinton's the One—Like It or Not," *Denver Post*, April 12, 1992, p. 4I.

24. All exit poll data from Associated Press, "Voter Dissatisfaction Dampens Clinton's Victory Parties," *Colorado Springs Gazette Telegraph*, April 8, 1992, p. A4.

25. Sandy Grady, "Clinton's the One—Like It or Not," *Denver Post*, April 12, 1992, p. 4I.

26. David Broder, "Republican Strategists Look with Glee at Bill Clinton's Character Flaws," *Denver Post*, April 10, 1992, p. 15B.

27. Rowland Evans and Robert Novak, "Clinton Busy Explaining Himself into Nomination," *Colorado Springs Gazette Telegraph*, April 11, 1992, p. B11.

28. David Maraniss, "A Question of Character: Despite His Success, Clinton Remains Defined by Doubts," *Washington Post National Weekly Edition*, April 20-26, 1992, p. 6.

29. Kenneth T. Walsh with Matthew Cooper and Susan Dentzer, "Thinking About Tomorrow: The Clinton Era Begins," *U.S. News & World Report*, November 16, 1992, pp. 32-33.

CHAPTER 15

1. R. W. Apple Jr., "Wisconsin Has Mixture to Give Clinton Trouble," *New York Times*, March 26, 1992, p. A15.

2. Robert S. Boyd, Knight-Ridder News Service, "Democrats Still Show Strong Distaste for Clinton," *Denver Post*, April 8, 1992, p. 6A.

3. John E. Yang, "Buchanan Will Shift Focus of Campaign," *Denver Post*, March 31, 1992, 8A.

4. Associated Press, "Sweep in Maine Locks up GOP Nomination for Bush," *Denver Post*, May 3, 1992, p. 6A.

CHAPTER 16

1. "A Challenger's Rise and Fall," *Time*, July 27, 1992, pp. 32-33.

2. There was at least one political columnist who, even at the height of Perotmania in mid-April of 1992, predicted that his independent candidacy would soon fade in popularity. See Ben Wattenberg, "Perot Won't Long Retain Wide Support," *Colorado Springs Gazette Telegraph*, April 15, 1992, p. B5.

3. For a lengthy account of Perot's youth and business career, and a typical example of the sort of favorable reporting that was done on Perot at the start of his independent campaign for president, see Alan Farnham, "And Now, Here's the Man Himself," the cover story in *Fortune*, June 15, 1992, pp. 68-74.

4. Some questions were raised in the press about the extent to which Ross Perot really was involved in the freeing of his employees in Iran. See William

Gaines and Mike Dorning, "The Myth of Perot's Iran Rescue: Daring Raid—or Just a Good Book," *Chicago Tribune*, July 9, 1992, p. 1.

5. "A Challenger's Rise and Fall," *Time*, July 27, 1992, pp. 32-33.

6. Responsible news media speculated quite openly that there was a real possibility of a Perot victory in November. The following quote is typical of how this idea was usually expressed. "[Perot supporters] think that Mr. Perot can win it all . . . in November, and as spring turns to summer an extraordinary number of other Americans are beginning to think so too." "Beginner's Luck?" *Economist*, May 30th, 1992, pp. 24-25.

CHAPTER 17

1. Tom Baxter, Cox News Service, "Nomination Process Is Clinton's Chief Rival," *Colorado Springs Gazette Telegraph*, April 8, 1992, p. A4.

2. R. W. Apple Jr., "The Voters' Message: Very Murky," *New York Times*, April 8, 1992, p. A1.

3. Associated Press, "Pennsylvania Provides Next Dem Battleground," *Denver Post*, April 8, 1992, p. 8A.

4. Katharine Seelye, "Clinton Victory Is Expected in Pa., but Voters Show Little Enthusiasm," *Philadelphia Inquirer*, April 26, 1992, p. A1.

5. Robin Toner, "Clinton Rolls over Brown 2-1 in Pa.," *Denver Post*, April 29, 1992, p. 2A.

6. Brown's speech in Portland was observed by the author. See also Foster Church and Dan Hortsch, "Brown, Clinton Woo Voters," *Portland Oregonian*, May 19, 1992, p. A1.

7. Paddy McGuire, state director, Clinton for President Committee, interview by the author, Portland, Oregon, May 19, 1992.

8. Dan Balz, "In Medias Res: If You Can't Beat 'Em, Bypass 'Em," *Washington Post National Weekly Edition*, May 25-31, 1992, p. 12.

9. Debbie Howlett, "Perot Write-Ins Steal Show," *USA Today*, May 21, 1992, p. 1A.

CHAPTER 18

1. R. W. Apple Jr., "In California, Primaries End With a Whimper," *New York Times*, May 26, 1992, p. A10.

2. Calculated from data provided in Rhodes Cook, *Race for the Presidency: Winning the 1992 Nomination* (Washington, DC: Congressional Quarterly Press, 1991), pp. 3, 102.

3. Associated Press, "California Gets a Green Light in Drive for Earlier Presidential Primary," *Colorado Springs Gazette Telegraph*, February 15, 1990, p. A8.

4. George F. Will, "Early Primary Won't End Democratic Tug of War," *Colorado Springs Gazette Telegraph*, February 21, 1990, p. B7.

5. Rowland Evans and Robert Novak, "Democratic Rule Changes Benefit Jackson, Not Party," *Colorado Springs Gazette Telegraph*, March 14, 1990, p. B9.

6. R. W. Apple Jr., "In California, Primaries End With a Whimper," *New York Times*, May 26, 1992, p. A10.

7. Robin Toner, "Clinton Off Course," *New York Times*, May 28, 1992, p. A11.

8. David S. Broder, "Before the Revolution," *Washington Post National Weekly Edition*, June 8-14, 1992, p. 4. Also see R. W. Apple Jr., "Throngs Wanted Perot Vote," *Denver Post*, June 3, 1992, p. 7A.

9. R. W. Apple Jr., "He's Not on California Ballot, But Perot Dominates the Race," *New York Times*, May 24, 1992, p. A1.

10. Adam Nagourney, "'I Have a Vision, You're Part of It': Clinton Reaches out to Gay Community," *USA Today*, May 20, 1992, p. 4A.

11. "1992 Democratic Primary Results," *Congressional Quarterly Weekly Report*, July 4, 1992, p. 69.

CHAPTER 19

1. David S. Broder, "When Winning Isn't Everything," *Washington Post National Weekly Edition*, June 8-14, 1992, p. 12.

2. For further information on regional primaries, see William Crotty and John S. Jackson 3d, *Presidential Primaries and Nominations* (Washington, D.C.: Congressional Quarterly Press, 1985), p. 228, and Nelson W. Polsby and Aaron Wildavsky, *Presidential Elections: Strategies of American Electoral Politics*, 5th edition (New York: Charles Scribner's Sons, 1980), pp. 229-230.

3. For strong advocacy of a national primary, see Martin P. Wattenberg, "When You Can't Beat Them, Join Them: Shaping the Presidential Nominating Process to the Television Age," *Polity*, Spring 1989, pp. 587-597. For a thoughtful discussion of the national primary as compared to the current sequential system, see Larry Bartels, *Presidential Primaries and the Dynamics of Public Choice*

(Princeton, NJ: Princeton University Press, 1988), pp. 281-282, 285-293. Also see Nelson W. Polsby and Aaron Wildavsky, *Presidential Elections: Strategies of American Electoral Politics*, 5th edition (New York: Charles Scribner's Sons, 1980), pp. 223-229.

4. William G. Mayer noted that New Hampshirites now speak about the Granite State holding the first presidential primary as if it were "the very Pillar of American Democracy." His view, which is also the author's, is that the undue influence of the New Hampshire primary and the Iowa caucuses can best be limited by altering the remainder of the primary and caucus calendar. Mayer recommends against taking on the almost impossible political task of getting New Hampshire and Iowa to give up their favored positions. William G. Mayer, "The New Hampshire Primary: A Historical Overview," in Gary R. Orren and Nelson W. Polsby, *Media and Momentum: The New Hampshire Primary and Nomination Politics* (Chatham, NJ: Chatham House Publishers, 1987), pp. 33-37.

CHAPTER 20

1. "A Challenger's Rise and Fall," *Time*, July 27, 1992, pp. 32-33.

2. Robin Toner, "Perot Makes Major Parties Do Some Major Rethinking," *New York Times*, June 4, 1992, p. A11.

3. "Campaign Notebook," *Colorado Springs Gazette Telegraph*, May 11, 1992, p.A3.

4. Howard Fineman, "Perot's Patriot Games," *Newsweek*, May 25, 1992, p. 34.

5. John Mintz, "Nobody Here But Us Country Boys? Yeah, Right," *Washington Post National Weekly Edition*, June 1-7, 1992, p. 13.

6. "Campaign Notebook," *Colorado Springs Gazette Telegraph*, July 3, 1992, p. A3.

7. Howard Fineman and Ginny Carroll, "How to Run Against Perot," *Newsweek*, June 1, 1992, p. 48.

8. Michael Kelly and Stephen Lebaton, "Perot Detective Describes Inquiry into a Rival Computer Company," *New York Times*, July 8, 1992, p. A1.

9. John M. Broder, "Ex-Adviser: Perot Couldn't Pay the Price," *Denver Post*, July 20, 1992, p. 1A.

10. "A Challenger's Rise and Fall," *Time*, July 27, 1992, p. 32.

11. "Campaign Notebook," *Colorado Springs Gazette Telegraph*, May 22, 1992, p. A3.

12. Andrew Rosenthal, "Quayle: Perot 'Temperamental Tycoon' Who Hates Constitution," *Denver Post*, June 13, 1992, p. 5A.

13. Howard Fineman and Ginny Carroll, "How to Run Against Perot," *Newsweek*, June 1, 1992, p. 48.

14. "Campaign Notebook," *Colorado Springs Gazette Telegraph*, May 23, 1992, p. A3.

15. Fred Brown, "Feeling Grows That Perot's Fading Fast," *Denver Post*, July 16, 1992, p. 17A.

16. John Hanchette, Gannett News Service, "Perot Demands Loyalty in Writing, Backers Say," *Denver Post*, July 11, 1992, p. 1A.

17. "A Challenger's Rise and Fall," *Time*, July 27, 1992, pp. 32-33.

CHAPTER 21

1. For a good description of national party conventions when they really did nominate the party candidates for president, see Paul T. David, Richard M. Goldman, and Richard C. Bain, *The Politics of National Party Conventions* (Washington, D.C.: Brookings Institution, 1960).

2. Although they were not the first to use the term, Polsby and Wildavsky describe contemporary national conventions as "ratifying" conventions. Nelson W. Polsby and Aaron Wildavsky, *Presidential Elections: Contemporary Strategies of American Electoral Politics*, 7th edition (New York: The Free Press, 1988), pp. 143-161.

3. For a thorough description of the mayhem at the 1968 Democratic National Convention, see Chapter 9, "The Chicago Convention: The Furies in the Street," in Theodore H. White, *The Making of the President 1968* (New York: Pocket Books, 1970), pp. 321-389.

4. For a full discussion of the various attempts to reform the Democratic Party in the 1970s and their lasting effects, see Nelson W. Polsby, *The Consequences of Party Reform* (New York: Oxford University Press, 1983). For a discussion of the effects of Democratic reforms on the national convention, see Byron E. Shafer, *Bifurcated Politics: Evolution and Reform in the National Party Convention* (Cambridge, MA: Harvard University Press, 1988).

5. See Chapter 7, "Confrontation at Miami," in Theodore H. White, *The Making of the President 1972* (New York: Bantam Books, 1973), pp. 209-255.

6. Jack W. Germond and Jules Witcover, *Blue Smoke and Mirrors: How Reagan Won and Why Carter Lost the Election of 1980* (New York: Viking Press, 1981), pp. 191-196.

CHAPTER 22

1. Quotes from the 1992 Democratic Platform can be found in E. J. Dionne Jr., "Clinton's Platform is Perched on the Politics of Inclusion," *Washington Post National Weekly Edition*, June 6-12, 1992, p. 14.

2. David E. Rosenbaum, "Democratic Platform Shows Shift in Party's Roots," *New York Times*, July 14, 1992, p. A9.

3. Germond and Witcover argue that the Sister Souljah incident won Bill Clinton the votes of many southern Whites and northern blue-collar workers in the November general election. They quote Kevin Mullaney, a North Philadelphia electrician: "The day [Clinton] told off that . . . Jackson is the day he got my vote." Jack W. Germond and Jules Witcover, *Mad As Hell: Revolt at the Ballot Box, 1992* (New York: Warner Books, 1993), p. 304.

4. E. J. Dionne Jr., "Clinton's Platform Is Perched on the Politics of Inclusion," *Washington Post National Weekly Edition*, June 6-12, 1992, p. 14.

5. Karen De Witt, "1985 Crusade by Tipper Gore is Likely to Help 1992 Ticket," *New York Times*, July 10, 1992, p. A9.

6. Gwen Ifill, "Clinton Chooses Gore," *Denver Post*, July 10, 1992, p. 1A.

7. Susan Yoachum and Jerry Roberts, "Ticket Targets South, West," *Denver Post*, July 10, 1992, p. 1A.

8. William Safire, "Clinton Shuts Down Dissent at Convention," *Colorado Springs Gazette Telegraph*, July 17, 1992, p. B11.

9. Knight-Ridder News Service, "Ohio Delegation Makes It Official," *Colorado Springs Gazette Telegraph*, July 16, 1992, p. A1.

10. Sandy Grady, "Democratic Convention's Seams Sealed," *Denver Post*, July 14, 1992, p. 7B.

11. Richard L. Berke, "Democrats Hope to Persuade Voters to Tune In to Tradition," *New York Times*, July 6, 1992, p. A1.

12. Jeff Greenfield, "Are We Watching a Theme Park Convention?" *Denver Post*, July 16, 1992, p. 7B.

13. Richard L. Berke, "Democrats Hope to Persuade Voters to Tune In to Tradition," *New York Times*, July 6, 1992, p. A1.

14. Knight-Ridder News Service, "It's Nominee Clinton Now," *Colorado Springs Gazette Telegraph*, July 16, 1992, p. A1.

15. Margaret Carlson, "Just a Couple of Hicks With 40 Million Viewers,"

Time, January 18, 1993, p. 27. Stephen J. Wayne describes this process of having show business professionals "produce" a national convention as "Scripting the Convention as Theater." Stephen J. Wayne, *The Road to the White House 1992: The Politics of Presidential Elections* (New York: St. Martin's Press, 1992), p. 161.

16. "Clinton-Gore 'Buscapade' to Cover 1,000 Miles," *Denver Post,* July 18, 1992, p. 18A.

CHAPTER 23

1. See Tom Morganthau, "The Quitter: Why Perot Bowed Out," the cover story in *Newsweek,* July 27, 1992, pp. 28-30. Also see Gerald Rafshoon, "Why I Left Perot," *Washington Post National Weekly Edition,* July 20-26, 1992, p. 28, and Rowland Evans and Robert Novak, "What Did Perot Have in Mind in Beginning?" *Colorado Springs Gazette Telegraph,* July 21, 1992, p. B5.

2. Carl Cannon and Kristin Huckshorn, Knight-Ridder News Service, "True Grit Up 'n Quit but Why?" *Denver Post,* July 17, 1992, p. 2A.

3. John Mintz and David Von Drehle, "The Day Perot Pulled the Plug," *Washington Post National Weekly Edition,* July 27-August 2, 1992, p. 9.

4. Laurence I. Barrett, "Perot Takes a Walk," *Time,* July 27, 1992, p. 32.

5. For a thorough analysis of the Perot economic plan and its political problems, see Jodie T. Allen, "Perot Took Aim At the Deficit, Then Took Off," *Washington Post National Weekly Edition,* August 3-9, 1992, p. 24.

6. John Mintz and David Von Drehle, "The Day Perot Pulled the Plug," *Washington Post National Weekly Edition,* July 27-August 2, 1992, p. 9.

7. Debbie Howlett, "Perot Loses Rollins," *Denver Post,* July 16, 1992, p. 17A.

8. Molly Ivins, "The Rise and Fall of Ross Perot," *Denver Post,* July 19, 1992, p. 4-I.

9. David S. Broder, "With Gore and Without Perot," *Washington Post National Weekly Edition,* July 27-August 2, 1992, p. 4.

10. Perot's brief campaign for president may have been most significant in its effect on the Clinton campaign. Clinton campaign advisers later argued the Perot campaign drew President Bush's and the media's critical fire exactly at the time Clinton needed to get out of the public eye and "recover from the press's critical coverage of his private life." See Robert Sherrill, "The Nitty Ditty Nitty Gritty Election," a review of *Mad as Hell: Revolt at the Ballot Box, 1992,* by Jack W. Germond and Jules Witcover, *Washington Post National Weekly Edition,* August 30-September 5, 1993, p. 35.

CHAPTER 24

1. "GOP Seeking Cure in Houston," *Denver Post*, August 17, 1992, p. 1A.

2. Richard Morin, "Bush in the Land of Way Down Under," *Washington Post National Weekly Edition*, August 17-23, 1992, p. 37.

3. Associated Press, "Ex-Bush Adversary Jumps on President's Bandwagon," *Colorado Springs Gazette Telegraph*, August 18, 1992, p. A3.

4. Wire Services, "Reagan Looks at Triumphs in Past, Future," *Denver Post*, August 18, 1992, p. 1A.

5. Thomas B. Edsall, "The Republicans' Value-Added Strategy," *Washington Post National Weekly Edition*, August 24-30, 1992, p. 15.

6. Associated Press, "Ex-Bush Adversary Jumps on President's Bandwagon," *Colorado Springs Gazette Telegraph*, August 18, 1992, p. A3.

7. Observed by the author on network television.

8. Observed by the author and everyone else who watched the 1992 Republican National Convention on network television. See also Richard Morin and Maralee Schwartz, "Trust and Parry Politics," *Washington Post National Weekly Edition*, August 31-September 6, 1992, p. 13.

9. "Inc." *Chicago Tribune*, August 21, 1992, Section 1, p. 22.

10. Observed by the author on network television.

11. Jack Nelson and James Gerstenzang, "Bush Rallies His Troops," *Denver Post*, August 18, 1992, p. 1A.

12. Wire Services, "Reagan Looks at Triumphs in Past, Future," *Denver Post*, August 18, 1992, p. 1A.

13. Observed by the author on network television.

14. Robert S. Boyd and Carl M. Cannon, Knight-Ridder News Service, "Bush Wins GOP Nomination, Makes It a Family Affair," *Denver Post*, August 20, 1992, p. 1A.

15. All quotes from President Bush's acceptance speech are from Robin Toner, "Bush Promises Across-the-Board Tax Cut and an Economic Revival in a Second Term," *New York Times*, August 21, 1992, p. A1.

16. Richard Morin and Maralee Schwartz, "Trust and Parry Politics," *Washington Post National Weekly Edition*, August 31-September 6, 1992, p. 13.

17. Thomas B. Edsall, "The Republicans' Value-Added Strategy," *Washington Post National Weekly Edition*, August 24-30, 1992, p. 15.

18. Molly Ivins, "A Feast of Hate and Fear," *Newsweek*, August 31, 1992, p. 32.

19. Virginia Culver, "Bush Must Win Colo., Editor Says," *Denver Post*, September 19, 1992, p. 2B.

20. Howard Kurtz, "Are Reporters Letting Clinton Off Easy?" *Washington Post National Weekly Edition*, September 7-13, 1992, p. 12.

21. "Polls Continue to Vary," *New York Times*, September 10, 1992, p. A11.

CHAPTER 25

1. The idea of holding the national convention prior to the presidential primaries rather than after them has been proposed in the past decade in a wide variety of forms. See Thomas E. Cronin and Robert D. Loevy, "The Case for a National Pre-Primary Convention," *Public Opinion*, December/January 1983, pp. 50-53. For a longer and more detailed version of the Cronin-Loevy proposal, see Thomas E. Cronin and Robert D. Loevy, "Putting the Party As Well As the People Back in President Picking," in Kenneth W. Thompson, ed., *The Presidential Nominating Process*, Volume I (Lanham, MD: University Press of America, 1983), pp. 49-64. The Cronin-Loevy proposal was linked to a national presidential primary rather than preserving the current sequential primary and caucus system. See also Martin P. Wattenberg, "When You Can't Beat Them, Join Them: Shaping the Presidential Nominating Process to the Television Age," *Polity*, Spring 1989, pp. 595-597.

2. Martin P. Wattenberg agrees that the delegates to a preprimary mini-convention should be "party leaders," although he does not limit his definition of party leaders to elected officials as my proposal does. Martin P. Wattenberg, "When You Can't Beat Them, Join Them: Shaping the Presidential Nominating Process to the Television Age," *Polity*, Spring 1989, p. 595.

CHAPTER 26

1. Cathleen Decker, "Clinton Tours South by Bus, Acknowledges Fear of Perot," *Denver Post*, October 27, 1992, p. 11A.

2. Bill Turque, "The Art of the Advance," *Newsweek*, September 28, 1992, p. 22.

3. Joe Klein, "On the Road Again," *Newsweek*, August 17, 1992, pp. 31-33.

4. Joe Klein, "On the Road Again," *Newsweek*, August 17, 1992, pp. 31-33.

5. Richard L. Berke, "Clinton Tour Makes Big News," *Denver Post*, August 9, 1992, p. 5A.

6. Joe Klein, "On the Road Again," *Newsweek*, August 17, 1992, pp. 31-33.

7. Author's notes, remarks by Richard L. Berke, New York Times, The Colorado Symposium on the Presidential Election, University of Colorado at Colorado Springs, December 11-12, 1992.

8. Author's notes, remarks by Stephen Hirsh, ABC News, The Colorado Symposium on the Presidential Election, University of Colorado at Colorado Springs, December 11-12, 1992.

CHAPTER 27

1. "A Silver Bullet," *Newsweek*, Special Election Issue, November/December 1992, pp. 82-83.

2. Michael Wines, "Baker Returns, Bringing Tried-and-True Tactics," *New York Times*, August 24, 1992, p. A1.

3. Katharine Seelye and Reed Karaim, Knight-Ridder News Service, "Clinton, Bush Both Lay Claim to Truman Mantle," *Denver Post*, September 8, 1992, p. 1A.

4. Michael Wines, "$8 Billion Directed to Wheat Farmers and Arms Workers," *New York Times*, September 3, 1992, p. A12.

5. Ann Devroy, "Bush, Going the 'Extra Mile,'" *Washington Post*, September 28, 1992, p. A1.

6. Judy Keen, "Wheedling, Needling on Tracks of Bush Trip," *USA Today*, September 28, 1992, p. 11A.

CHAPTER 28

1. For a thorough history of the electoral college as it has evolved over the years, see Neal R. Peirce and Lawrence D. Longley, *The People's President: The Electoral College in American History and the Direct Vote Alternative*, rev. edition (New Haven, CT: Yale University Press, 1981).

2. There are a number of political analysts who defend the electoral college precisely because it does overrepresent large states. "Originally designed to check popular majorities from choosing presidents unwisely, the electoral college later on provided a 'check' on the overrepresentation of rural states in the legislative branch by giving extra weight to the big state constituencies of the president." Nelson W. Polsby and Aaron Wildavsky, *Presidential Elections: Contemporary Strategies of American Electoral Politics*, 7th edition (New York: Free Press, 1988), p. 284.

3. For a good discussion of how candidates for president have sought to put together electoral college majorities in the past, see "Building a Winning Geographic Coalition" in Stephen J. Wayne, *The Road to the White House 1992: The Politics of Presidential Elections* (New York: St. Martin's Press, 1992), pp. 191-195. Writing in 1991, Wayne argued that nominating a southerner was one of the few options the Democrats would have in 1992 in hopes of building a winning majority in the electoral college.

4. For a book-length treatment of this issue, see Judith Best, *The Case Against Direct Election of the President: A Defense of the Electoral College* (Ithaca, NY: Cornell University Press, 1975). For a shorter and somewhat more personal evaluation, see Martin Diamond, *The Electoral College and the American Idea of Democracy* (Washington, DC: American Enterprise Institute for Public Policy Research, 1977). Polsby and Wildavsky devote an entire section of their book to "An Appraisal of the Electoral College" and conclude it would be best to leave things alone. Nelson W. Polsby and Aaron Wildavsky, *Presidential Elections: Contemporary Strategies of American Electoral Politics*, 7th edition (New York: Free Press, 1988), pp. 275-284.

5. Rochelle Sharpe, Gannett News Service, "Will of People Routed Through 538 Electors," *Colorado Springs Gazette Telegraph*, October 23, 1992, p. A1.

CHAPTER 29

1. Michael Kelly, "Those Chicken Georges and What They Mean," *New York Times*, September 30, 1992, A11.

2. Writing shortly after the 1988 presidential election, Michael Nelson described the tendency at that time of the South and other parts of the nation to vote Democratic for Congress but Republican for president as "split-level realignment." Michael Nelson, "Constitutional Aspects of the Elections," in Michael Nelson, ed., *The Elections of 1988* (Washington, D.C.: Congressional Quarterly Press, 1989), pp. 195-206.

3. "A Base of Support for the Democrats?" *New York Times*, August 3, 1992, p. A11. "Battleground States," *Washington Post National Weekly Edition*, August 31-September 6, 1992, p. 12. "A Competitive Campaign Map," *New York Times*, September 7, 1992, p. 8. David S. Broder, "Which Way Will the Votes Swing?" *Washington Post National Weekly Edition*, September 14-20, 1992, p. 4. Ann Devroy and Dan Balz, "For the Bush Campaign, It's Now a Numbers Game," *Washington Post National Weekly Edition*, October 12-18, 1992, p. 13. Nexis and Associated Press, "The Presidential Race State by State," *Colorado Springs Gazette Telegraph*, October 23, 1992, p. A1.

4. Nexis and Associated Press, "The Presidential Race State by State," *Colorado Springs Gazette Telegraph*, October 23, 1992, p. A1.

5. Steve Daley, "Midwest Key to White House," *Chicago Tribune*, September 6, 1992, p. 1.

6. Howard Kurtz, "The Candidates' Ad Campaigns Go Their Separate Ways," *Washington Post National Weekly Edition*, September 28-October 4, 1992, p. 13.

7. Michael Kelly, "Those Chicken Georges and What They Mean," *New York Times*, September 30, 1992, A11.

8. Leslie Phillips, "Hopefuls May Spend Record $300 Million," *USA Today*, October 23, 1992, p. 1A.

CHAPTER 30

1. Jeff Thomas, "Bush Touches on Economic Vision," *Colorado Springs Gazette Telegraph*, September 16, 1992, p. A3.

2. Author's notes, Bush Rally, Inverness Industrial Park, Arapahoe County, Colorado, September 15, 1992.

3. Jennifer Gavin and Robert Kowalski, "Bush Brings Colo. No Surprises," *Denver Post*, September 16, 1992, p. 1A.

4. The photograph was on display, for the remainder of the *Forever Plaid* run, in the lobby of the Galleria Theater, Denver Center for the Performing Arts, Denver, Colorado.

5. Author's notes, panel discussion on "The 1992 Campaign," The Colorado Symposium on the Presidential Election, University of Colorado at Colorado Springs, December 11, 1992.

6. Author's notes, Clinton Rally, Civic Center Park, Denver, Colorado, September 17, 1992.

7. Robert Kowalski, "Clinton: 'We Can Do Better,'" *Denver Post*, September 18, 1992, p. 1A.

8. Jeff Thomas, "Clinton: Vive la Difference," *Colorado Springs Gazette Telegraph*, September 18, 1992, p. A1.

9. This list of politically relevant lyrics from music played at the Clinton rally was provided by Augustus W. Janeway, a political science major at Colorado College in Colorado Springs.

10. The photograph was on display, for the remainder of the *Forever Plaid* run, in the lobby of the Galleria Theater, Denver Center for the Performing Arts, Denver, Colorado.

CHAPTER 31

1. Charles R. Babcock and Michael Isikoff, "The Off-and-On Candidate With His Personal War Chest," *Washington Post National Weekly Edition*, October 5-11, 1992, p. 14.

2. Chuck Raasch, Gannett News Service, "It's a Go For Perot," *Colorado Springs Gazette Telegraph*, October 2, 1992, p. A1.

3. Kevin Sack, "Perot, in TV Talk, Dissects Economy," *New York Times*, October 7, 1992, p. A1.

4. Sandy Grady, "Only Ross Perot Has the Megabucks and Megabrass To Go For It Twice," *Denver Post*, October 5, 1992, p. 7B. Barbara Demick, Knight-Ridder News Service, "Ross Perot Spends His Way into History," *Denver Post*, October 30, 1992, p. 20A.

5. Richard Morin, "The Night of the Living Non-Candidate," *Washington Post National Weekly Edition*, September 21-27, 1992, p. 37.

6. "The Second Coming," *Newsweek*, Special Election Issue, November/December 1992, pp. 86-87.

7. Cathleen Decker, "Clinton Tours South by Bus, Acknowledges Fear of Perot," *Denver Post*, October 27, 1992, p. 11A.

8. Robin Toner, "Two Camps Regard a Perot Revival With Less Fear," *New York Times*, September 30, 1992, p. A1.

CHAPTER 32

1. For a detailed history of presidential debating in the United States, with a particular emphasis on the effect of radio and television broadcasting on presidential debates, see Kathleen Hall Jamieson and David S. Birdsell, *Presidential Debates: The Challenge of Creating an Informed Electorate* (New York: Oxford University Press, 1988). For a shorter study that includes transcripts of highlights from presidential debates, see Joel L. Swerdlow, ed., *Presidential Debates: 1988 and Beyond* (Washington, D.C.: Congressional Quarterly Press, 1987).

2. Theodore H. White gave this evaluation of the impact of the television debates on the 1960 presidential election: "When they began, Nixon was generally viewed as being the probable winner of the election contest and Kennedy as fighting an uphill battle; when they were over, the positions of the two contestants were reversed." See Chapter 11, "Round Two: The Television Debates," in Theodore H. White, *The Making of the President 1960* (New York: Pocket Books, 1961), p. 349.

3. See Chapter 40, "The Second Debate: Eastern Europe," in Jules Witcover, *Marathon: The Pursuit of the Presidency 1972-1976* (New York: Signet, 1977), pp. 633-648.

4. See Chapter 13, "'There You Go Again,'" in Jack W. Germond and Jules Witcover, *Blue Smoke and Mirrors: How Reagan Won and Why Carter Lost the Election of 1980* (New York: Viking Press, 1981), p. 281.

5. "Face to Face in Prime Time," *Newsweek*, Special Election Issue, November/December 1992, p. 88.

6. All quotes from the first debate are from "Transcript of First TV Debate Among Bush, Clinton, and Perot," *New York Times*, October 12, 1992, p. A12.

7. Elizabeth Kolbert, "Bush Failed in Debate by Inviting Perot," *New York Times*, October 13, 1992, p. A11. "Report Card," *Colorado Springs Gazette Telegraph*, October 12, 1992, p. A1.

8. Bill Carter, "TV Ratings for First Debate Top Baseball Playoff Game," *New York Times*, October 13, 1992, p. A11.

9. All quotes from the vice-presidential debate are from author's notes, The Vice Presidential Debate, Atlanta, Georgia, October 13, 1992.

10. George J. Church, "The Long Road," *Time*, November 2, 1992, p. 43.

11. "Face to Face in Prime Time," *Newsweek*, Special Election Issue, November/December 1992, p. 91. Germond and Witcover believed this event to be so important in the 1992 presidential election campaign that they began their book with it. See Chapter 1, "Blowing the Whistle," in Jack W. Germond and Jules Witcover, *Mad As Hell: Revolt at the Ballot Box, 1992* (New York: Warner Books, 1993), pp. 9-14.

12. George J. Church, "The Long Road," *Time*, November 2, 1992, p. 43.

13. Author's notes, Third Presidential Debate, East Lansing, Michigan, October 19, 1992.

14. "Transcript of 3d TV Debate Between Bush, Clinton and Perot," *New York Times*, October 20, 1992, p. A12.

15. "Face to Face in Prime Time," *Newsweek*, Special Election Issue, November/December 1992, p. 91.

16. George J. Church, "The Long Road," *Time*, November 2, 1992, p. 43.

17. David S. Broder, "Saving the Best for Too Late," *Washington Post National Weekly Edition*, October 26-November 1, 1992, p. 4.

CHAPTER 33

1. For discussion and analysis of the 1992 presidential advertising campaigns, see F. Christopher Arterton, "Campaign '92: Strategies and Tactics of the Candidates," in Gerald M. Pomper et al., *The Election of 1992* (Chatham, NJ: Chatham House Publishers, 1993), pp. 96-101.

2. Richard L. Berke, "The Ad Campaign: Mixing Harshness With Warmth," *New York Times*, October 22, 1992, p. A12.

3. Elizabeth Kolbert, "The Final Ads: Tipoffs to Endgame Strategies," *New York Times*, October 20, 1992, p. A11.

4. "To the Wire," *Newsweek*, Special Election Issue, November/December 1992, p. 92.

5. "Perot Presents His Autobiography, Part I, in 30-Minute TV Program," *New York Times*, October 23, 1992, p. A12.

6. "Clinton Poll Lead Narrows," *New York Times*, October 29, 1992, p. A12.

7. Ann McDaniel, "Mourning in America," *Newsweek*, October 26, 1992, p. 33.

8. Andrew Rosenthal, "Bush Steps Up Attacks on Democrat's Character," *New York Times*, October 29, 1992, p. A1.

9. Michael Kelly, "As Race Looks Tighter, Theme Is Truth and Trust," *New York Times*, October 29, 1992, p. A1.

10. Richard L. Berke, "Volleys of Data Replace Blatant Attacks of 1988," *New York Times*, October 29, 1992, p. A12. Elizabeth Kolbert, "Bush and Clinton Customize Their TV and Radio Ads in the Swing States," *New York Times*, October 22, 1992, p. A12.

11. Personal observation by the author. See also Richard L. Berke, "Volleys of Data Replace Blatant Attacks of 1988," *New York Times*, October 29, 1992, p. A12.

12. Author's notes, *CBS Evening News*, October 30, 1992.

13. "Bush Possibly Knew of Arms Deal," *Colorado Springs Gazette Telegraph*, October 31, 1992, p. A3.

14. Mary Voboril and David Hess, Knight-Ridder News Service, "Political Hopefuls Sprint for Finish Line," *Denver Post*, October 31, 1992, p. 15A.

15. Germond and Witcover gave extensive coverage to the last-minute Iran-Contra charges, thus suggesting that they considered the charges to be one of the most important developments in the last week of the campaign. See Jack W. Germond and Jules Witcover, *Mad As Hell: Revolt at the Ballot Box, 1992* (New York: Warner Books, 1993), pp. 497-504. F. Christopher Arterton saw the Iran-Contra charges helping Clinton but attributed them to Clinton "luck" rather than campaign skill. See F. Christopher Arterton, "Campaign '92: Strategies and Tactics of the Candidates," in Gerald M. Pomper et al., *The Election of 1992: Reports and Interpretations* (Chatham, NJ: Chatham House Publishers, 1993), pp. 86-87.

16. Maureen Dowd, "On the Trail, the Contradictory Sides of Bush," *New York Times*, November 2, 1992, p. A1.

17. "Clinton Edges Farther Ahead," *New York Times*, November 2, 1992, p. A10.

18. "Presidential Candidates Draw Claws for Halloween," *Denver Post*, November 1, 1992, p. 1A.

19. *Newsweek*, October 19, 1992.

20. *Time*, October 19, 1992.

21. *Newsweek*, October 26, 1992.

22. *Time*, November 2, 1992.

23. Matthew Cooper, Kenneth T. Walsh, and Jerry Buckley, "Now, It's Down to the Wire," *U.S. News & World Report*, November 2, 1992, p. 28.

24. "So Many States, So Little Time," *New York Times*, November 2, 1992, p. A10.

25. The exact times for all these election-night results are from the author's notes on the CBS News television coverage.

26. "It's a Runaway!" *Denver Post*, November 4, 1992, p. 1A.

27. "The Vote for President," *New York Times*, November 5, 1992, p. B2.

28. According to exit polls, 42 percent of voters in the 1992 presidential election cited "Economy/jobs" as the issue that mattered most in deciding how to vote. "Health care" was a distant second at 20 percent of voters. Among those who said the economy was the most important issue, 52 percent voted for Clinton, 25 percent for Bush, and 24 percent for Perot. See Paul J. Quirk and Jon K. Dalager, "The Election: A 'New Democrat,'" in Michael Nelson, ed., *The Elections of 1992* (Washington, D.C.: Congressional Quarterly Press, 1993), pp. 80-81.

29. Author's notes, Richard L. Berke, *New York Times*, "Campaign Advertising," a session at The Colorado Symposium on the Presidential Election, University of Colorado at Colorado Springs, December 11, 1992.

30. David Broder, "Clinton Has a Chance to Show a Skeptical Country That Politics Can Work," *Denver Post*, November 5, 1992, p. 11B.

31. Thomas B. Edsall, "Clinton's Reelection Campaign Has Already Begun," *Washington Post National Weekly Edition*, January 11-17, 1993, p. 23.

32. Thomas Byrne Edsall, "Clinton, So Far," *New York Review of Books*, October 7, 1993, p. 6. Edsall argued in this article that, during his first half-year

in the White House, Clinton forgot he was "a different kind of Democrat," went too far to the political left, and rapidly lost support among the White middle class.

33. Gerald M. Pomper, "The Presidential Election," in Gerald M. Pomper et al., *The Election of 1992: Reports and Interpretations* (Chatham, NJ: Chatham House Publishers, 1993), p. 153.

34. John Kenneth White, "The General Campaign: Issues and Themes," in William Crotty, ed., *America's Choice: The Election of 1992* (Guilford, CT: Dushkin Publishing Group, 1993), p. 68.

35. For a thoughtful discussion of the new 1992 "talk show politics," see Philip Meyer, "The Media Reformation," in Michael Nelson, ed., *The Elections of 1992* (Washington, D.C.: Congressional Quarterly Press, 1993), pp. 98-101.

36. Joe Klein, "The Bill Clinton Show," *Newsweek*, October 26, 1992, p. 35.

CHAPTER 34

1. This proposal is somewhat unique in that it provides for the plurality winner to be elected president no matter how small his or her percentage of the vote. A number of other proposals for eliminating the electoral college require that, if the winner does not receive at least 40 percent of the vote, there will be a runoff election between the top two finishers. The American Bar Association made such a proposal in 1967. See Neal R. Peirce, *The People's President: The Electoral College in American History and the Direct-Vote Alternative* (New York: Simon and Schuster, 1968), pp. 191-192.

CHAPTER 35

1. Nelson W. Polsby, *Consequences of Party Reform* (New York: Oxford University Press, 1983), p. 72-75. Polsby described a nominating system in which elected officials of a political party have influence as "repertory theater." Many of the same actors (elected officials) come back every four years to play "leading roles" in the nomination of party presidential candidates.

2. There are a number of good descriptions of the historical evolution of the presidential nominating process in the United States. See Chapter 5, "The Development of the Presidential Selection System in the Twentieth Century," in James W. Ceaser, *Presidential Selection: Theory and Development* (Princeton, NJ: Princeton University Press, 1979), pp. 213-259; Chapter 1, "An Introduction to the Nominating System," in William Crotty and John S. Jackson 3d, *Presidential Primaries and Nominations* (Washington, D.C.: Congressional Quarterly Press, 1985), pp. 3-25; and Chapter 2, "From Back Rooms to 'Big Mo,'" in Larry M. Bar-

tels, *Presidential Primaries and the Dynamics of Public Choice* (Princeton, NJ: Princeton University Press, 1988), pp. 13-27.

3. Carl Ingram, "State Moves Presidential Primary to March," *Los Angeles Times*, October 6, 1993, p. A3. Also see Richard L. Berke, "California Guarantees Warm Primary Season," *New York Times*, September 23, 1993, p. A8.

BIBLIOGRAPHY

GENERAL WORKS

Alexander, Herbert E. "The Price We Pay For Our Presidents." *Public Opinion* (March/April 1989), pp. 46-48.

Arterton, F. Christopher. *Media Politics: The New Strategies of Presidential Campaigns.* Lexington, MA: D. C. Heath, 1984.

Ceaser, James W. *Presidential Selection: Theory and Development.* Princeton, NJ: Princeton University Press, 1979.

Crotty, William, ed. *America's Choice: The Election of 1992.* Guilford, CT: Dushkin Publishing Group, 1993.

Devlin, L. Patrick, ed. *Political Persuasion in Presidential Campaigns.* New Brunswick, NJ: Transaction Books, 1987.

DiClerico, Robert E., and Uslaner, Eric M. *Few are Chosen: Problems in Presidential Selection.* New York: McGraw-Hill, 1984.

Germond, Jack W., and Witcover, Jules. *Blue Smoke and Mirrors: How Reagan Won and Why Carter Lost the Election of 1980.* New York: Viking Press, 1981.

———. *Wake Us When It's Over: Presidential Politics of 1984.* New York: Macmillan, 1985.

———. *Whose Broad Stripes and Bright Stars? The Trivial Pursuit of the Presidency 1988.* New York: Warner Books, 1989.

———. *Mad As Hell: Revolt at the Ballot Box, 1992.* New York: Warner Books, 1993.

Goldstein, Michael L. *Guide to the 1992 Presidential Election*. Washington, D.C.: Congressional Quarterly Press, 1991.

Jamieson, Kathleen Hall. *Packaging the Presidency: A History and Criticism of Presidential Campaign Advertising*. New York: Oxford University Press, 1984.

Kessel, John H. *Presidential Campaign Politics*. 4th edition. Pacific Grove, CA: Brooks Cole, 1992.

McGinniss, Joe. *The Selling of the President 1968*. New York: Trident Press, 1969.

Moreland, Laurence W., Steed, Robert P., and Baker, Tod A., eds. *The 1988 Presidential Election in the South*. New York: Praeger, 1991.

Nelson, Michael, ed. *The Elections of 1984*. Washington, D.C.: Congressional Quarterly Press, 1985.

——— . *The Elections of 1988*. Washington, D.C.: Congressional Quarterly Press, 1989.

——— . *The Elections of 1992*. Washington, D.C.: Congressional Quarterly Press, 1993.

Polsby, Nelson W., and Wildavsky, Aaron. *Presidential Elections: Contemporary Strategies of American Politics*. 7th edition. New York: Free Press, 1988.

Pomper, Gerald M., et al. *The Election of 1984: Reports and Interpretations*. Chatham, NJ: Chatham House, 1985.

——— . *The Election of 1988: Reports and Interpretations*. Chatham, NJ: Chatham House, 1989.

——— . *The Election of 1992: Reports and Interpretations*. Chatham, NJ: Chatham House, 1993.

Popkin, Samuel L. *The Reasoning Voter: Communication and Persuasion in Presidential Campaigns*. Chicago: University of Chicago Press, 1991.

Robinson, Michael J., and Sheehan, Margaret A. *Over the Wire and On T.V.: CBS and UPI in Campaign '80*. New York: Russell Sage Foundation, 1983.

Rose, Gary L., ed. *Controversial Issues in Presidential Selection*. Albany, NY: State University of New York Press, 1991.

Runkel, David R., ed. *Campaign for President: The Managers Look at '88*. Dover, MA: Auburn House, 1989.

Spero, Robert. *The Duping of the American Voter: Dishonesty and Deception in Presidential Television Advertising*. New York: Lippincott and Crowell, 1980.

Steed, Robert P., Moreland, Laurence W., and Baker, Tod A., eds., *The 1984 Presidential Election in the South*. New York: Praeger, 1986.

Wayne, Stephen J. *The Road to the White House, 1992: The Politics of Presidential Elections.* 4th edition. New York: St. Martin's Press, 1992.

Weaver, David, et al. *Media Agenda-Setting in a Presidential Election.* New York: Praeger, 1981.

White, Theodore H. *The Making of the President 1960.* New York: Atheneum, 1961.

────── . *The Making of the President 1964.* New York: Atheneum, 1965.

────── . *The Making of the President 1968.* New York: Atheneum, 1969.

────── . *The Making of the President 1972.* New York: Atheneum, 1973.

Witcover, Jules. *Marathon: The Pursuit of the Presidency 1972-1976.* New York: Viking Penguin, 1977.

THE PRESIDENTIAL NOMINATING PROCESS

Barber, James D., ed. *Race for the Presidency: The Media and the Nomination Process.* Englewood Cliffs, NJ: Prentice-Hall, 1978.

Bartels, Larry M. *Presidential Primaries and the Dynamics of Public Choice.* Princeton, NJ: Princeton University Press, 1988.

Brereton, Charles. *First Step to the White House: The New Hampshire Primary 1952-1980.* Hampton, NH: Wheelabrator Foundation, 1979.

Cook, Rhodes. *Race for the Presidency: Winning the 1992 Nomination.* Washington, D.C.: Congressional Quarterly Press, 1991.

Cronin, Thomas C., and Loevy, Robert D. "The Case for a National Pre-Primary Convention." *Public Opinion* (Dec./Jan. 1983), 50-53.

Crotty, William, and Jackson, John S. III. *Presidential Primaries and Nominations.* Washington, D.C.: Congressional Quarterly Press, 1985.

David, Paul T., Goldman, Richard M., and Bain, Richard C. *The Politics of National Party Conventions.* Washington, D.C.: Brookings Institution, 1960.

Orren, Gary R., and Polsby, Nelson W., eds. *Media and Momentum: The New Hampshire Primary and Nomination Politics.* Chatham, NJ: Chatham House Publishers, 1987.

Plissner, Martin, and Mitofsky, Warren J. "The Making of the Delegates: 1968-1988." *Public Opinion* (Sept./Oct. 1988), pp. 45-47.

Polsby, Nelson W. *The Consequences of Party Reform.* New York: Oxford University Press, 1983.

Reiter, Howard L. *Selecting the President: The Nomination Process in Transition.* Philadephia: University of Pennsylvania Press, 1985.

Shafer, Byron E. *Quiet Revolution: The Struggle for the Democratic Party and the Shaping of Post-Reform Politics.* New York: Russell Sage Foundation, 1983.

————. *Bifurcated Politics: Evolution and Reform in the National Party Convention.* Cambridge, MA: Harvard University Press, 1988.

Squire, Peverill, ed. *The Iowa Caucuses and the Presidential Nominating Process.* Boulder, CO: Westview Press, 1989.

Stanley, Harold W., and Hadley, Charles D. "The Southern Presidential Primary: Regional Intentions With National Implications." *Publius* (Summer 1987), pp. 83-100.

Thompson, Kenneth W., ed. *The Presidential Nominating Process.* Volume I. Lanham, MD: University Press of America, 1983.

Wattenberg, Martin P. "When You Can't Beat Them, Join Them: Shaping the Presidential Nominating Process to the Television Age." *Polity* (Spring 1989), 587-597.

Winebrenner, Hugh. *The Iowa Precinct Caucuses: The Making of a Media Event.* Ames, IA: Iowa State University Press, 1987.

PRESIDENTIAL DEBATES

Jamieson, Kathleen Hall, and Birdsell, David S. *Presidential Debates.* New York: Oxford University Press, 1988.

Swerdlow, Joel L., ed. *Presidential Debates: 1988 and Beyond.* Washington, D.C.: Congressional Quarterly Press, 1987.

THE ELECTORAL COLLEGE

Best, Judith. *The Case Against Direct Election of the President: A Defense of the Electoral College.* Ithaca, NY: Cornell University Press, 1975.

Diamond, Martin. *The Electoral College and the American Idea of Democracy.* Washington, D.C.: American Enterprise Institute for Public Policy Research, 1977.

Peirce, Neal R., and Longley, Lawrence D. *The People's President: The Electoral College in American History and the Direct Vote Alternative.* Revised edition. New Haven, CT: Yale University Press, 1981.

PRESIDENTIAL VOTING ANALYSIS

Black, Earl, and Black, Merle. *The Vital South: How Presidents Are Elected.* Cambridge, MA: Harvard University Press, 1992.

Dent, Harry S. *The Prodigal South Returns to Power.* New York: John Wiley, 1978.

Ladd, Everett Carll. *Where Have All the Voters Gone? The Fracturing of America's Political Parties.* 2nd edition. New York: W. W. Norton, 1982.

Lubell, Samuel. *The Future of American Politics.* 2nd edition, revised. Garden City, NY: Doubleday, 1956.

———. *The Hidden Crisis in American Politics.* New York: W. W. Norton, 1970.

Nie, Norman H., Verba, Sidney, and Petrocik, John R. *The Changing American Voter.* Enlarged edition. Cambridge, MA: Harvard University Press, 1979.

Phillips, Kevin P. *The Emerging Republican Majority.* New Rochelle, NY: Arlington House, 1969.

———. *The Politics of Rich and Poor: Wealth and the American Electorate in the Reagan Aftermath.* New York: Random House, 1990.

———. *Boiling Point: Republicans, Democrats, and the Decline of Middle-Class Prosperity.* New York: Random House, 1993.

Scammon, Richard M., and Wattenberg, Ben J. *The Real Majority.* Capricorn edition. New York: Coward, McCann & Geoghegan, 1971.

Swansbrough, Robert H., and Brodsky, David M., eds. *The South's New Politics: Realignment and Dealignment.* Columbia, SC: University of South Carolina Press, 1988.

INDEX